ACKNOWLEDGEMENTS

This book is dedicated to *anyone* and *everyone* who has been dazed and confused by the diet and processed-food industry. It is utterly exhausting—both mentally and physically—going from one diet disaster to another, so bravo to you for moving away from the pack and seeking an end to your *dirty* dieting ways. Here's to finally *cleaning* up your diet and becoming the ultimate version of you.

Disclaimer
The advice and strategies contained herein may not be suitable for every individual. It is very important for anyone reading this book or interested in trying any dietary recommendations to consult a qualified health professional before making any changes in diet and lifestyle, or before taking vitamin and/or food supplements. While all care is taken with the accuracy of the facts and procedures in this book, the author accepts neither liability nor responsibility to any person with respect to loss, injury, or damage caused, or alleged to be caused directly or indirectly by the information contained in this book. The purpose of this book is solely to educate and inform. For any medical advice you should seek the individual personal advice and services of a medical professional.

Abundant Health Systems, Inc.

Printed in Canada by Friesens Corp.

www.DirtyDiets.com

TABLE OF CONTENTS

I was working with a very large sports nutrition company at the time, helping them create protocols that would allow their sports-related supplements to help athletes overcome this overtraining spiral and get back to what they love to do as quickly as possible. It turned out that after much experimentation, one of those protocols greatly helped the athletes recuperate rapidly. Aside from this, almost every athlete would notice a spike in their metabolisms to the point that no matter how much they ate—as long as they stuck to the recommended foods and optimal timing of those foods I had outlined in the protocol—they would get and stay super lean.

I soon had an epiphany that if I could take this same protocol and tweak it so the everyday non-athlete could apply it, what would this mean to the current "go from one fad diet to another" population? And so my *Dirty Diets* was born. I started to have so much success with my protocol that I decided to move away from specializing in sports nutrition and move toward nutritional research that could benefit anyone who wanted to look, feel, and perform their very best.

Over those 20 years or so, I have further tweaked my protocol to the point that almost anyone who tries it is able to see quick but sustainable results. *Dirty Diets* is not a diet, as it is not a short-term solution. *Dirty Diets* is actually a program that anyone can follow with very little effort because it does not incorporate things like calorie counting and cravings for fat-forming foods like heavy starches disappear within the first few days to a week of applying it.

I learned very early on that no one enjoys counting calories and no matter how fantastic a diet may seem, if you are constantly battling the craving demons, you will eventually fail – no exceptions. There is only so far your willpower is going to take you and besides, life is about living and being happy, not about depriving yourself of great food.

By reeducating your metabolism to become super-efficient all day long, and even while you sleep, you will ensure that your very own body fat is the target of your metabolism's efforts. This can be achieved by creating the proper environment for your genes to make the necessary machinery and stimulate hormones through the right food choices, the timing of your meals, and a few other alterations along the way.

Since I wrote my international bestselling book, *Fat Wars*, over ten years ago, thousands of individuals around the globe, just like you, were able to finally experience the success they so desperately craved. I have since been able to further amend those principles so they are even more effective today. In fact, I now teach a portion of the *Dirty Diets* program to fourth-year students in a master class at Boucher Institute of Naturopathic Medicine, one of the leading naturopathic universities in North America, in order to arm these graduating doctors for the obesity-laden world that awaits them.

But in order to share my life's work with you and help you finally win your own personal war with the bulge, I am a big believer in first helping you understand *why* you are presently in this situation to begin with, so you never have to repeat these same mistakes again.

Your Weight is Over

My goal is to defang the diet industry and bring the power back to where it belongs – to you. Along the way, I'm going to reveal the barriers most people have when trying to lose weight. Most of the blocks are obscured by an absurd obsession with calories.

But mostly, I'm going to empower you with my *Dirty Diets* proven techniques that actually work for the long haul.

We'll start in Chapter 1, with exposing the calorie delusion and you'll be introduced to an incredible new area of science called "epigenetics" and how it pertains to your tummy. Then we'll move to Chapter 2, where you'll find out how we got so fat and we'll also do a clean sweep of diet myths that are so pervasive they're considered conventional wisdom (even by health care professionals). This is where we'll begin the process of exposing the diet industry's favorite tool: the "Lite" food. Chapter 3 will discuss the psychology of weight and reveal the single largest barrier to sustained weight loss – your mind. Then, it's time to take a look inside the body to see how the dozens of chemical messengers, known as hormones, work behind the scenes to orchestrate our weight, appetite, and health. I promise you'll not only find this understandable, but highly interesting.

In Chapter 4, I will draw your attention away from the number on the bathroom scale and onto a significantly more important determinant of weight loss success – body composition. Chapter 5 will discuss one of the most important factors when it comes to metabolic success, your body mass. Chapter 6 unveils the most common stumbling blocks to sticking to healthy eating - your multifaceted appetite. Be sure to keep reading for Chapter 7, when you'll see for yourself the extraordinary impact sleep has on weight and appetite.

We'll discuss in Chapters 8 and 9 the differences in the physiology, psychology, and perception of weight gain and loss in men and women and the influence of male and female hormones on the body's weight regulation systems.

Many health experts point to childhood obesity as a more worrisome sign of the times than adult obesity. That's why I've dedicated Chapter 10 to parents who are looking for ways they can avoid or reverse obesity from swallowing their children.

Part II of *Dirty Diets* is dedicated to uncovering the truth about the macronutrients: protein, carbohydrates, and fats. Along with calories and "lite" foods, it's these three concepts that tend to be most misunderstood among the dieting community. You'll see there's nothing inherently "bad" about any of these nutrients, it's just the wrong choices from each category we make and the way we combine them that's harmful.

We get practical as I arm you with information you can use immediately in your life. Starting with Chapter 14, there's going to be a paradigm shift in what it means to be fit, and a crystal clear image of a healthy lifestyle will replace the lite food-induced fog. Chapters 15 and 16 will give you newfound insight into the role drugs and supplements can play in shedding fat. I've written Chapter 17 dedicated to how your mind impacts fat loss and gain in "Think Lean, Be Lean."

The book concludes with Part III and a set of simple and to-the-point principles that will put an end to measuring food or counting calories to give you lifelong success with your metabolism, your mind, and your health.

Slowly, but surely, you'll be moving out of a mindset of frustration, perplexity, and mystery to one of satisfaction, clarity, and confidence. It's time to stop the diet industry's stranglehold on your life and wallet. For most, the shift from lite foods back to real food—or what I like to call *clean* food—will be long overdue. But whether you've got five or fifty diets under your belt, and as more and more lite foods wiggle into our culture, now is the time for real change.

DIRTY DIETS

PART I

CHAPTER 1 – Searching for Silver Bullets and Magic Potions

Julie quickly walked by the plate glass windows that lined the sidewalk on her way to work. This used to be her favorite part of the day when she could take a glance at her fierce reflection. "That's right," she'd think as she looked at the people all around her. "I still look hot. Call me a cougar; it's okay." Over time, Julie toned down the morning pep talk to just feeling good that she was still wearing clothes that fit her curves instead of giving into loose-fitting pastel drapes. It's like being in a parade surrounded by rushing Easter eggs, she would think, never seeing the inches creeping up around her own waistline.

But Julie's self-confidence started to shrink in direct proportion to how much her thighs expanded until she stopped paying attention to her reflection at all. She noticed men no longer told her she couldn't possibly be over forty. She loved that line and always answered confidently, "This is what forty-two looks like." The checkout girl at Wal-Mart had even carded her once when Julie was buying wine. When was that, she thought? Two years, no... three years ago?

Over time, Julie's glimpses at herself started to get shorter and shorter until she started looking away altogether. That was just after the New Year and all of the holiday parties. She had been invited out every weekend for over a month, but made herself a promise to only take "a taste" of everything at each party. No big bites, except for the crab puffs. You just can't waste good crab meat.

She observed the crowd of people moving along with her, all of them trying to get to work on time. Everyone seemed exhausted just getting down the sidewalk. She wondered, "Do I look like that? Is that heavy breathing mine? I can remember when I had better excuses for breathing like than simply trying to get to my cubicle at work."

Most of her fellow commuters also had a little something extra spilling out of the top of skirts and pants; a little more jiggle in the back. "Geez, that lady even has muffin top calves," mumbled Julie, as she watched the woman who had stuffed herself into a pair of boots teeter by. "I thought shoes were the one thing that always fit."

Julie laughed to herself as she slipped another bite of the chocolate granola bar into her mouth when she didn't think anyone was looking. Her mother was always tsk-tsking at her for eating in public, but the bars were perfect for Julie's on-the-go life. They were small, so she let herself eat two. She kept them hidden in the bowl of apples in the kitchen where her husband would never think to look.

Between trying to get to the office, working, and then taking little Simon to his tae kwon do classes, it's a wonder she ate at all. Besides, she'd been eating healthier. All last week she brought some of those frozen meals for lunch. Didn't they say "lite with only 300 calories" right on the cover? Sure, they gave her gas and wouldn't you know it, usually during a meeting, but she was sure everyone thought it was Stanley from accounting. And, these pants still fit, she thought. The pale blue ones with the elastic top that matched the floral blouse she was wearing. They were nice linen pants and with the blouse overtop no one could tell there was no zipper or button and just a band of elastic. They were all the rage, said the sales lady, when Julie had gone in search of more comfortable slacks. The old ones were starting to make her feel more like she was wearing Spandex three sizes too small instead of comfortable cotton, especially toward the late afternoon.

Julie had reluctantly tried the pants on, wondering if she was becoming too much like her mother until she saw how they looked like dress pants. She bought them in five different colors. At the cash register, there were two other women buying the same kind of pants.

They're popular, thought Julie as she'd hurried to work, comfortable as could be. But then, Julie had a different thought. "I deserve better," she said, too quietly at first for anyone to hear. "I deserve better," she said, a bit louder, as the parade of commuters turned to see who was causing a commotion. "I deserve better, and I'm the only one who can do anything about it," she said to the man next to her.

Julie stopped in her tracks and took a good, long gaze at herself in the windows. It was hard to acknowledge that she'd not only let herself get pudgy, but she was downright fat. And, as Julie looked around she realized most of the people around her had the same bloated, round bodies. "How did this happen?" asked Julie. "We didn't all used to look like this." Julie felt like she had just woken up from a sad nightmare and was finally able to see the truth.

Of course, she realized that in this day and age being over-fat has become the norm.

Are You Over-Fat?

Over-fat? What the heck does that mean? Today, weight is all people talk about on TV or during our lunch break. From the time we are old enough to watch adults nervously weigh themselves on the bathroom scale as they hope maybe this time the numbers will have moved in the right direction, losing weight has been easy to talk about, but difficult to achieve. Weight loss is all most of us ever think about, which is why we are inundated by what is commonly referred to as the "weight loss" industry. However, the truth is, weight has very little to do with how we look, feel, or perform. Believe it or not, there is even good weight on our bodies that we can't afford to lose – it's called muscle and it weighs—one cubic inch for one cubic inch—more than fat.

Muscle is the main metabolic engine of the body, and without enough of it, we can find ourselves on perpetual dieting merry-go-rounds. Unfortunately, you never hear any dieters discussing where they expect the majority of their weight loss to come from when they find themselves at the start of their fifth, tenth, or God-knows-what-number diet they are presently on. This is why research shows that on most fad diets, we lose almost equal portions of fat and muscle. Losing muscle dooms most dieters to regain all they've lost, plus a few extra pounds. Not good.

Let's face it, fad diets are nothing more than short-term solutions to what is commonly known as a lifelong problem – it's called obesity. Time to wake up and smell the bacon. We're fat, people. To just say we are "overweight," or we "weigh too much," or "I need to lose some weight," is never going to solve the problem. When we go on diets, most of us become nothing more than reduced versions of our former fat selves. We fit into smaller clothes, but we are no closer to being fit and healthy. I coined this phenomenon as The Smaller Fat Person Syndrome, in my bestselling book, *Fat Wars*, over ten years ago. It's time to change our perception of reality because we are a nation of over-fat people. We are not over weight.

Fat and Blind

Julie is far from alone. Even though many people believe you become fat when your weight rapidly swells like a balloon, the reality is that most people accumulate body fat just like Julie – little by little, year by year, until suddenly, they're over-fat and trying not to look at their reflection or wondering why the stairs are harder to climb. Piling on fat at the rate of a few ounces a month makes accurately determining whether you are out of shape a legitimate challenge. Northwestern University researchers in Chicago, Illinois, recently found that about one quarter of obese people either don't realize their size or don't admit to it on a questionnaire.

We often hear about obesity in the news, and we know it's a growing health problem, yet we use a different pair of eyes when we gaze at ourselves. I call it "fat blindness." We have become so fat that researchers now say the problem of obesity, particularly in western countries, outweighs the issue of starvation. As a planet, we're eating ourselves into early graves and have reversed the trend of modern science to elongate the lifespan. The tendency toward obesity has gotten to the point where the current youth of North America are the first generation expected to have a shorter lifespan than their parents.

Some years ago, when I decided to stop formulating nutritional products for other companies and start my own line, I created a group of cutting-edge products under the Fat Wars brand. It was a no brainer. After all, well over one hundred and fifty thousand individuals had read *Fat Wars* and experienced what proper metabolic eating was all about. Needless to say, these people were believers in the Fat Wars philosophy, so why wouldn't they naturally try my Fat Wars products?

Well, I quickly learned a difficult lesson—one which almost cost me my business. No one likes to admit they're the fat one in the crowd. The Fat Wars logo was a major deterrent, and even though most people who shopped in health food stores had either read or heard of Fat Wars, no one wanted to walk up to a health food store counter with a bottle of something that mentioned anything to do with fat. It was like carrying around a massive sign with an arrow pointing right at you saying, "Hey, look at me, I'm fat."

So many retailers told me even though they knew the products were great, when they tried to bring them to the attention of their customers they were met with the exact same response, "Why would I buy that? I'm not fat!" Ain't denial a punch in the pudgy gut?

The *New England Journal of Medicine* published a study that confirmed the slow, but steady weight gain denial phenomenon. They found that people tend to put on a pound or two during the gorging period commonly referred to as "the holidays," just like Julie. But because no one can seem to rid themselves of those extra pounds, it becomes permanently tacked onto their weight. The extra bulk is almost always in the form of pure lard.

Could it be that Grandma's Thanksgiving pumpkin pie is the cause of this obesity epidemic you've been hearing about? Unfortunately, our situation is much direr than our inability to abstain from a second slice of pie – yes, even Grandma's. If you've turned on a TV anytime since the Clinton administration, you won't be surprised to hear that we're fatter than at any other time in history – and by an enormous margin. The average North American male has tacked on 20 extra pounds since the 1960s and now tips the scales at 180 pounds instead of 160 pounds (similar patterns are noted for women, as well). While the amount of people classified as overweight or obese (as determined by body mass index*) remained steady from 1950-1980, rates of overweight and obesity suddenly doubled in the 1980s.

Getting to Know the BMI

*Body mass index (BMI) is the ratio of height to weight. It's measured by dividing your weight in kilos or pounds by your height in meters or inches squared. In general, a BMI less than 20 is considered to be extra lean, 20 to 25 is seen as ideal, 25 to 30 is clinically overweight, while anything above 30 is called "obese." However, keep in mind that the BMI is one of those grey areas because it puts all weight into the same category—without judging whether the source of the weight is good and bad. Although it works more or less for the majority of people, it only does so because the majority of our population has let themselves go. Never confuse what is deemed normal with what is considered healthy. To be "normal" in North America is to be over-fat and unhealthy. I know that's not the nicest statement, but then again, the truth is not always warm and fuzzy. Maybe warm and deep-fried.

Contrary to popular belief, people didn't abruptly transform from lean and muscular to flabby and rotund once the 80s hit. Weights have been steadily inching upward since World War II. This newfound weight gain was widely considered a positive phenomenon by health experts as it nudged many underweight folks into healthy weight ranges. However, like the out-of-control portion sizes, our steady increase in weight never peaked – instead it's accelerated.

Here's the twist to my story. It may come as a surprise to learn that the number of people who are classified as overweight has barely budged over the last 20 plus years. The Center for Disease Control's (CDC) National Health and Nutrition Examination Survey (NHANES) found the percentage of overweight people has actually *decreased* since 1988. It's not that people are getting leaner though, far from it. The reality is we're getting so fat that we're being pushed into higher and higher categories of fatness. We are becoming Super Fat. During the same time period that overweight rates dropped, obesity rates catapulted upwards. Obesity went from rare to commonplace, afflicting about one in ten to nearly one third of all adults. Just as troubling is the fact that "extreme obesity," a BMI greater than 40, has more than doubled.

The Excess Calories Delusion

The question that may be bouncing around in your head is, "What happened?" I'll fully explore the answers in the next chapter, but it helps to have at least a basic understanding of how we got into this predicament. As you'll see, there are many so-called "causes" of obesity whose impact is either largely overstated or just a flat out myth. Like the idea that body weights suddenly shot up in the 80s and 90s, and wasn't a byproduct of a 50 year trend. These misconceptions about the origins of obesity make cracking this case much more challenging than it has to be. But awareness is often the first step to solving a big problem.

Although many lay the blame on TVs, computers, and general laziness (typically called the less offensive "sedentary lifestyle"), numerous studies have found that we burn about the same amount of calories as we did before this mess began. Modern conveniences that have been around for a while, like washing machines, escalators, and oil heaters have partially or completely replaced washboards, stairs, and labor-intensive fire-burning stoves, with the expected result being fewer calories burned while doing chores and work. Also, it's often reported that we now spend about 20 minutes more per day plopped in front of the TV than we did in 1975 – another well-known "cause" of weight gain. However, we've largely made up for this caloric gap with what scientists call "leisure time physical activity," known to most people as exercising. Our health conscious, although horribly misguided, population spends more time walking and playing sports than fifty years ago (although this is still much less than most experts recommend). And yet, we're still super-sized.

For the source of the problem, we have to look no further than what's going into our mouths. Not surprisingly, in the last few decades, our entire culture of eating has completely transformed. We spend less time cooking and enjoying our food than ever before. Highly-processed, calorie-rich foods are everywhere. Perhaps most significantly, the two primary barriers to food, time and effort, have all but vanished. Indulging in a sweet treat like baking a cake from scratch, something that was once a relatively time-consuming act, has been replaced by a thirty-second purchase with a credit card. What is the result of our abundance of highly available food? We eat a lot more of it, more often.

Contrary to popular belief, portion sizes haven't grown as much as we think (or perhaps at all). Films like *Super Size Me* (2004) have given us the impression that we're fat because our sparse dinner plates of yore are now overflowing with mountains of greasy fare. While the billions of gargantuan fast food meals handed out through drive-thru windows in the last couple of decades have definitely lent a hand, it's not the excessive calories these foods contain that are responsible for making us fat. In fact, since the mid-1970s, the calories we eat per meal haven't changed. What has changed is the composition of the nutrients in what we shovel down our gullets and how that composition affects the way our body uses fat for energy.

As you'll learn in an upcoming chapter, the foods we choose to consume have an incredible impact on various hormones that tweak the genes of our metabolic machinery to express themselves by either setting the internal environment for copious amounts of fat to be manufactured (for the next famine) or stimulating the body to use that fat as energy—in which case you don't just end up looking better, you feel better as well. In other words, the sum total of all the calories you consume doesn't always dictate whether you are going to be Super Lean or Super Fat, but the expression of your genetic codes does and that expression is highly dependent on the composition of those calories among other things.

Epigenetics and Your Fat Cells

If breakfast, lunch, and dinner are the same size they were 40 years ago, what's going on here? Besides the fact that we are snacking on the wrong types of foods, the calories from our three square meals might be the same, but what those meals look like has completely changed. Meals that were once made up of real food are now low-fat/high-carb monstrosities of their former selves. Refined carbs, mostly from processed corn, not lean forms of protein or healthy fats, are now the centerpiece of our diet. This unprecedented onslaught of refined carbs has forced the pancreas of almost every North American to work overtime—producing extra insulin after we sit down to eat a meal. Not only that, but the foods we're eating between meals aren't allowing our out-of-breath pancreas a breather. Data from the Continuing Survey of Food Intake shows that snacking on highly-processed foods is one of the most important shifts in our eating patterns over the last twenty five years. The end result of this constant carb assault is a tired pancreas, an out of control appetite, and a much fatter you.

Believe it or not, the problem isn't so much how we've waddled here; it's the hole we've dug ourselves into we're trying to escape from.

Speak to almost any anthropologist and he/she will tell you that 99.9% of our genetic structure (or the human puzzle) developed in the wild, thousands of years ago. As some Paleolithic experts have said in the past, "We are in a sense living with Fred Flintstone bodies, but we're in a George Jetson world." During those thousands of years, the human body developed countless adaptations to mold human physiology to the environment around them.

Epigenetics refers to the long-term alterations in the potential expression or outcome of a cell that are not necessarily heritable. This book was originally named *Sell You Lite*, as much of its message is about the mass confusion surrounding the diet industry and how much of its deception is both making and keeping us fat. After a lot of back and forth thinking, I decided to go with *Dirty Diets* because that is, in fact, what the great majority of people are on these days: dirty and destructive diets as opposed to eating *clean* and in a way that best supports an optimal metabolic rate that is conducive to continual fat release.

As the book evolved, I wanted the reader to also understand there is a major genetic component of obesity and more importantly, how that component is influenced by the environment in which we live in and create for ourselves. The reality is we are largely in control of whatever environment we live in—at least in this day and age. In other words, perception equals reality. The 1902 literary classic by James Allen, *As a Man Thinketh*, sums it up best. The book begins with the following statement:

> *Mind is the Master power that moulds and makes,*
> *And Man is Mind, and evermore he takes*
> *The tool of Thought, and, shaping what he wills,*
> *Brings forth a thousand joys, a thousand ills: —*
> *He thinks in secret, and it comes to pass:*

Environment is but his looking-glass.

The science of epigenetics has shown us that we are a byproduct of our environment, which is not always a good thing, as a poor self-image along with the wrong diet often breeds a less than optimal mind and body. Let's also not lose sight of the fact that agriculture is a very recent phenomenon in human history —and even more so, the introduction of "so-called" diet foods. Needless to say, our rapid 30 plus year switch to highly refined, sugary, starchy lite crap flies in the face of millennia-old physiology — especially the signals that regulate how our bodies use fat or store it.

To combat our bulging waistlines, we have, by and large, turned to a set of food-like substances, exercise gizmos, gurus, and empty promises known as the diet industry. What a billion dollar industry it is with a nation of overweight (really over fat) people desperate to do (and pay) just about anything to slim down. Sure enough, we're handing over more and more of our money for weight loss programs, diet foods, and supplements every year. Smack dab in the middle of a recession, North Americans scraped the bottom of their piggy banks to shell out over $80 billion dollars last year on weight loss programs (a figure that trumps the US budget for education, social assistance, and healthcare, combined).

Far from helping, the diet industry is a primary cause of the obesity challenge. Paula Franken, a medical practitioner and the general manager of Lighten Up, a group aiming to help people slim down without dieting, said, "Dieting is a business with enormous financial interest in making sure it continues." The diet industry has more in common with Wall Street than Main Street. Many experts agree with Franken's theory that the diet industry is what *Business Week* calls a "big fat lie" - a system designed for you to fail and keep coming back to buy more tools. But what if we could turn that around? With the guidelines in *Dirty Diets*, we can. Keep reading.

Paying More to Stay Fat

The facts are, there is a direct correlation between how much we dole out on fad diets and how fat we are. In other words, as the diet industry grows, so do our waistlines. A snapshot comparison of our wild spending on diets and modern obesity statistics should make it clear to you that our failure to remedy the era of fat has little to do with willpower or effort, and everything to do with our approach. Our strategy for shedding pounds has been a complete reliance on whatever the diet industry tells us to do. So, why is it we only got fatter?

While it's impossible to pin down exactly what the diet industry message is, as it seems to change like the weather, there's one mantra this perverse industry loves more than any other: *Diets are hard, we make them easy.* They tell you that in order to maintain a healthy weight without them; you just have to commit to a lifelong regimen that's bland, time-consuming, and altogether painful. It's no wonder the alternatives they present have such irresistible appeal, and we're willing to pay them, over and over again.

Have you ever noticed that whatever they're pushing doesn't work for long? It's the only consistent measure of an industry that continues to fail its clients. Even though the Federal Trade Commission (FTC) reports that a quarter of all US men and half of all women are trying to lose weight, they either fail to lose the weight or can't keep it off.

A statistic that seems to get thrown around quite a bit is "95% of all diets fail." Actually, research suggests the performance of most diets is much worse than the paltry 5%. It doesn't seem to matter what kind of diet you follow, low-carb, low-protein, or low-whatever, the same story rings true time and time again: people drop about 10-20 pounds (and remember, they're losing fat *and* muscle) within the first few months, only to have it fly back on again as we tip-toe back to our old ways of eating (sometimes with extra bites for good measure). A large-scale clinical trial by Harvard researchers that was designed to figure out which diet worked best ended up becoming more noteworthy for the study's inability to keep people from gaining the weight back—despite screening for highly-motivated and well-educated participants.

As one dieting guru from years past used to say, "Stop the Insanity!" So why don't we just stop opting-in to this futile and vicious cycle of yo-yo dieting? Many believe after a dozen or so failures under our belts, we're so frantic for a solution that we turn off our rational brain that's chiming in to remind us of how crazy we are for jumping on yet one more fad-diet. And, like any industry, the diet machine has million-dollar marketing and research and development teams working night and day concocting ways to trick you into forking over your cash in exchange for their latest and greatest product. It kind of sounds like the pharmaceutical industry when you think of it. They attack us where it hurts most: our ego.

CHAPTER 2 – Why Lite Never Means Lean

Lois loves to make lists. She has one of all the things she's going to eventually buy, including a sunshine yellow or baby blue Coach™ purse , a Toyota® Prius just like Leonardo DiCaprio's, a wedding tiara, and a condo with a balcony that overlooks a pool. So far, all she has is a knockoff Coach™ bag in brown pleather, a bright red, used Dodge Neon, and an efficiency apartment that looks into the parking lot, but it's a start.

There's already a size 8 wedding dress carefully preserved in plastic, hanging in her closet back behind her heavy winter coats. She still has a few details to work out before she can wear the dress, like going down from an 18 to an 8, a size Lois hasn't seen since college. Then, she needs her boyfriend, Roger, to pop the big question. But Lois is certain both things will happen because she has a plan.

If she can get back to a size 8, she figures that will make the second plan—Roger down on one knee—a little easier. Sure, Roger's been plumping up right alongside her and kneeling down may be a little tricky these days. Lois has put them both on a new diet strategy. Step one is lots of lite snacks in between meals to cut down on cravings. It's working like a charm. "I don't miss the candy I used to eat at all," she says to the mirror as she investigates whether or not her waist band has any more give to it yet. She has to push her belly back just a little to wedge a finger into the top of her skirt.

Lois also has a list for her career with "Get a corner office" as the number one item, written in big letters in her favorite silver sparkle pen. The numbers two through ten detail which friends she'll promote and which ones will get the axe once her raise comes through. She keeps that list in the bottom of her purse underneath an emergency stash of cereal bars for when she misses lunch. A couple of the names are regularly moved from promote to axe and back again.

Her favorite list, though, is about Roger, and all the ways she's going to improve him. That list is already up to 139 points. Number two, after proposal, is for Roger to get back into those tight Lee® jeans he could wear when they first met. "How is he ever going to fit into an Armani tux with a belly like that?" she muses. Roger is ignorant of her lists and Lois means to keep it that way. She plans to hide it away in her bathroom, which will be just off the future master suite with the required balcony, after they're married.

Lois is always on the lookout for more helpful hints from the pages of *Cosmopolitan* or from sitting in the lunchroom with her two best friends, Susie and Diane. They usually dish dirt about men and work over a hot bag of popcorn. "I only get the brand that has antioxidants added in," Lois tells her friends. Later, she opens her desk drawer to hunt for a caramel rice cake. She had started locking the drawer after she noticed a few of her snacks were missing. Whoever is stealing from her is definitely on the axe list forever. "Don't mess with my snacks when I'm hungry."

As she munches on her simple, lite diet snack, she muses, "Ooooh, maybe I can get Roger to take me through the drive-thru tonight. I'll only get the salad with the ranch dressing and a Diet Coke®. Maybe some small fries won't hurt."

Turn Off the Lite

It happens every day across North America: drive-thrus are jam-packed with hungry commuters on their way home from a long hard day at work. When people are that tired, it's just easier to stop for a quick meal that someone else cooks instead of taking the time to prepare something at home. It's only a matter of time before one of those commuters—the one with the growling, empty belly—makes a fast-food employee giggle as he pulls up to the microphone and says, "I'll have a Double Quarter Pounder with cheese, extra-large fries, an apple pie... and a *Diet* Coke®." While it may sound ridiculous, this misguided customer firmly believes the Diet Coke® will absolve him of his fast food sins. If only eating lite foods were the diet equivalent of a pencil's eraser—canceling out our dietary splurges and missteps.

Today, all of the foods that come in and out of our lives are like the animals on Noah's ark. There are two of every kind: a "normal" version and a "lite" version. You'll find lite ketchup, lite dog food, and even "Spam® Light" (as if we ever knew what was in regular Spam® in the first place). Our appetite for lite foods has expanded every year along with our waistlines, the rate of morbid obesity, and the bank accounts of diet food marketers.

How did we get so fat so fast? There's a lot of finger pointing to go around, from our overindulgence in artificially-sweetened liquids like diet soft drinks or faux lemonade to imbalances in the bacteria that grows in our gut and even something as obscure as a viral infection. However, the latest research indicates that three groups, in particular, shoulder most of the blame. It all started with a consensus vacuum in the scientific community that continues to this day and it led to the official stances of government and leading health authorities to be based on faulty or nonexistent data. Counterintuitive as it may seem, it's probably best to ignore most weight loss "experts" because, as you'll see, they're just as confused as everyone else.

Inaccurate Food Labels

The emergence of so-called lite foods is what really turned North America into what Brian Wansink, the Director of the Food and Brand Lab at Cornell University, calls, "A country of low-fat foods and high fat people." The infiltration of these packaged lies has ended up being the number one obstacle to our efforts to combat the rising tide of obesity. Billions of dollars have been spent to develop and distribute cutting-edge psychological trickery, which over a period of only thirty years, has fundamentally shifted the way we view our relationship with food, a bond that originally took generations to develop or change.

Shining the spotlight away from food itself and onto individual aspects or ingredients has duped an unsuspecting public into thinking junk food can be instantly transformed into something healthy by adding a single nutrient. For example, one of the diet industry's favorite targets is calories, (something research has shown is nearly impossible to track) instead of the food's source or its level of processing. They also play on everyone's ignorance—experts and the general public alike—by amplifying the results of preliminary research into bold, new health claims.

Every month, there's a new food to avoid or another one that promises to be the next weight loss miracle. The impact of the marketing trickery on the public has led to the food industry being put "on trial" by regulatory groups like the FTC. Misleading information combined with detrimental health effects has labeled food marketers, "the tobacco industry of the new millennium," according to former chair and professor of Nutrition, Food Studies, and Public Health at New York University, Dr. Miriam Nestle.

To understand how a group of corporations out for financial gain have superseded the influence of health experts, we need an appreciation of just how confused our experts have become. In fact, confusion may be an understatement. The shared knowledge of what causes weight gain, and especially what's effective in the treatment of it, is more akin to a physicist's ability to understand distant solar systems, if not more limited.

Keeping It Off

When noted obesity researcher, Albert J. Stunkard, MD, approached the podium of the New York Academy of Sciences to sum up the most current efforts to combat obesity, he proclaimed, "Most obese persons will not stay in treatment for obesity. Of those who stay in treatment, most will not lose weight, and of those who do lose weight, most will regain it." That was 1958. We are all hardwired to hold on to our habits. That's why it's important to be careful what habits we encourage as a nation.

What's Your Default?

As I will delve into a little deeper in the next chapter, your brain is basically a Pattern Recognition Storage System. What this means is your brain will always seek out the path of least resistance in order to bring you back to a place of familiarity as this is what is experienced as comfort. In other words, what is familiar to us becomes most comfortable to the brain and the brain works to fall back upon this as often as possible. Yes, even if that comfort is your excess body fat.

It's hard to believe we are quite literally hardwired to default back to the familiar because it is the most obvious place of comfort, even if it is the most destructive (i.e. obesity). Knowing about your brain's default switch is a key to understanding that you are literally in control of your body either storing or burning fat; especially through the messages we receive from our environment, both external and internal.

A half-century later, despite billions of dollars and hours spent on the Holy Grail of weight loss—an approach where people lose weight and keep it off—the obesity epidemic continues unabated. Recognizing the obesity epidemic as one of the greatest public health threats ever facing humanity, scientists have become determined to crack the obesity code. However, as you can deduce from the dismal success of most diets, we're far from anything that could be considered progress.

It's not for a lack of trying: billions of tax dollars have been spent on obesity research. Obesity research centers have popped up in universities around the globe. Entire nutrition departments have shifted research away from areas like vitamins and minerals to focus wholeheartedly on the new disease—obesity, without even giving a second thought to the possibility that at least part of the problem may lie in the lack of these essential nutrients the body—and metabolism—so desperately needs. To give you an idea of the money being thrown at this issue, the National Institute of Health (NIH) has invested a staggering $100 million dollars on just three large-scale research studies.

What golden-fried nuggets can we glean from this remarkable effort? Despite newspaper headlines frequently promising one weight loss breakthrough after another, the reality is much less hopeful. In 1997, a group of ambitious British researchers tried to make sense of the piles of weight loss studies. The first thing they noticed was the fundamental elements of study design, such as randomization and following subjects over a time period long enough for meaningful results, were relatively nonexistent. After sifting through 10,000 research studies, one by one, they were disappointed to find that only 97 fit their criteria for research quality. Not to be deterred, these scientists analyzed the data from those 97 studies. In a mind-boggling declaration, the authors proclaimed, "...much uncertainty remains over the most effective interventions for the treatment of adult obesity." Unfortunately, thirteen years of additional research hasn't been able to close the gap. A 2008 review concluded, "More research is urgently needed to extend the body of evidence."

Again, 97 studies with contradicting results that finally concluded with "uncertainty" undoubtedly sum up the kind of data that experts have to rely on when making recommendations. It's no wonder that many patients are confused about what works and what doesn't because doctors and dietitians don't know either.

A lack of a unified message from health care professionals – people that we've been raised to trust – has led to desperation and bewilderment for all parties. One thing is clear; more laboratory research isn't going to solve this growing problem. Nutrition professor, Martijn Katan, Ph.D., from the Institute of Health Sciences at VU University in Amsterdam, puts it best. "We do not need another diet trial; we need a change of paradigm."

The Low-Fat Movement

How did a scarcity of conclusive data become corrupted to the point that David Kritchevsky, Ph.D., one of the most influential researchers on diet and health of the 20th century, can accurately summarize our view on dietary fat as, "...we no longer fear God or the Communists, but we fear fat?"

The low-fat movement, which has only recently begun to be questioned, started out without much consideration toward obesity, which was somewhat rare until the late 1970s. Rather, the low-fat movement was created to eradicate the new killer of North Americans after World War II: heart disease. However, in the last 30 years, the US and Canadian governments and the food industry have essentially teamed up to spread the message that fat is "bad" for both weight and general health, but with what evidence and more importantly, at what cost?

For the first time since Upton Sinclair published *The Jungle*, we were afraid of food. A handful of pivotal decisions have painted fat as the dietary equivalent of a nutrition super villain. It's a nutrient so dastardly that it's believed to cause not only heart disease and cancer, but obesity as well. Surprisingly, the anti-fat campaign did not begin with a landmark research study or outspoken scientists, but with a senator.

In 1968, South Dakota's George McGovern initially formed his Select Committee on Nutrition and Human Needs to fight a problem almost unheard of today: eradicating malnutrition in the US. As malnutrition became replaced with over-nutrition, the focus of the committee gradually shifted toward the emerging threat of heart disease. A report entitled, *The Soft Science of Dietary Fat* concluded, "McGovern's staff members - they almost single-handedly changed nutritional policy in this country and initiated the process of turning the dietary fat hypothesis into dogma."

Unscientific Science

In a series of critical steps, this committee spun the science into a concept that anyone off the street could latch onto: *fat is bad for you*. It began when McGovern's committee was put in charge of crafting a new set of dietary guidelines for Americans. Who did McGovern choose to dictate the official American stance on diet and health? Did he choose a top scientist, a highly-respected professor of nutrition, or a panel of elite cardiologists? Not quite. The individual chosen for the task of writing the 1977 "Dietary Goals for the United States," a document meant to embody contemporary scientific thought on diet and health, was none other than a *Providence Journal* beat writer with no scientific or nutritional expertise whatsoever. Worse yet, the report was based almost entirely on one man's anecdotal observations. Harvard researcher Mark Hegsted, Ph.D., who was a strong believer in the connection between fat and heart disease, ignored the sizeable group of scientists who weren't convinced that fat had much, if anything, to do with heart health.

How the consensus of a single scientist and a journalist became the mouthpiece for the entire scientific community for the next three decades is not abundantly clear. Many blame the media with their magnetic attraction to simplicity. Some hold politicians responsible for perpetuating the dubious connection between high fat intake and health before the data was there to back it up. Others feel that the scientific community holds the most accountability because they spent billions of research dollars trying to manufacture a connection that simply didn't exist. It just goes to show that with enough money, you can make anyone believe almost anything.

A Food Pyramid Based on Lies?

Letting go of blame for a moment, there's no doubt that fat-phobia only accelerated in the decades to come. Of course, the mascot of the ridiculous myopic view of fat is the much-maligned food pyramid.

The United States Department of Agriculture (USDA) Food Guide Pyramid and Canada's Food Guide to Healthy Eating (yes, the one with the colorful rainbow design) were both released to the public in 1992. These are the same food guides that close to 80% of people can instantly recognize and they more than illustrate the government's commitment to fat-phobia. They're also the same ones that cause millions of people to scratch their heads in disbelief as they stand on their bathroom scales crying out, "I don't get it! I followed that food pyramid's guidelines to a tee."

As you may recall from the US pyramid, "fats, oils, and sweets" are all lumped into a single category that appears at the very tip of the pyramid, meaning we should eat them "sparingly." The pyramid actually has the gall to present images of saltine crackers, rice, and white pasta at its large base, while spurning high-fat, yet incredibly healthy foods like extra virgin olive oil and nuts, to imprisonment within the pyramid's short tip. You may wonder how grains ended up becoming the literal foundation of the American diet. While many cry foul about the USDA's links to agribusiness, it had more to do with a process of elimination based entirely on grains than limited fat composition. Heck, we had to eat *something*, didn't we?

Another strike against fat was its well-known caloric density. Pound for pound, fat has more than double the calories of protein or carbohydrates (fat has nine calories per gram, while protein and carbohydrates have four). When doctors and nutritionists began looking around and noticing people getting fatter, common sense dictated that reducing fat would be the easiest way to decrease calories due to the calorically-dense property of fat. Actually, pinning fat as not only the cause of heart attacks, but obesity as well was a tidy way to tie in two messages together and kill two birds with one greasy stone.

But, it turned out that it was scientists and public health officials who were dense. This narrow-minded view of fat and weight ignores the pivotal contribution that dietary fat plays in the health of our bodies. For example, our brain is predominantly made up of fat, which means you and I are actually *fat heads*.

Preliminary research suggesting that low-fat diets helped people drop pounds ignored the simple and long-standing belief that any diet which restricts calories should, in fact, induce weight loss. It turns out, the composition of the foods we consume, such as protein, carbs, and fats, may actually be more important than the total number of calories coming from our food choices. For instance, studies using well-designed testing methods have shown that the relative composition of protein, carbs, and fats in the diet does matter, and reducing fat may be the worst way to go. A 2006 study published in the *Archives of Internal Medicine* compared a battery of weight loss diets and found that a low-fat diet performed the worst. "Most of us would have predicted that if we can get the population to change its fat intake, with its dense calories, we would see a reduction in weight," said nutrition researcher William Harlan, MD. "Instead, we see the exact opposite."

Regardless of fat's actual impact on weight, it's fair to say that the fat-phobia message has sunk in. Since the Dietary Goals for the United States and Canada went public, our intake of calories from fat has dropped from 40% to 36%. Of course, this modest reduction in fat intake has coincided with an explosion of obesity and diabetes, the likes of which the world has never seen.

The Bulging Lite Industry

With fat demonized as the cause of North America's number one killer, as well as our bulging waistlines, it wasn't long before food manufacturers, armed with a virtual mandate from public health officials, created a very lucrative new market – *light foods*. Light or "lite" foods are nothing new. In fact, it didn't take long for food companies to see dollar signs every time a new fat-phobic study was reported in the news, and the media was only too eager to play along.

Back in 1982, the *New York Times* published a frighteningly prophetic article headlined, "How the 'Light' Foods Are Conquering America." It's fair to say that in the over 30 years since that article was written, lite foods completely crushed our meager defenses and ultimately conquered us.

Houdini of Nutrition

The stranglehold of lite foods has only become tighter as more lite foods enter the marketplace every year. There are 17,000 new food products every year, many of which are classified as "lite" foods. More than a simple results-by-volume approach, the food industry has even refined their techniques to increase their effectiveness. In essence, the lite products fool us by preying on the weaknesses of three body parts most crucial to food evaluation: the mind, mouth, and eyes.

Despite natural skepticism, the lite food smoke-and-mirror trickery is successful in making us believe that the processed food industry will lead us to a tasty salvation. Indeed, research shows that while we may be wary of health claims, we tend to ultimately trust the vast majority of them. For a fighting chance against the over-hyped adjectives and misleading claims, you must have a salient understanding of just how far the makers of lite foods go to hoax you.

The first thing that should set off alarms is if a food is advertised as "new." Forgetting for the moment that the healthiest foods out there were created millions of years ago and not by man, the promotion of a food's youthful age fools us by stimulating our evolutionary desire to seek novelty. For our thrill-seeking brain, there's nothing new and exciting about a grape. On the other hand, a brand new lite product jam-packed with a so-called "super food" speaks directly to our intense desire to find the next big thing. Not only does this claim drive us to buy, but it drives us to eat more of the product. It's a feat with a double whammy that many food marketing tricks are designed to elicit. For a yet to be understood reason, people eat more when there's a perception that there are lots of different versions of food in the marketplace (i.e. a lite version of a mainstream food). Researchers have found that simply presenting a few extra jelly bean flavors caused people to eat 69% more of the candy. Simply put, variety induces overeating, and lite foods add a layer of variety to almost every food we've grown up with.

Subtly, and not so subtly, lite products also suggest that, by their nature of being new, they are inherently more advanced than everything else out there. As *New York Times* bestselling author, Michael Pollan, points out in, *In Defense of Food: An Eater's Manifesto* (Penguin, 2009), we eat about 40% of our calories from only three sources: wheat, soy, and vegetable oil, all of which were never part of our metabolic evolution. Any newfangled product is simply a recomposition of these three foods with a benign amount of the nutrient flavor of the month thrown in for good measure. While lite foods may be low in calories, they are some of the most intensely processed products in the food supply.

Madison Avenue's Marketing Magic

For us to look past the hodgepodge of artificial ingredients and additives, marketers' favorite trick is to plaster food packaging with words we associate with health and leanness -"lite" being the epitome of this tactic. Speaking of lite foods, when did "lite" ever become a real word? When food companies plastered it on the front of every packaged food they legally could, that's when. It's as if by shortening the "light" we know and love by one letter the healthy quality is more profoundly felt. Of course it is, it's new.

More than anything else, lite foods take full advantage of the fact that most people are too darn busy, stressed, and overwhelmed with options to closely investigate the food packages in front of them. We don't flinch when confronted with a lite food because we take "lite" to mean it is good for our health and weight. It settles the debate right there on the spot: *this will make me thin because it's "lite."* And let's not forget that when a food is "lite," we get to eat loads more of it because there is no way we can become fat from a lite food. Unfortunately, North America is bulging at the seams with people who have put that theory to the test.

"Lite" isn't the only buzzword marketers use to trick us into thinking their product will help us drop pounds. Adjectives abound on today's food labels. As soon as you walk through the doors of your local supermarket or grocery store, you're inundated with health claims at every turn: "reduced fat," "low fat," "no fat," "less sodium," "whole grains," "omega-3's," "good source of fiber," "natural," etc. It's only a matter of time before a health claim will be found on literally every single food item on the shelf. Of course, even though the FDA regulates the claims that appear on packaging, through the ingenuity of marketers, most health claims generally amount to nothing and are the processed food equivalent of lipstick on a pig (unless of course you're Miss Piggy).

Minimum Requirements

It would require an entire book to divulge the true meaning of every health claim out there, from "reduced fat" to "lower calories" to "excellent source of x and y." The claim that best epitomizes the deception is the claim that a food is "healthy." Can't argue with that can you? After all, the government allows it and when does the government ever lie? This seemingly black and white term, which by law, states that the food must contain no more than three grams of fat (including one gram of saturated fat) and 60 milligrams of cholesterol per serving. The food must also contain ten percent of the daily value of one of these nutrients: vitamin A, vitamin C, calcium, iron, protein, or fiber.

Pretty straightforward, right? Those sound like fairly unremarkable benchmarks for a food to meet to receive the FDA official stamp of healthiness. However, using their guidelines, dozens of foods most dieters should avoid like the plague, including soft drinks (yes, even if they're vitamin and mineral fortified), pass the healthy litmus test while some of the healthiest foods on Earth (salmon, flaxseed, spinach, or almonds anyone?) don't make the cut. Perhaps the greatest beneficiary of the FDA's misguided fat-phobic labeling rules has been lite foods, which tend to be high in sugar and low in fat. Needless to say, they've taken this competitive advantage and run with it.

Food manufactures are having a field day with product labeling. It's helping them move items off the shelf, and more importantly, shift eyeballs and attention away from the bland produce section and into the center aisles where the action takes place. Bogus health claims are causing palatable swings in the way we spend our food dollars. Since 1978, the time that lite foods started to become mainstream, we have spent 180% more of every dollar at the grocery store on processing and marketing and less and less on fresh fruits and vegetables—the *real* health foods.

Obviously, the marketing doesn't start and end within the confines of the grocery store. The images and messages we see on TV, on the internet, and in print gradually shape our beliefs about what will help us be thin and trim. Seven billion dollars are spent every year to convince us to buy one food over another. The battle for a slice of our food budget isn't between a Special K® protein bar and a can of beans. It's between two slightly different lite versions of the same basic highly-processed concoction. Unfortunately, foods proven by research to facilitate weight loss might as well be invisible. Just 2% of all food advertisements are for fruits, veggies, whole grains (the real ones), and legumes. The medium also plays a part in the overexposure of lite foods. Seventy-five percent of food marketing is on television, which leads me to ask: When was the last time you saw a commercial during the NFL™ championship game for a tomato?

FDA Oversights

You may picture a lab coat wearing scientist peering judgmentally at every food label with a magnifying glass before it hits your local grocery store shelf. Not so. We're living in the food label equivalent of the Wild West where rules are sparse and enforcement is practically nonexistent. Even the "rules" that currently exist are being broken every day due to the lack of oversight. According to a report by the Center for Science in the Public Interest, "While the FDA has devoted more money to dietary-supplement issues, its resources for key nutritional health, food labeling, and fraud programs have been cut by more than half over the last decade." Harvard researchers have found that "countries with more food laws have lower levels of obesity." Lite foods mislead consumers every day. You really have to cross the line to get caught. It took the cereal Cheerios® comparing itself to statin medications (think Crestor® and Lipitor®) for the control of high blood pressure for the FDA to step in and finally call a halt to their advertising claims.

Serving Sizes

If you're able to machete your way through the jungle of bogus health claims, you just might reach the nutrition facts label on the side of a packaged food. If you're like most people, your eyes tend to drift toward calories and total fat. The especially health conscious consumer might even take a gander at fiber or protein. Regardless, most people skip right over the most crucial area of any nutrition facts label: the serving size.

Food manufactures love to manipulate the serving size to make a food's caloric content have an air-like quality. Most serving sizes are well below what most people are willing to eat. A great example of this is in a box of Snackwells® reduced fat cookies (and oh boy, are they tasty). A quick once-over before you dig in gives you the impression that you're about to eat a mere 110 calories. However, because the serving size is a paltry pair of quarter-sized cookies, you're much more likely to eat a typical eight cookies—or 440 calories. In reality, you will soon learn that it doesn't matter how many calories a food has in a serving. What matters is how many calories you actually end up eating and, more importantly, where those calories are coming from.

It turns out that how much we eat at a sitting is to a great extent determined by the health claim on the label. The more lite foods we eat, the better we feel about the decision. A Quaker Oats© spokesman calls the emergence of lite foods a "nothing-to-lose situation" and added that replacing real food with lite food "allows people to cut down on calories while still enjoying their food and not reducing volume."

The Lite Halo Effect

When referring to lite foods, "nothing-to-lose" should be more aptly phrased "unable to lose." We now know that lite foods lead to the "lite halo effect" – eating more of a food just because we perceive it as healthy. Researchers know that what harms us the most about lite foods isn't the simple fact that it forces our hand away from a claim-less apple to a low-fat diet bar, but it's what we do once we've bought it. We eat a lot more of it.

An unscientific, but illustrative study shows it doesn't take much for us to dramatically change the way we view food once it has a health claim slapped on it. *New York Times* writer John Tierney teamed up with a French scientist to see how influential health claims were in assessing calories—even if the assertion was completely unrelated to calories. To do so, Tierney set up shop in Brooklyn's über health-conscious Park Slope neighborhood and asked passers-by to evaluate the calories in a picture of an Applebee's® Oriental Chicken Salad. While the volunteers tended to actually overestimate the caloric contribution of the meal by about 70 calories, this all changed with the addition of a health claim-tagged food.

When volunteers saw the same meal with two trans-fat free crackers added to the picture, their judgment became notably skewed. Instead of estimating that the salad and cracker combination contained more calories than the salad alone because the crackers added about 100 calories, the volunteers actually underestimated the calories in the meal. Counterintuitively, adding food caused a 270-calorie estimation swing in the wrong direction.

Cornell University researchers also set out to see if the lite halo effect is something that influences our perception and our behavior. The scientists split a set of 250 people into two groups. One group received a hefty bowl of standard M&M's® and another received the same bowl, but this time with the title of "low-fat" M&M's®. Everything was identical between the two sets of M&M's®, including the fat content. The only thing that separated the two groups was whether they were told that the M&M's® in the bowl in front of them were low-fat or normal.

The influence of two seemingly innocuous words surprised even the researchers. People ate dramatically more of the candy if it was considered to be low-fat. Regardless of weight, the low-fat claim turned plain old M&M's® into a catalyst for overeating. However, the light halo effect hit the very people who needed it the least the hardest. Those who were overweight, and presumably trying to lose weight, ate 50% more M&M's® when the M&M's® were paired with a low-fat label. This effect was dampened for people of normal weight. Also, the simple act of describing M&M's® as low-fat caused people to think they ate half of what they actually put into their mouths. Not surprisingly, the overweight participants performed the worst at the serving size estimation.

What causes our senses to frazzle in the face of two simple words that you'd think we'd be desensitized to by now? According to the authors of the M&M's® study, three factors are at play:

First, when we see a food as low-fat, we also see it as having fewer calories. Our perception here is right on because low-fat and lite foods generally have fewer calories than the standard version of that same food. Therefore, you might assume that because the low-fat food has fewer calories, an extra few handfuls of lower-calorie M&M's® ends up balancing out. When the M&M's® researchers put that theory to the test, they found that assumption to be false. Low-fat foods, even if they are lower in calories, coerce us into eating 10% more total calories than if we went with a so-called normal version of the same food.

Secondly, when we see a food as "lite," we adjust our perception of serving size accordingly. While ice cream made with pure sugar and cream may unconsciously prod us into ordering a small cone, the lite version seems to hypnotize us into splurging on a triple scoop and in the process letting loose the small kid within us (or stealing the kid's cone beside us).

Finally, the third factor that seems to have the most weight is that low-fat foods make us feel less guilty about eating them. Guilt is known to be a more prevalent emotion in North American eaters than those in Europe or Japan. Every time we make a decision, particularly in the realm of food, a battle ensues. The area of your brain hardwired for immediate gratification implores you to go for it and chow down on that blueberry muffin. In opposition, your long-term planning centers remind you that while the muffin might be tasty now, it's going to end up as an extra layer of flab. In our minds, the low-fat label instantly transforms a food from a guilt-laden flab promoter to God's gift to your waistline. What was once a fattening treat is now something that's not just neutral, but with enough health claims, actually good for us even though the actual food hasn't changed one bit.

The Lesson

The moral of this story is that health claims should be ignored. All that's required for a health claim to appear on a package is some ingenuity from savvy marketers and food scientists who are willing to do a thirty second internet search for a single flawed research study to prop up the claim.

Lite foods make you gain weight, not lose it. The reality is that fat loss is multi-factorial and calories-in versus calories-out is a gross generalization and one that is often wrong. How else can you explain the fact that olive oil—a food that's one of the most calorically dense on the planet and is consumed by the gallons in the Mediterranean— has been independently associated with healthy weight?

By now, you must realize that micromanaging calories by turning to lite food is not exactly a wise choice. If anything, as the M&M's® study showed us, eating a food based on calories alone makes a bad situation worse.

The link between your mind and your weight goes much deeper than health claim trickery. In fact, new research is shining a light on the fact that the brain, and not the stomach or mouth, is the primary roadblock to most people's success.

In the realm of epigenetics, the expression of our genes can shift toward fat accumulation when too many of the wrong foods are consumed too much of the time. From the research, one can argue that "lite foods," or "low fat," and "no fat" foods are wrong when it comes to the genetic expression of our metabolic machinery. Simply put, these foods are messing with our inherent program and creating havoc with our metabolisms. The main problem is that our mind ultimately controls what we will and will not become. New science shows that it is also within our ability to change the program and in the process the expression of the genes that can ultimately control the fate of our 30 billion fat cells.

So, you see, it's quite simple. It's all up to you and no one else.

CHAPTER 3 – Leave the Fat Suit on the Hanger

Megan lunges for the paper as it emerges from her computer printer. She's so excited she can't stop fidgeting in anticipation, waiting to read the magic words that will be on the page. One of her Facebook friends posted that new diet they found online, and from what Megan already knew about it, this one was finally going to be the perfect one for her. "This time is going to be different," she says, trying to mentally delete the other twelve diets she attempted before this one. The Bathroom Diet is definitely going to do the trick, she thought. Look at how thin the girl is in the picture.

She grips the information in her hand and her eyes hurriedly read over the directions. This diet instructs you to move into your bathroom. Don't worry; you won't be alone because your computer, TV, and a stack of magazines can come with you. The philosophy of this diet is that it can't fail because there's nothing edible in the bathroom except plenty of calorie free water and the constant reminder of your inflated figure reflected in the mirror and on the bathroom scale. Your food cravings will simply flush away. "It's a fool proof plan," Megan remarks as she fantasizes about her new, trim body. For an entire week, Megan adjusts to life in her bathroom. The dripping sink is a bit annoying, but she's never been cleaner or leaner. The convenience of the shower and the scale has made sure of that.

"How long is this one going to last?" asks her husband, Mark. While he understands his wife's desire to be healthy and trim, he's a little perturbed that she's on yet another diet, and this one takes her away from him. The last one had her eating cheese all day, another one had her on nothing more than miracle wafers, and then there was the one where she drank water with hot pepper sauce. Those other regimens also had Megan stuck in the bathroom all day long, but for entirely different reasons. Heaven forbid if *he* needed to use the bathroom. "Go use the one down the hall," she says to him, wondering why men never appreciate all the effort women go through.

With ten pounds of weight finally gone, Megan starts to spend every other night in her comfy bed curled up next to Mark again, instead of a cold tile floor covered with pillows and blankets. As the days pass, she shuffles out of the bathroom and onto her much more relaxing living room couch with an increasing frequency to watch TV. Eventually, as she starts spending most of her time outside of the four walls of the bathroom, her weight creeps back up.

Fed up with her backwards progress, Megan blames herself for a lack of willpower. Instead of seeing how absurd it is to make up a diet based on a certain room in her house, Megan turns her anger and frustration inward and loses hope. That is until her old college roommate sends her an e-mail about the new Psychic Diet. This is one where you pay a woman in Louisiana to tell you which of your past lives was traumatic enough to cause your present life situation. Megan is stoked again and has a new spark in her step. She hopes to lose a few pounds and also find out if she was anyone interesting or famous in her previous lives.

Obesogenic Society

Losing weight and keeping it off is often referred to as "effortless," "simple," "automatic," and "easy" by fad-diet experts, diet books, exercise videos, gyms, and the lite foods industry. If the ability to not only drop pounds but also stop them from ever coming back is so easy that it can be offered in exchange for $19.95, then why can't everyone seem to do it?

The answer, of course, is that maintaining weight loss is far from easy. If it were that simple, the statistics I showed you in the preceding chapters wouldn't exist and medical journals wouldn't report long-term weight loss as "exceptional." But the question remains: why do we get fat again and again? Scientists claim we live in an "obesogenic" society; one that makes obesity inevitable. According to them, today's modern world has created a "collision of the genome" – where our primitive hardwiring is at odds with our food-plenty and exercise-deprived world.

Once again, this brings us close to the epigenetic story and the role our environment plays in our present situation. Our inability to adapt to this new environment has been compared to a polar bear being thrust into the desert. Just as the polar bear adapted over millions of years to cold, our bodies adapted a long time ago to a food-scarce world designed to keep on the fat in order to save us from the impending calorie-deprived setting.

Considering today's food-abundant world, this theory assumes that being fat is like death and taxes: a sure thing. These experts say the only time we can ever get thin is when we work our tails off long enough to fight society's strong pull toward fatness. Eventually, however, we tire from swimming upstream and let the tide of our calorie-ridden world take us under.

Why You Eat

Another group of doctors and dietitians feel that weight maintenance issues stem from a lack of knowledge. Volumes of medical journals have been written about the fact that the "right" weight maintenance knowledge is some sort of missing link. Indeed, millions of dollars are spent on public health messages imploring us to stop smoking, eat more vegetables, and to go for daily strolls in the park. The mentality is, *if only people knew what to do, the problem would go away.*

As was the case of dietary fat, the experts are wrong again. *Dirty Diets* calls many of these weight regain assumptions into question – citing research, case studies, and chunks of wisdom from psychologists who specialize in weight issues.

We've already established that we don't have to keep handing the diet industry a cut of our monthly paycheck to become thin and healthy, which may lead to a fatter wallet. If the diet industry doesn't have the solution, then the $80 billion dollar question is, who does?

You do!

Despite the deck being stacked against you in certain uncontrollable ways, an emerging body of research has uncovered that when it comes to sustaining our weight loss success, we're our own worst enemy. In other words, it's not a matter of *what* you eat, but *why* you eat.

Those people you know who lost weight and never looked back? They may talk non-stop about the merits of marathon gym sessions and vegetarian diets, but there's something deep inside their brain, cells and genes that made the switch and allowed their weight loss results to last longer than your average *American Idol* contestant.

Blame it on Your Subconscious Mind

When I say deep inside the brain's cells and genes, I mean it. Deep within us lays our subconscious mind, which is the decision-making part of the brain you can't hear that acts without your permission. For most people, it's the subconscious mind that derails diet results more than any reduced-fat cake could ever hope to do. Simply put, most people sabotage their diet's success. Yes, you do and in the process you activate the wrong genes that are responsible for keeping you fat.

I'm going to warn you, this isn't the typical diet book self-help talk. This isn't another tired discussion about calories or grams of fiber either. It's about your deepest, darkest fears and self-defeating psychological issues. Perhaps you chase after fad diets because you know they won't work. The fact that you regain all the weight you lost might actually be because you aren't ready to deal with the real problems in your life. In other words, you aren't willing—or able—to shed the protective blanket you've become so comfortably snuggled up in all these years. Deep stuff.

Your first reaction to hearing this may be, "That's crazy. I want to change and I've worked my butt off to lose every pound I've ever lost, why would I purposely try to put it all back on?" As hard as it may be to believe or accept, being fat has its upsides. All the dieting, calorie counting, food weighing, and low-fat snack munching has afforded you the necessary distraction so you never had to ask yourself, "Is my fat attached to me or am I attached to my fat?"

Dr. Eddie Selby, Ph.D., a clinical psychologist from Florida State University, has often been referred to as a "self-sabotage" expert. Dr. Selby speaks for many psychologists when he says, "Most of the time, there are a number of positive factors that play a role in self-sabotaging behaviors." Our conscious mind tends to dwell on the drawbacks of being fat: "I can't fit into my jeans," "I'm a heart attack waiting to happen," etc. On the other hand, there's a certain level of psychological gain from being fat that oftentimes goes completely undetected.

Comfort Fat

The most noteworthy thing about fat is that the layers of it on our body provide us with a protective mechanism—a blanket of sorts—to shield ourselves from the rest of the world. Many of us wish to be invisible, and because this isn't possible, we turn to the next best thing: being fat. Because obesity is stigmatizing, the part of our brain that seeks societal withdrawal is actually drawn to the possibility that being fat equals being ignored. While fat-induced anonymity is true in a broad, society-wide sense, it also applies to intimate relationships.

While loved ones bring unique opportunities of joy, companionship, and camaraderie, they also force us to connect and open up – two things that leave us open to the possibility of rejection and judgment. For those with a low sense of self-worth, obesity allows them to forgo close relationships to avoid rejection or emotional hurt. It has been documented in various studies that many people gain weight to prevent sexual or romantic advances and that this avoidance stems from the fear of loss or as remnants of abuse. The weight is like a nightclub bouncer keeping meaningful interpersonal attachment from getting in.

Others use their weight as a unified excuse for failure. You may assume that weight is the only thing holding you back from health, wealth, and happiness. Therefore, weight loss is the panacea you need. The media perpetuates this mindset as it often portrays thin people as happier and better off than their fatter counterparts. However, the subconscious mind knows your situation isn't as cut and dry as that. It realizes your circumstances are the result of hundreds of mitigating factors, many of which have nothing to do with how much you weigh. This is why countless people get depressed after losing weight. They realize their hopes and dreams weren't dependent on one factor and they have to finally face the decisions they made that got them to where they are. It's a lot easier to point the blame at a single factor than to face reality.

Certain people may actually fail at dieting as an attention-seeking behavior, oftentimes as a reflection of a low self-worth. The ups and downs of dieting are something many people can relate to. Dieting battle scars bring on a lot of pity from others. Self-worth issues like these, which can originate from unsupportive or abusive loved ones, often cultivate self-fulfilling prophecies. Our world tends to unfairly associate weight with worth, so not being able to "cut it" or "fit in" and instead staying fat reinforces the idea that we're just not good enough.

Food as a Distraction

One of the most common uses of being fat is as a distraction. Dealing with deeply-rooted, painful issues isn't easy. It's much easier to distract yourself. Food is one of the best ways to divert attention away from the hard questions. Steven Stosny, Ph.D., author of *Love Without Hurt*, calls this "core value eating," which is eating in order to drown out emotional pain. He says, "The connection between core hurts and high-energy, high-sensory food is irresistible." Because food stimulates our mind, taste buds, and requires an appreciable amount of time to think about, prepare, and enjoy, food may be the perfect distraction. We put our box of chocolate chip cookies in the closet right alongside our skeletons.

Dieting—especially work-heavy fad diets—are another detour from emotional confrontation. A mind focused on the pounds on the scale isn't thinking about the parents that were never quite supportive enough. Once the weight comes off; however, the focus inevitably shifts and it opens a Pandora's Box of emotional issues.

The behavior that feeds these self-sabotaging actions is emotional eating, which is consumption without regard to hunger signals. Everyone emotionally eats at one point or another in their lifetime. If you think about it, our society is centered around meals and food (can you imagine serving water on Thanksgiving or inviting your neighbors over just to talk). Research shows that people who weigh the most are much more likely to eat in response to their internal mood. If this sounds familiar, if emotional eating supersedes hunger-oriented eating, that's a red flag that self-sabotage is at play.

One of the most successful women of all time, Oprah Winfrey, has struggled mightily with emotional eating. "How can I hide myself?" are words you wouldn't expect to hear from one of the most visible people on the planet. Yet, that's how she felt in 2009 when her weight ballooned to over 200 pounds. "What I've learned this year is that my weight issue isn't about eating less or working out harder, or even about a malfunctioning thyroid. It's about my life being out of balance... I don't have a weight problem, I have a self-care problem that manifests through weight," Winfrey said. Like many others, her decision to eat transcended physical needs and served other purposes.

Emotional Eating

Why do we emotionally eat? A study published in Qualitative Health Research found that people's drive to emotionally eat is "not about the food." Even though sugary foods have a magnetic-like attraction to painful emotions, the food itself isn't the driving force. In order to maintain the fat that's essential as a prop for our coping mechanism, we have to eat more than our stomach tells us we require. But emotional eating can also serve another important purpose: substituting as a loved one. When psychologists study the emotions people experience after they've lost weight, a consistent theme is that many of them are mourning the "loss of a friend." In some ways, food is more reliable than a loved one.

It's not uncommon for overweight people to project the values they look for in another human being onto food. Food is commonly referred to as "reliable," "comforting," and even "understanding" – all things we crave in the ones we love. When we lack emotional attachment or a strong social circle, for example, we literally fill the emptiness we feel inside with food.

The pattern of emotional eating is quite predictable. Let's face it; most people don't emotionally eat carrots. For that matter, when we are under emotional duress, we tend to over-consume the very foods that make us fat and keep us in that state. When emotions drive our eating decisions, entire bags of cookies and chips are left in the wake. Mental health professionals call this binge eating disorder (BED), which is a clinically-diagnosed condition afflicting up to 20% of people who struggle with weight. Along with easing emotional pain, BED derails the progress of healthy, new lifestyle changes, causing many to give up and revert back to old habits.

Science backs up the idea that BED and emotional avoidance go hand-in-hand. French researchers have independently correlated *alexithymia* (a mental state characterized by an inability or unwillingness to express emotions) with BED. The study's authors theorized that people binge to "avoid performing psychic work." In a way, our unexpressed emotions are literally being drowned out by the food-focused voices in our head telling us to overeat, as well as the self-deprecating voices that punish us for doing so.

The After-Effects of Bariatric Surgery

How do we know that weight regain comes about because we sabotage our success, and not just because of the obesogenic environment we live in? Studies on the emotions of bariatric surgery patients give us tremendous insight into the mentality that develops from someone having a completely new body, but being stuck with the same mind. Because it isn't physically possible for bariatric surgery patients to regain their weight until about a year post-op, they're forced to face their issues. Sure enough, when many of them lose weight, previously unknown psychological issues sprout up.

Bariatric surgery (which includes gastric bypass and banding) is now one of the most common surgeries in North America. It almost always causes rapid weight loss that's irreversible until months or years down the road. Along with the surgery's well-documented physical risks, new studies are shining light on the emotional trauma these patients undergo. A recent study in the journal *Archives of Surgery* found the suicide rate after bariatric surgery to be at least five times that of the general population. Research has also found that people who have had bariatric surgery are more likely to be depressed. Imagine that, you're unhappy because you're walking around with extra weight, and yet when it's gone, you're even unhappier than before.

Are You Emotionally Ready to be Healthy?

How do we know this isn't a chicken or the egg phenomenon? Couldn't these people have been depressed before going under the knife? A study published in the *Journal of the American College of Nutrition* found that one-third of pre-operative bariatric patients, who had no previous signs of depression, suddenly became depressed in the weeks after their surgery. Why would these people, who had weight, not mental problems, and voluntarily embarked on a positive, life-changing experience seeking a new lease on life, be so sad? It boils down to the fact that the mental issues were always there; they were hiding the fat. Once the fat disappeared, these issues could no longer cower behind food or dieting-obsessed thoughts and suddenly appeared front and center.

An article in *Bariatric Times*, written by Dr. Cynthia Alexander, a psychologist who specializes in the area of bariatric surgery, examined the realities of people losing their scapegoat along with their fat. "In my groups, I see a subset of people dealing with the reality that the surgery does not do all the work, and these postoperative patients are struggling once again to control emotional eating. This realization can lead to feelings of depression." People who have undergone bariatric surgery teach us that fat loss is a noble goal, but it isn't a miracle that will turn every facet of your life around.

Think about the many times you've heard stories of people who were down and out with mere pennies in the bank, and then, all of a sudden, they cashed in a lottery ticket worth millions only to blow all the cash in record time to find themselves once again penniless. These people will insist that no one showed them how to live with money; therefore, they reverted back to what made them most comfortable inside, which is being broke. The point is, money doesn't buy happiness any more than a slim physique does. It just makes it easier to enjoy life if you are ready for it.

As I previously mentioned, your brain is a Pattern Recognition Storage System that almost always defaults back to what is most familiar, even if it is something harmful, as in the case of excess fat.

We know emotional issues lie behind dieting failures. Whether it's for comfort, distraction, or companionship, food is an incredibly accessible and effective way to drown out the voices in our own head. We don't call them "comfort foods" for the fun of it. The weight that accompanies emotional eating only helps create a lard-laden moat between us and the rest of the world. If your diet demons continue to pull the strings behind the scenes and steer you toward failure, all of your efforts will eventually crash and burn.

I placed this chapter early in the book because I want to give you the tools and skills to get your mind ready for the new and improved body you're about to mold. Of course, our self-defeating binge eating sessions are orchestrated from the subconscious mind – making it more difficult to pinpoint why you're constantly setting yourself up to fail. As weight-loss specialist and author, Loree Taylor Jordan, proclaims, "No matter how motivated you think you are, none of your reasons for losing weight will work for you if the subconscious reasons for keeping the weight are stronger." Take heart, though, later on in *Dirty Diets*, I'm going to give you the special tools you need to reprogram your subconscious mind and reset that faulty default switch.

The First Step is Awareness

As with any self-help program aimed at getting to the heart of an issue, the first step is awareness. It's going to take a little work. Okay, make that a lot of work. Jeffrey Willber, Ph.D., a psychologist, whose specialty is helping people identify and destroy their underlying emotional issues, calls these issues "fattitudes." He calls the self-discovery process an "unnatural act" for people who are fat. He's right on when he says, "Overeaters live their life in self-protective ignorance for so long that stopping and facing directly what lies inside is a terrifying change." Terrifying, challenging, and even painful, yes, but it's also necessary. The only way to lose fat for good is to squash the self-defeating behaviors that are causing the fat in the first place.

Therapy is one option. For those who scream, "I don't need a shrink," consider for a moment just how deeply ingrained these eating habits and attitudes are. It may take an expert to help you dig them out so they see the light of day. Therapy can also help you overcome alexithymia – giving you a calorie-free outlet for your repressed emotions. In fact, a study done by researchers at the University of Birmingham in England found that therapy sessions aimed at combating emotional eating were more successful at long-term weight loss than most calorie-cutting programs (no big surprise here). I'm not going to coerce anyone into a therapy session, but because of the tremendous boon therapy can have on your mental and physical health, it's something you may wish to consider.

Self-Monitoring

Luckily, you don't have to rely on a therapist to do some soul-searching. One of the best ways to bring awareness into your eating choices is by daily self-monitoring. Make it a habit to write down the feelings, emotions, circumstances, and events that occur when you eat— especially when you overeat. It won't take long for patterns to jump off the page – giving you a whole new perspective on why you couldn't stop yourself from finishing that entire pint of Ben & Jerry's™ ice cream in one sitting.

Another pen and paper exercise, recommended by Eddie Selby, is to record the rewards of fatness. I've already presented many of these possibilities, from withdrawal to sheer distraction. However, everyone is different, and you might have your own underlying reasons for being fat. Shifting focus away from the apparent negatives and onto your personal benefits may reveal why you've been sabotaging your own efforts.

Exercises like this can bring out the "core hurt eating" that's underlying dieting letdowns. Ultimately, the goal is to replace your hurt eating with "core value eating." With core value eating, you substitute the focus of eating away from weighing every lettuce leaf, counting calories, and tracking every grams of fat and onto improving the health of your mind and body. Honestly, it took years for these experiences, attitudes, and behaviors to manifest, so it will take a fair amount of time to reverse them. Improvement can be made on a daily basis. It's a journey and not a destination.

Finally, one of the most insightful things you can do is become super-aware whenever you "relapse" from healthy eating. Please remember this is different than relapsing from a fad diet, which tend to be so overly restrictive that it's actually healthy to stop. When a person slips and gorges on five slices of pie, they get angry with themselves for the over-indulgence. If this happens, try to look past the anger and ask yourself *why* you reverted to old habits. Is it more comfortable? Is it deflecting uncomfortable emotions? And, of course, the most pressing question of all is: do you really want to stay fat?

Cheerleaders or Saboteurs

Because no man or woman is an island, it's helpful to look at those around you. Is your spouse, best friends, or favorite co-worker a cheerleader in your life or a saboteur who will stop at nothing to see you fail? Surprisingly, the people we surround ourselves with can also have their own stake invested in your fat. Their own subconscious mind, with another set of issues and problems, may guide your loved one's hands to interfere with your new healthy frame. After all, misery enjoys company.

Why would people you love do this to you? Long ago, Charles Horton Cooley developed the looking-glass theory, which says we judge ourselves largely by subconsciously comparing ourselves to the people around us. For someone close to you, a new and improved body may bring out insecurities and anxiety that you'll be more successful and worthy of attention, leaving them in the dust. Also, if you become one size smaller that makes them one size closer to you. They lose the comparison game. It's important to take note of how the people in your life change when you do. Part of the reason you always bounce back toward fatness may have been that you have a team of people who will stop at nothing to take you off your newly-crafted path.

Social Support and Personal Accountability

I'm sure most people close to you legitimately have your back and are nothing but a reservoir of support. While programs like Weight Watchers® have serious flaws (like the focus on calories over food choices), research shows that their social support keeps people on track.

Brown University researchers took a set of people who recently lost 40 pounds and put them into three groups: one received a newsletter, another got internet support, while the third group met with a counselor face-to-face. They wanted to see which method would help keep the weight from returning, as it always seems to do. Over the course of a year and a half, the group that met with a real person regained less than half the weight (and just five total pounds). Face time, or personal accountability, works.

Self-Image

Another study, this one published in the *Journal of Consulting and Clinical Psychology*, concluded that people who received typical weight loss counseling along with support from a friend had a 40% better chance of keeping weight off than those who went at it alone. While some people have it out for us, more times than not, leaning on someone supportive helps keep the fat boomerang at bay.

The late Dr. Maxwell Maltz, one of the most widely-known and highly-regarded plastic surgeons of our time, once wrote in his mega bestselling book, *Psycho-Cybernetics*, "When you change a man's face, you almost invariably change his future."

But this alteration occurs on a much deeper level than mere cosmetics. It also takes place in personality, behavior, and sometimes even basic talents and abilities.

Dr. Maltz noted that some patients—*no matter how physically altered they are through surgery*—showed no change at all in personality. It was as if nothing had changed, and that in their minds, they still remained scarred or ugly. Dr. Maltz later went on to discover that a person's "self-image" or the true way in which the individual perceived themselves, is the real key to a person's personality and behavior.

We need to change the program (our perception of the environment) before we can ever hope to change our reality. The fat clinging to your body will always serve as a warm, comforting, protective layer unless you do the work necessary to transform your psyche. As you'll see in the next chapter, the emotionally driven eating decisions you make have tremendous biological implications on the hormonal messages that ultimately determine whether you're thin or fat.

CHAPTER 4 – The Skinny on Fat—Why You Store It and How to Burn It

I didn't want to be the one to bring this up, but your pancreas is insisting. It has something it needs to get off your chest. With a job, a mortgage, and a 46" plasma screen TV, you might not think you need to give a second thought to the football-shaped organ that sits in your abdomen, but you should before it's too late. Your pancreas is tired, stressed-out, and overworked. You know, I think I'll just let it say what it needs to say:

"Hi, it's me, your pancreas. Since the day you were born, I've been producing insulin for you when you needed it. No questions asked. Not to get all sentimental on you, but it's been an honor making your insulin all these years. But for a while now, things have been getting a little out of control and I'm starting to feel a taken advantage of. Sure, we've had some tough times before now. Remember when you downed a dozen Hershey bars at summer camp after that snooty girl Hillary said your new bathing suit was so-last-year? That was a doozy of a day.

"You're an adult now, so I'm going to be frank with you. I can't handle all these dirty carbs you're grazing on. Who are we kidding? You're practically swallowing them whole every day. And don't even get me started on those alleged diet bars dipped in fructose. Those are the worst.

"Don't try to tell me I'm exaggerating or am wrong. I can tell by the cinnamon-glazed rice cakes that just came through, you clearly are not paying attention to my cries yet. So allow me give you an idea of my typical workday lately. I'm working diligently, making sure your digestive enzymes are all primed and ready for the next delivery, when suddenly I hear the alarm signal from the upper GI tract screaming out, 'sugar's coming!' I'm not going to lie to you. There were more than a few four-letter words that slipped out when I heard that warning. At that point, I know my day is about to go into overtime because I have to hit the assembly line and pump out insulin like there's no tomorrow.

"Now, you've had a particular hankering for those lite foods as of late, which means you've gotten your hands on yet another fad diet from one of those women's magazines, I presume. It's too much. Insulin signaling is all messed up and I'm a full-out stress case. I don't know if I can keep going on this way. To make a long story short, whether I want to or not, I may have to quit.

"I'm not sure if you know this or not, but when I shoot out a shipment of insulin to you, what happens afterwards is out of my control. I don't want to make you fat, flabby, and tired all the time, but I can't help it. I know I have grease-tinted blood on my hands, but it's not my fault that the insulin I make tells the rest of the body to store fat.

"What I'm trying to say to you is to please cool it with all the lite foods. They're giving me a nervous breakdown and they're making you fatter, not thinner. Honestly, I've been looking at some open positions elsewhere with less demanding hours. I don't want it to come to that, though. If you'll just replace those lite foods with ones that contain actual nutritional value, I'll be happy to stay on as your pancreas."

Cavemen Don't Diet

Flashback 50,000 years: your grey cubicle is suddenly transformed into the green Savannah of our caveman ancestors. Everything is radically altered from the world you know today—and nothing is more different than how we eat. In this environment, even the most ardent present day follower of a Paleolithic diet would be out of his or her element.

Besides the fact that you'd be hard pressed to find a 'lite' version of a gazelle, one of the first things you'd notice is a severe shortage of carbs. You might expect to slowly wither away and die from not getting a bite of bread, rice, or pasta after a few weeks, but truth be told, humans subsisted—and even thrived—on a carb-less diet like this for 50,000 years. Unlike today, with sugar and starch available on every corner, carbs were in short supply, at least by our modern day standards. Stone Age humans largely sustained themselves on meat, which composed 50% of the diet, eggs, vegetables, nuts, and if they were lucky, whole grains and fruits.

One man who takes the hunter-gatherer lifestyle to heart, John Durant, the author of *The Paleo Manifesto: Ancient Wisdom for Lifelong Health,* appeared on *The Colbert Report* a few years back. He proposed a hypothetical situation, which flipped the script on the typical zoo situation and made us the ones in captivity. Durant said that whoever was in charge of the human exhibit would, "Replicate their natural habitat as much as possible... you feed raw meat to the lions, you feed rodents to the snakes. And the same principle applies to human beings.

We are happiest and healthiest when we eat the types of foods that hunter-gatherers ate in the wild." I'm not recommending some sort of "Paleo" caveman diet here; however, I am recognizing that our bodies have remained essentially unchanged over the last 100,000 years or so, giving some clues about what you should be putting into your mouth every day.

In fact, 99.9% of human physiology developed in the wild, thousands of years ago. As numerous Paleolithic experts have said in the past, "We are living with Fred Flintstone bodies in a George Jetson world." During those thousands of years, the human body developed countless adaptations to mold human physiology to the environment around them. Don't forget, we are a product of our environment.

Agriculture is a very recent phenomenon in human history, and even more so, the introduction of lite foods. Needless to say, our rapid 30 year switch to highly refined, sugary, starchy, lite crap flies in the face of millennia-old physiology, especially the signals that regulate fat storage.

Remember, our goal is not just to lose weight, but to lose fat and gain muscle. Calories do have an impact on fat accumulation and loss, but much less than most people think. Obviously, if you stuff yourself with 1,000 more calories than you need every day, fat is going to eventually pile on, no matter what those 1,000 calories look like. On the other hand, the macronutrient (fat, carbs, and protein) compositions of the meals you eat ultimately decide whether you're chubby or lean. That's because the macronutrient ratio of a meal has a tremendous impact on the genes regulating the hormones which control the fate of your 30 billion or so fat cells.

The Gatekeeper of Fat Storage

How does food tell your body to store fat or burn it? Fat loss and accumulation are largely controlled by continual hormonal messages. Hormones are the body's tiny, chemical messengers that rush throughout, telling cells to grow, shrink, open, morph, and even die. When it comes to fat metabolism, a handful of hormones work in concert as a silent orchestra telling the body to either store or release fat. As you'll see, lite foods and the majority of diets the public believes will help them lose weight, end up stimulating the wrong hormonal messages.

The hormone that has the greatest impact on body fat is *insulin*. If you're like most people, you first heard about insulin because you knew someone who had diabetes. Everyone needs insulin to live. That's because insulin's chief role in the body is to bring glucose into cells, thus giving them much needed energy. Without insulin, you don't last long, which was the case for type 1 diabetes patients in the years before insulin therapy was discovered. Luckily for most of us, special beta cells in the pancreas produce the insulin we need to get nutrients from our blood into the cells where they belong.

But insulin's role in the body doesn't end there. When it's not shuttling glucose into cells, insulin is telling the body to store food as fat, shut down fat oxidation (burning), and start building new fat cells—lots of them. Insulin has an especially dramatic influence on enzymes called *lipases*. Lipases are like little Pac Men who run around your body releasing fat from its cushy containers so it can be shuttled into muscle cells to get burned off. Yippy!

When insulin levels are high, they instruct the body to hit the "off" switch on lipases, putting them into a holding pattern until further notice. In fact, the most prominent lipase involved in fat-burning is called *Hormone Sensitive Lipase* or HSL for short. HSL is the premiere key holder that unlocks those fat storage containers which make you leaner. Unfortunately, the more insulin that's present, the less HSL is available to release fat for energy and the end result is you become fatter. Not so yippy.

Not only that, but at the same time insulin is blocking fat-burning, it's creating an internal environment ripe for fat storage. Insulin activates another lipase enzyme called *Lipoprotein lipase* or LPL for short. LPL produces brand new fat cells and orders existing ones already living inside your body to open up so they can accept some new cargo: huge wads of pure fat. It's next to impossible for the body to store fat without a certain amount of insulin floating around.

As you can see, insulin is something we need, but we don't want too much of it. Otherwise, we end up with a body that acts as a 24/7 fat-storing factory.

Almost any food, or even the mere thought of it, can cause insulin release, but carbohydrates are the primary drivers when it comes to a flood of insulin. High-carb foods, especially those of the highly processed (yes, lite versions as well) and refined variety, cause glucose levels in your blood to skyrocket. However, the body doesn't work very well when glucose gets too high, so it sends out a stream of insulin to stem the rising tide of glucose. Sure, a spike of insulin gets glucose back under control, but it has the unfortunate side effects of turning the vast majority of that glucose into newly formed fat.

On the other hand, when insulin levels are under control, the body swiftly transitions into fat-burning mode. Normal insulin levels cause lipases to spring into action. Also, a hormone often viewed as insulin's opposite, *glucagon*, starts to rise. Glucagon travels around the body, ordering fat cells to relax and let go of the fat they're clinging to.

It's accurate to view eating and lifestyle as a hormonal event. In a primitive dietary world made up of fresh produce (including roots, shoots, seeds, and nuts) and wild game meat, our hormones were never a problem. In other words, there weren't many, if any, obese cavemen or ladies. If a caveman was lucky enough to stumble upon a beehive filled with honey or a bush sprouting plump berries, insulin was there to process the carbohydrates properly. But for the most part, the diet that our pancreas was designed for only called insulin into action on a part-time basis.

Our modern-day avoid-fat-at-any-cost dieting, forces our pancreas to work double or triple shifts. The human body was simply not designed to metabolize all these carbs. The real kicker is that because of our ravenous appetite for insulin-stimulating lite foods, the weight we've been accumulating over the last few decades is pure, unadulterated fat, which isn't just unsightly, but it brings with it a whole host of health issues.

The Consequences of Carbs

For years, scientists hotly debated what was making us so fat and unhealthy. They basically settled on two primary areas:

1. One side claimed it was pure thermodynamics: we eat more calories than we burn; therefore, we're packing on pounds.

2. The other side pointed to the fact that we're getting our calories from completely different foods that were never part of our evolutionary existence. Therefore, the body has great difficulty in metabolizing these foods properly.

In 2004, researchers from Case Western Reserve University documented the transformation of the North American diet since the early 20th century and concluded that both sides were right. We're eating more calories, but the reason we're eating more is that we're downing more and more carbs. In fact, 80% of the extra calories we swallow nowadays are in the form of refined carbs (the other 20% is a reflection of the marginal fat and protein content of highly-refined carbs.)

The researchers discovered that carbohydrate intake is higher than at any other time in human history. They found that in a 25 year period, "An increased consumption of dietary carbohydrates from 48% to 54%... and a relative decrease in dietary fat from 41% to 37% of total energy intake" had occurred. While a 6% increase in carb intake might not knock your socks off, the consequences should. "During the same period, the prevalence of type 2 diabetes increased by 47% and the prevalence of obesity increased by 80%, indicating a significant positive correlation between the percentage of energy from refined carbohydrates and the prevalence of type 2 diabetes and obesity." Three decades of carbs galore swiftly resulted in practically everyone in North America walking around with sky-scraping insulin levels and bulging waistlines. The deal we've made to exchange fat for highly refined carbs is a trading blunder that rivals the famous barter by Native Americans that gave Manhattan to the Dutch for $24 in beads.

The Case Western study suggests that fat-phobia made us fat, but their data doesn't reveal a cause and effect – it's just a correlation. However, dozens of others have filled the research gap finding time and time again that a high-carb, low-fat diet messes with your hormonal environment and makes fat accumulation inevitable.

The Low-Fat Failure

A study published in *The Journal of Clinical Endocrinology & Metabolism* compared the effects of two diets on not just weight loss, but also on fat loss. Like many other studies, they found that a low-fat diet induces the same amount of weight loss as a diet composed of moderate carbohydrates and a particular healthy fat: *monounsaturated* fat. Fortunately, these researchers were sharp enough to dig a bit deeper. While on the surface, everyone lost the same amount of weight. However, what that weight was made of was entirely different. The low-fat group lost twice as much muscle mass and half the fat as the moderate carb group.

Why did the low-fat group actually get fatter as the number on the scale dropped? You guessed it; their insulin levels were constantly sky-high. Research published in the *American Journal of Clinical Nutrition* looked at the effects of these same two diets on insulin levels. As expected, the macronutrient ratio didn't make much of a variance in terms of weight loss, but insulin levels couldn't have been more different. Even though insulin levels are expected to decrease when someone loses weight, the insulin levels of the low-fat group actually *increased*, no doubt because of an onslaught of non-stop carbs.

University of Pennsylvania Medical Center scientists had similar findings: feeding bushels of carbs to overweight people throws their insulin signaling completely out of whack. The group that restricted their dietary fat watched their insulin levels rise like an elevator, even as the pounds came off.

I've said it once, and I'll say it again, the goal isn't just losing weight – it's losing fat. Losing fat is impossible if you work against your body's natural design. And if you're unfortunate enough to go against the grain for too long, the end result is the debilitating condition known as type 2 diabetes.

The Type 2 Diabetes Cause, Effect, and Consequences

Type 2 diabetes is a disease whose prevalence has climbed 765% over the last 60 years, which tells us a lot about the long-term ramifications of around-the-clock elevated insulin levels. The 21st century view of type 2 diabetes is that it's an endpoint of a sugar-coated, insulin-mediated vicious cycle.

The cycle starts when one shuns fats in favor of carbs in any form. The unavoidable insulin rush this brings on—over time—makes cells less sensitive to the effects of insulin, a condition known as insulin resistance. This means that you need more insulin to do the same job. Sadly, the surplus of insulin commands your body to manufacture and hoard fat as quickly as humanly possible. The inflammation produced directly from the body fat you're amassing actually interferes with insulin signaling even further – forcing your pancreas's beta cells to shoot out insulin like a machine gun. Even though beta cells work harder than security holding back a hundred screaming tweens at a One Direction concert, they can only do so much. Ultimately, beta cells succumb to what's known as beta cell burnout – they can't keep up with the insulin demands anymore. It's then, and only then, that true type 2 diabetes sets in.

Not All Carbs Are Created Equal

Even though research has associated a high carb diet with swelling insulin levels and type 2 diabetes, it's inaccurate to shove every single carb under the same "insulin-magnet" umbrella. Certain carbs cause insulin spikes while others barely make a dent. Scientists have worked hard to categorize carbs based on what's known as their glycemic index (GI) – the impact a carb source has on glucose (and therefore insulin), levels. A food with a high GI instigates beta cells to produce boatloads of insulin while foods with a low GI do just the opposite. Needless to say, you want the vast majority of your carbs to be in the form of *low* GI carbs.

Measuring GI

The GI uses a scale measurement from 0 to 100. The index measures the speed at which carbohydrates break down and put sugar into the bloodstream. Some break down quickly during digestion, causing a drastic rise in blood-sugar levels. These have the highest glycemic index rating. Glucose, at a dose of 50 grams, is used as the benchmark and is given a rating of 100 because it raises blood sugar super-fast. Other carbohydrates are ranked in relation to glucose (at the same dosage of 50 grams). The glycemic index measures the increase in your blood glucose over a period of two or three hours following a meal.

To develop a glycemic index rating for a particular carbohydrate, 50 grams of the food is consumed, and then the subject's blood-sugar level is measured. If the carbohydrate raises blood sugar quickly, it's given a high number on the glycemic index. Measurements of fewer than 55 are considered low glycemic.

Foods you already know are unhealthy, like white—and even brown—flour breads, corn chips, and jelly beans find themselves, not surprisingly, in the high GI camp. However, because of the clever labeling tactics we discussed in Chapter 2, diet food companies can get away with insulin-spiking murder with what they put into lite foods. Because lite foods gladly sacrifice fat for sugar, their effects on insulin are nothing short of disastrous. And all the while, you unwittingly think you're eating a healthier version of your favorite foods.

Take one of the most heavily-marketed diet foods in the world – Special K® cereal. Because processed cereals like this are low-fat and low-calorie, many desperate dieters pack their pantries with pallets of these convenience foods. However, if cereal manufacturers like Kellogg's® (who produce Special K®) were actually forced to replace their "so-called" health claims with the true glycemic index those cereals contain, I suspect sales would plummet.

It is important to understand that different countries can offer different glycemic indexes of the same product brand. For example, Kellogg's Special K® breakfast cereal in North America (Kellogg USA) has a GI roughly 15 points higher than the Kellogg's Special K® in Australia (Kellogg Sydney, Australia) and the Kellogg's Special K® breakfast cereal in France (Kellogg France) is once again even higher than that found in the North American brand.

Special K® that is sold throughout the USA and Canada has a glycemic index of around 70; however, that number jumps to 84 for those purchasing the cereal in Europe. To put that into perspective, sugary cereals that most dieters wouldn't touch with a ten-foot pole are actually lower. For instance, Honey Smacks®, a cereal that has the word "honey" right in the title has a GI of 55, and Fruit Loops® checks in at about 69. Unlike the health claims splashed on the packages of lite foods, the numbers don't lie.

HFCS – From Bad to Worse

Any highly-refined carb, from white bread to pure sugar, taxes the pancreas and stimulate an insulin torrent, but high fructose corn syrup (HFCS) is in a class by itself. HFCS, a compound that our body was *never* designed to deal with, makes up 10% of the average North American's total calories. Studies show that HFCS sits in front of cells, blocking insulin's action. This means your body has to pump out even more insulin to counteract the negative effect of HFCS.

Of course, HFCS is a favorite filler to overpower the synthetic taste of cardboard-like low-fat and lite foods. To make matters worse, the most heavily-processed version of HFCS, made up of 90% fructose, is produced specifically for use in lite foods.

Research presented in the *American Journal of Clinical Nutrition* in 2004, showed a direct correlation between the use of high-fructose corn syrup and the present epidemic of obesity in North America. The report went on to say that the increase of high-fructose corn syrup foods and beverages—especially soft drinks—far exceeds the consumption of any other food or food group. But why would a sugar as natural as fructose seem to cause so many problems with our fat cells?

Fructose found naturally in fruit is far from the same thing as industrialized fructose. High-fructose corn syrup is highly processed from cornstarch (containing anywhere from 55 to 90 percent fructose). It no longer contains the natural metabolites our bodies need to process it properly. Unlike whole natural fruit (not fruit juice) that contains fiber, high-fructose corn syrup has been documented in human studies to raise both blood sugar and insulin – easily placing the body into a fat storage mode and setting the stage for obesity and type 2 diabetes.

Numerous published studies using rodent models show that rats fed fructose develop insulin resistance in a relatively short period of time (just a few weeks). In fact, NASA neuroscientist, Dr. Michael Schmidt, notes these effects are so predictable that many scientists now use fructose to induce these conditions in animals so they can study drugs that might correct them.

The problems with fructose don't end there. Research from the National Institute on Aging (NIA) in Baltimore, Maryland, shows fructose is more *lipogenic* (fat forming) than any other sugar or starch. It also causes greater elevations in blood fats (triglycerides and cholesterol) than other carbohydrates. Excess fructose consumption has resulted in increases in blood pressure, uric acid, and lactic acid. Research shows that those suffering from high blood pressure, high insulin, high triglycerides, non-insulin-dependent diabetes, and postmenopausal women are more susceptible to the negative effects of fructose than other individuals.

The insidious side of industrialized fructose should not be ignored any longer. Check the labels on food products you buy. You'll do your health a favor by avoiding fructose at all costs. Your belly and life may depend on it.

The Power of Acceptance

Eating a potato and being a couch potato have similar effects on insulin levels. Being a lump on a log slowly deteriorates the cell receptors responsible for interacting with insulin, resulting in laziness-induced insulin resistance. Studies show that changing your diet without changing your sluggish lifestyle has only a paltry effect on insulin, and therefore, fat loss.

Later chapters will provide you with the tools for serious fat shedding, but I don't want to leave you in suspense. I'm going to give you a sneak preview on how you can manipulate your internal hormonal environment so your body is no longer a storage depot, but a fiery, fat-burning furnace.

Like any 12-step program, the first step is acceptance by acknowledging the incredible importance of insulin on how you look in the mirror. Then, you have to admit that downing fistfuls of carbs at every meal creates havoc with your body's metabolic systems (i.e. insulin secretion and insulin sensitivity). You must also recognize that lite foods are nothing but sugar-bombs in disguise. Now it's time for the real fun, which is learning the truth about burning off unwanted fat.

Obviously, before we can burn fat, we have to obliterate the packaged junk foods we call lite foods. While you're at it, do away with the majority of refined carbs in your diet. This means that the white bread, packaged cereals, and sugar-packed foods have to go. Don't get me wrong, I hate the whole "avoid this and that" message as much as anyone else, but it's a necessary evil of permanent fat loss.

The Power of Protein

You're probably asking yourself, "Okay, that's a long list of foods I have to stay away from, but what about foods I *can* eat?" While we're on the subject of carbs, it's time to replace the "bad carbs" you've thrown away with judicious amounts of "good carbs." This means limited amounts of whole grains (especially the sprouted variety), beans, fruits, and as many fibrous vegetables as you can sink your teeth into.

Next, it's time to start eating protein at regular intervals throughout the day. Protein has a number of giant advantages over carbs. The two most important are that a high-protein meal only marginally nudges insulin levels and that protein is incredibly satiating – reducing the risk of carb-laden binge sessions. Purdue University researchers found that upping protein intake above the norm helps people hang on to precious muscle mass – even as the weight flies off. Protein keeps insulin in check and provides your body with plenty of the building blocks it needs to maintain and build muscle as you lose fat. Don't worry; protein is so important to fat loss that I cover it thoroughly in its own chapter later.

Eat Fats to Lose Fat

You don't have to read between the lines of this book to realize I think fat-phobia is a joke. However, like carbs, certain fats can be cleanly placed into different categories based on their remarkably differing effects on body fat. First off, saturated and trans fats, commonly called "bad fats," live up to their moniker. That's because these two fats are more likely to end up on your waist, and less likely to be burned off. Therefore, you want to eat two specific types of fats: *monounsaturated* fats (abbreviated as MUFA) and omega-3's. I'll go over how these fats work in terms of fat-burning in a later chapter also, but start carving this message into your brain: fats are not the enemy – healthy fats blunt insulin levels and combat fat storage.

Don't worry, I'm not some crazed Atkins disciple, suggesting you should use two slabs of meat instead of bread for your sandwiches, but the research is clear: limit carbs to fibrous sources, eat copious amounts of high-quality protein, and throw in some healthy fats and you'll watch your body burn off fat and replace it with muscle. As I've stated countless times in my seminars and books, I believe in a balanced approach to macronutrients. You should aim for every meal to be a healthy mix of fibrous carbs (approximately 40%), high-quality protein (approximately 30%), and healthy fats (approximately 30%).

The only way to build muscle—which is your new reason for changing your habits because it makes fat loss a breeze—is to get off your butt and start exercising. Not any exercise will do – weight-baring exercise is the ideal stimulus for boosting insulin sensitivity and building new muscle tissue.

And speaking of Atkins, the next chapter unveils what happens to your body when you get myopically focused on fad diets and weight loss and ignore the metabolic engine of the body – muscle.

CHAPTER 5 – Smaller Fat People

Every New Year's Day, Jack sets his sights on a new goal. He takes an item from his bucket list and tries to start off the year with a big bang. Last year, he wanted to learn how to SCUBA dive, but never got farther than the second lesson at the community pool when he threw up underwater. He was pushing off from the shallow end when suddenly the pizza-in-a-pocket he had wolfed down on the way to class came back with a vengeance.

"The information on the box said it was healthy," he said sheepishly, as he offered to clean out the pool. His stomach let out a low growl, probably embarrassed for him.

The teacher took a look at the extra pounds around Jack's waist and suggested he was perhaps more of a landlubber. Jack wanted to point out that walruses do just fine in the ocean, but he figured that particular comparison wouldn't earn him any favors.

The previous year, Jack started the New Year by trying to train for a 10k run in thirty days. He was hoping he'd turn out to be a natural and would be able to build his way up to a full marathon. "That'll be great bragging rights," he said, as he posed in front of the mirror, picturing the buffer, leaner version of himself walking by that cute girl in the office.

His first step was to buy a pair of those high-end neon orange running shoes he saw on that buff dude at the relay and try them out in the store so the salesman could watch his perfect gait. It made him feel official. He was a runner.

However, for the first two weeks of training, things at the office were frenetic and he ended up working late every night, eating fast food at his desk. "Okay, I'm not losing weight, but I'm saving money. Besides, I got the burrito with the low-fat sour cream." His stomach let out an audible gurgle as his manager passed by and asked, "Did you say something, Jack?"

"No, sir. Have a good night," Jack said, hoping his stomach didn't talk back anymore to his boss.

By race day, Jack had only gone out for a couple of practice runs. He figured he was enough of a man to tough it out for the actual event. After the starting gun sounded, Jack only made it as far as the sixth kilometer when he keeled over and threw up on a little old lady's new pink Nikes her grandchildren had bought her just for this race. He tried to apologize, but all that came out was a low warble as the last of his pre-race breakfast burrito evacuated his body. He didn't know what had gone wrong. He'd heard it was important to load up on carbs before races.

So, this year, Jack is determined to lose fifteen pounds by the end of January, and he's decided to be smarter and actually buy a diet plan. As he peers at his round reflection in the mirror he says, "Not eight pounds, not twelve pounds, not fourteen and a half pounds. This year I'm losing exactly 15 pounds." He remembered the words of the motivational speaker on that PBS special, "Be as precise as possible when you set goals, as the conscious mind doesn't deal in thereabouts."

He picks up the new diet book and smiles at the picture of a giant cabbage with healthy people posed in front of it. He was feeling more fit already. When he sees that one of the guys on the cover is wearing the same running shoes he bought, he nods with pride. "It must be a sign," he thinks.

The cover says in bright green letters, "New and Improved Cabbage Soup Diet: You too can lose excess weight on just cabbage soup, fruit, and even an occasional piece of steak for only 30 straight days!" Jack feels excited as he reads all of the nice things Mary from Atlantic City and Bob from Milwaukee have to say about their results.

Jack's best friend, Barbara, notices the book on Jack's counter. She knows the previous results from Jack's bucket list, so, naturally she's a little worried the list might eventually be the cause of Jack kicking the bucket. Barbara is a research assistant at a nearby university and she sneaks Jack in after hours to let him use the nutrition department's scale that's been proven accurate to the tenth of an ounce. He steps up on the scale and looks away for a moment as he mentally prepares for his unveiling. On the far side of the room, he notices a strange-looking device that seems like something out of *Star Trek*, the prequel.

"What the heck is that?" Jack blurts out, hoping to distract Barbara from the numbers on the scale.

"It's called a Bod Pod. It tells you your body fat percentage," replies Barbara. Her plan is working perfectly. She knows about Jack's love of shiny, new gadgets and she's hoping she can lure him into learning how to become healthy without losing a limb or a vital organ.

"I want to try it," he says. After stripping down to his underwear, Jack sits inside the chamber while Barbara works away at the attached computer. "Your body fat is at thirty percent," Barbara informs him as he withdraws from the pod.

"That's not bad, right?" Jack asks. "Now, let's see what a little cabbage soup will do."

Barbara rolls her eyes, but she knows better than to try and stop him.

A month later, Jack is back at the lab. He gets on the scale, itching with anticipation. Amazingly, he's dropped 15 ½ pounds. That's more than his goal! "It was worth forcing all that cabbage soup down my throat after all," he thinks to himself. It's the first item from his list to ever really work. As Jack begins to feel like a new man, Barbara fears the worst.

"Why don't you give the Bod Pod another go," she suggests. He agrees, but is exacerbated when he sees the results.

"I can't believe it!" he exclaims. "My body fat percentage has gone *up* to thirty-four percent? How can I be fatter if I just lost all that weight?"

"Exactly!" says Barbara. "Now, I've got a few truths for you, old buddy."

Where's the Weight Coming From?

"Lose 20 pounds for $20!" shouts one of Jenny Craig's® latest marketing campaign promises. The diet industry is notorious for turning pounds into cash cows, but you'd be hard-pressed to find a diet program that actually guarantees fat loss. Why? In no uncertain terms, it's harder to lose fat—which should be the real goal—than to lose weight. Actually, losing weight is pretty simple. Just go on a ridiculously low-calorie juice fast for a few days, start running on the treadmill while watching the 11 o'clock news, and bingo! All of a sudden, you're ten pounds lighter than you were a few days ago.

We've been trained to equate weight loss with a healthy body; therefore, we celebrate the minus ten pounds achievement. You know who else celebrates? The dude at the health food store. You know him. He's the fad diet pusher who lived up to his end of the bargain by selling out of the newest fad diet program, the Juice-Fast Miracle Diet so he can collect another check. It's a win-win situation, right?

Wrong. Fortunately for you, I'm not your typical diet guru. I know that on the surface you might think you're getting a great deal, but if you're interested in being trim and healthy, you're actually getting ripped off. That's because fad diet programs don't have the all-important body composition on their radar screens.

"I call this alchemy," Dr. Jules Hirsch, MD, from Rockefeller University, once said, "It's making gold out of ignorance." I couldn't agree with him more.

Over a decade ago, I coined the phrase "smaller fat people" and the "smaller fat person syndrome." Despite well over ten years of research and thousands of success stories later, I still get the occasional funny look when I bust out my now-famous phrase. That's because most people are so obsessed with the number that stares back at them from the bathroom scale that they don't think what that weight consists of is what matters the most. They want weight loss and they want it now. There's no shortage of programs and books that'll give it to them. The problem is 99.9% of these programs actually set you up for failure because they make you a smaller, but fatter, version of your former self (the smaller fat person syndrome).

You may be perplexed by the idea that the number on the scale could keep going down while your body fat goes up. If you're losing weight, what does it matter where it came from? Coaching legend, Vince Lombardi, once famously proclaimed, "Winning isn't everything; it's the only thing." The same rule applies here: *fat loss isn't everything; it's the only thing.*

It's fat that interferes with insulin signaling, forcing your overtaxed pancreas to work so hard that it poops out. It's fat that causes inflammation, which wreaks havoc on your heart and mind and your ability to lose fat. It's fat that makes clothes stick to your curves like glue. Make no mistake, fat is public (and personal) enemy number one – not the number that flashes back at you from that newfangled scale you bought from Amazon.com.

That's not the entire story. It's not just about fat; it's about muscle, too. This is something that weight, and even BMI, gets wrong.

When I presented the chilling obesity statistics in Chapter 1, you may have wondered how government researchers determine whether someone is fat or not. I'm sorry to say that your tax dollars don't always go toward the most accurate methods of gathering stats that will really benefit you.

The researchers' standard is to use BMI, which is the ratio of height to weight. Typically, BMI is a fairly good indicator of how fat someone is, but not always.

A research study published in the journal, *Nutrition,* shed some light on BMI's shortcomings. In a mixed group, scientists calculated the BMI (I listed a chart regarding so-called underweight to overweight below) using a technique called bioelectrical impedance to nab the body composition, and then compared the BMI with the subject's overall body fat percentage. Needless to say, the scientists found that a person's weight and body fat have little to do with one another.

BMI	Weight Status
Below 18.5	Underweight
18.5 – 24.9	Normal
25.0 – 29.9	Overweight
30.0 and Above	Obese

The researchers found if your BMI is really high, as in over 35, you probably have a high body fat percentage to match. That's to be expected. However, they also found many people who think they're thin and trim with a normal or slightly high BMI, were actually considered *obese* based on body composition (percentage of body fat). In fact, a third of men and nearly *half of all women* with a normal to slightly high BMI were actually overly fat. Results like these have led National Public Radio (NPR) to smear BMI as nothing but "mathematical snake oil." Despite the intense focus on the scale, it turns out that pounds don't carry much weight.

The Metabolic Engine

If BMI doesn't matter, then what does?

Muscle Matters.

Unfortunately, many women I speak to are actually afraid of muscle.

They think that having more muscle on board will make them look like a long-haired version of Arnold Schwarzenegger, at least in his heyday. It's yet another unfounded fear. While you're dealing with fat-phobia, you might want to drop muscle-phobia, too. Neither one of them are doing you any favors.

For every man, woman, and child, muscle is the metabolic engine of the human body. The amount of muscle you have on board—and how active that muscle is—determines how much fat you're potentially going to burn. I say potentially, because there are other factors that come into play (i.e. diet) that need to drive the fat into the muscle before it is burned. Muscle tissue is akin to getting more furnaces to burn more fuel. Thousands of metabolic furnaces, called *mitochondria,* live in almost every muscle cell, so fat-burning potential climbs rapidly when you adhere to a program that allows you to build and activate muscle tissue. In fact, replacing a few pounds of fat with new muscle is akin to doing an extra treadmill session—or two—daily without having to do the work. Any way you look at it, more calories are going to get burned.

How does adding a pound or two of muscle give you such a gigantic fat-burning edge? It's all about the way the body uses calories. Even though most people think you only burn calories when you're exercising, the vast majority of the calories you burn off in a typical day happen while you're not really doing anything. This is known as your resting metabolic rate (RMR). In fact, 60-70% of all calories burned happen outside of your gym's walls.

Your RMR becomes even more important when you realize that the body's preferential source of calories is body fat. While carbs are often referred to as the body's "fuel," as long as your insulin levels are under control, the body actually uses about 60% of all resting calories in the form of pure body fat. In other words, if you view your body as an engine, it burns off more fat while idling throughout the day than it does when you hit the gym and put the pedal to the metal. But when you're muscular, it's like you're revving the engine all-day, burning off fat like there's no tomorrow—especially if you're eating the right foods to make that magic happen.

Low-Calorie Catastrophes

That means the worst thing you can do to your metabolic engine is rely on yo-yo diets. When your weight goes up and down like a roller coaster, your muscle and fat switch sides like a seesaw. As a result, muscle gets stripped from your frame and fat sneaks in to replace it. This is exactly what scientists find when they investigate very low-calorie diets – the medical profession's version of a fad diet. These diets "work" by giving people between 800-1,200 calories per day to live on; however, I've even seen diets that go as low as 500 calories.

As expected, people drop enormous amounts of weight in a short period of time. The patient sees the number on the scale take a sudden nosedive, and he gives the doc his payment along with a pat on the back. But when researchers actually look at *what* was lost, they find that precious muscle was eaten away while a good amount of body fat remained, stoically clinging to the subject's midsections (aka: the smaller fat person syndrome).

Modern Day Famines

Why does this happen? For the answer, we have to go back to our days of hanging out in the jungle. Forget 30 minutes or your pizza is free. Back then, dinner wasn't exactly guaranteed. Many anthropologists believe humans lived in periods of oscillating feast or famine – in other words they didn't know when their next meal was coming. When times were good and food was plentiful, we designed a nifty storage system for excess calories – body fat. In fact, we evolved to manufacture between 30 and 40 billion of these fat storing containers (fat cells) that have almost a limitless ability to expand.

But when food was scarce, the body kicked-in adaptive mechanisms to make sure it didn't fade away like a teleporting actor from *Star Trek*. Collectively, these adaptations are usually called "starvation mode." Even though you'd be hard pressed to find a legitimate starving person in North America, when most of the calories your body's accustomed to suddenly vanish, your body doesn't know there's a McDonald's on every corner (which isn't exactly a bad thing) – it thinks you're in big trouble.

The first thing the body does is turn down the dial on your RMR. With calories suddenly hard to find, you can't afford to waste a single one. In other words, the fat-burning engine stalls. Also, because muscle is so metabolically active – burning calories all day every day – your body begins to view muscle as excess cargo. Because a fat cell burns about 80% less calories than a muscle cell, your body prefers to keep fat on board, and is perfectly willing to drop energy-expensive muscle. If the tiny amounts of calories you're "allowed" to eat on the fad diet happen to be   predominantly   high-sugar,   low-fat   foods,   then   the   fat retention/muscle loss program accelerates. This means fat-inducing insulin levels and a body keen on storing (not burning) massive amounts of fat.

When you count, ration, and cut calories, your body goes to great lengths to make you smaller and fatter. Most North Americans follow similar eating patterns. For months at a time, they overeat super-processed foods and refined carb sources. In a frantic stab at making up for past indiscretions, they starve themselves into losing massive amounts of weight as fast as their bodies will let it go. There's no grey anymore – it's either all-out stuffing yourself with insulin-happy foods or putting the brakes on eating altogether. In essence, you're unknowingly manipulating your body in such a way that it stores as much fat as humanly possible. Talk about running the wrong program.

So are you doomed to a life of lard no matter what the weight is that you fight tooth and nail to get down to? Hardly.

By changing your internal metabolic environment so your body clings to fat-torching muscle and loosens its grip on fat, you can actually build muscle as you lose weight. Accomplishing this feat can finally be a reality. I'm about to share with you some top-notch research that is about as simplistic as it comes. Ready?

Stop counting calories. Focus on a macronutrient ratio of no more than 40% fibrous carbs, 30% protein, and 30% healthy fats. When you exercise, think high intensity and short duration and include strength and interval training (as in sprints or Burpees).

We're a nation obsessed with calories. We constantly hear commercials for low-calorie yogurts, breakfast cereals, and TV dinners. Of course, these companies fail to mention the fact that a good amount of the calories in foods like lite yogurts, are from HFCS and sugar. It's time to stop obsessing over calories and start taking note of what it is you're putting in your mouth. The composition of the foods you eat, not calories, is what makes a difference – right down to your genes. It's time to realize the solution to obesity is not doing more math. All that causes is extra stress, which makes you even larger.

I discussed the incredible importance of the glycemic index on insulin levels in the last chapter. It turns out that all of the insulin released as a result of high GI lite foods can make or break body composition. Dutch researchers followed a group of free-living people (people outside the lab) over a year's time, tracking everything they ate.

They found the factor that correlated closest with how fat someone became over the year was the glycemic index of the foods they ate. Unbelievably, for every ten-points a person went up on their average GI intake, their body fat percentage followed suit, going up 2%. At first glance, 2% may not seem like much, but consider this: if you weigh 190 pounds and did nothing else but lower the average GI of the foods you ate by 25 points (which you can do blindfolded), you could expect to shed nearly ten pounds of pure fat. Do I have your attention now?

Protein is the next piece of the fat loss puzzle. Purdue University researchers recently put two groups—both of which were looking to lose weight—on separate diets: one with 30% of their calories coming from protein and another with about half that, and a higher carb intake. They found that the extra bit of protein preserved twice as much muscle mass. Since your muscles are made up of almost pure protein, it's important to get plenty of it if you want the muscles to stay put and metabolically active.

While you're adding a bit of protein to your diet, throw in some fat. I hope the chapters leading up to this one have wiped your brain clear of fat-phobia, but if not, maybe this study published in the journal, *Nutrition,* will finally push the last throes of low-fat brainwashing out of your head. Researchers put people on either a run-of-the-mill low-fat diet or a diet chock full of healthy monounsaturated fats. Despite identical protein intake between the groups, the one that chewed the fat lost more of it. Not to mention the fact that they preserved seven times more muscle mass than their low-fat counterpart, insuring they were more likely to keep the fat off in the future. The concept that fat makes you fat can now be considered officially dead.

However, my favorite study has to be the one that appeared in the *American Journal of Clinical Nutrition.* The group that put this study together investigated a diet with a macronutrient count of 44% as carbohydrate, 27% protein, and 29% as fat – almost the exact ratio I've been touting for eons (what, did you think I made this stuff up). Not surprisingly, this macronutrient intake suppressed insulin levels and kept precious muscle glued to their frames.

Timing is Just as Important

It's not only what you eat; it's also how often and at what intervals throughout the day. There's been a lot of buzz about eating more frequent, smaller meals to lose fat, but unlike other diet trends, this one is right on target. If you're like most people, your meals are all over the place. You may have breakfast when you wake up, eat a late lunch, and grab dinner on the way home – all the while going seven, eight, or maybe even 12 hours between meals. Piling up hours between eating actually puts your body into a "mini-starvation mode."

On the other hand, eating a small, but nutritious meal every 2 ½ – 3 ½ hours keeps insulin levels from swinging wildly between extreme highs and rock-bottom lows. It's important to remember that the body isn't very good at processing huge amounts of protein at one sitting and likes to get an adequate dose of protein at regular intervals. That's because protein isn't stored in the body like fat and carbs. This means more muscle for you. Also, by eating smaller meals more frequently, you avoid blood sugar crashes that induce fatigue, irritability, and insulin-creating sugary binge sessions.

Doesn't this all sound like it's too-good-to-be-true marketing BS: *eat more often, weigh less.* But in this case, you're actually spreading your calories evenly throughout the day and not simply eating five or six meals of the size you've grown to see as normal. Making the switch from two to three heavily-laden plates to five or six smaller meals is one of the simplest and most effective ways to rev up your fat-burning machinery.

Now that we've established the average ideal macronutrient ratio for fat-burning and the best times to eat, it's time to discuss an area of fat loss that has more misunderstandings than your typical call to tech-support: exercise (We will discuss exercise in more depth in Chapter 14.)

When you hear the word "exercise," it is usually followed by "treadmill," "jogging," "going to the gym," and "boring." Like the diet food industry, the exercise industry has invented gadgets and gizmos that hypnotize us into counting calories. When the treadmill or elliptical trainer shows that you burned 200 calories in an hour, and 60 minutes of strength training only burns about 50, you assume that cardio must be the best way to exercise for fat loss because it rids your body of the most calories. Again, our calorie fixation has led us astray.

Sure, there are great reasons for breaking a serious sweat on the treadmill, but if it's not paired with strength training, you can expect to lose muscle faster than a sombrero in a windstorm. Like money, muscle doesn't grow on trees. Only one stimulus can force the body to make new muscle: resistance (weight-bearing) exercise.

For the most part, cardio itself won't do the trick. A really interesting research study supports the notion that strength training can't be topped for fat loss. Researchers who had people strength train during a weight loss bout found that strength training didn't just offset the "inevitable" sag in RMR, but it actually pushed RMR upwards. What do you think the researchers found when they looked at body composition? You guessed it, more muscle and less fat.

However, all the strength training, meal timing, and macronutrient leveraging won't make much of a difference if you eat thousands of extra calories due to a psychotic appetite. In order for the advice in this chapter to become useful, you have to get control of two of the most hideous demons in the fat loss realm: hunger and cravings.

CHAPTER 6 – The Hunger Games

"Not again," Dr. Martin groaned as he watched the drug rep bring in bags with the Dunkin' Donuts® logo plastered all over them. Dr. Martin self-consciously tried to pull his lab coat over the flab that was peeking out from between the openings, but the material fell short of the expanse. Like many of the patients at his internal medicine clinic, he is trying and trying to lose weight, but has only managed to lose a little more self-esteem. Like almost all of his patients, he is failing miserably, over and over again.

"It's my damned sweet tooth," he says.

"It's your damned sweet teeth," says his receptionist, Madge. "You don't just have a sweet molar in there. Every tooth in your head is betraying you and I think your tongue may be in on it too."

Dr. Martin wants to argue, but just this morning he had to make a new hole in his belt. Madge has a point.

He cringes as he peers over the conference table overflowing with a smorgasbord of bagels, donuts, and top-heavy muffins. Ah, there's the lemon-filled powdered donut he really likes. If he doesn't take that one while he's thinking about it, it won't be there later.

"Don't do it," says Madge, who's a little worried about job security at the rate he's been eating. The drug rep stands in front of the table like a carnival barker, smiling at him, offering a napkin with the bright pink logo. "Don't trust a man who can resist his own poison," says Madge, pointing at the drug rep's thin physique.

Dr. Martin knows he should get out while he can, but he's too tired from late nights and early mornings. He can head down to the hospital's food court, although it isn't much better. He hasn't been able to resist the soft serve ice cream or the Chinese chicken salad with crunchy noodles.

"My empty stomach is only aching from a skipped breakfast," Dr. Martin rationalizes, and a donut *is* legitimate breakfast food.

"That's not real breakfast food," says Madge, startling the good doctor who has wondered more than once if Madge has found a way inside of his head.

The urge to eat floods his body from head to toe. The Hippocratic Oath doesn't seem to apply to himself as he gives in and stuffs handfuls of lemony, sugary goodness into his mouth as fast as is socially acceptable. Throughout North America that's now considered to be somewhere between not letting any crumbs hit the floor and the speed of light. Einstein would be proud of how we adapted his findings to our daily use.

"You are messing with my retirement plans," Madge says, snapping at him. "You keep this up and I'm going to be forced to pull the trigger. That's right! I'll tell your wife!"

Dr. Martin shudders at the thought of his wife finding out he'd been less than honest about his diet. He had been swearing that he hardly had time to eat anything during the day, which was basically true. However, he was leaving out that he managed to somehow cram things into his mouth when he found a moment, which wasn't often.

"Can you even taste it when you eat that fast?" Madge asks.

"Not really," thinks the doctor as he eyes the chocolate-oozing éclair.

Madge wedges herself between the table and Dr. Martin and crosses her arms menacingly over her chest. "I have plans to move to a nice little condo in Florida and I'm not going to let your lack of willpower and a few donuts stop me. I have a good solid seven years to go until retirement and then you can eat yourself into that early grave. Back away from the table or I will lick every one of these donuts even faster than you can get one more in that mouth."

Dr. Martin had seen how fast Madge could move once when a small child got loose in the clinic and was quickly scooping up supplies. The kid never heard her Aerosoles® coming.

That did it for now. He went back to his office, but he was still thinking about that second donut or perhaps a muffin. In a few hours, maybe he'll head down to the cafeteria for lunch after all. He knows that's a better plan although he is pretty sure he'll be getting the six-cheese stuffed manicotti special and topping it off with a little dessert.

He sincerely hopes Madge has a Plan B. "I just can't seem to stop," he says to himself as he slumps in his chair. "I can't believe medical school was easier than trying to lose this fat!" he cries out.

While his conscious mind yells at him to stop the destructive eating patterns, the rest of him is screaming, "Go for it!" To be fair, the hormonal signals the good doctor induced by staying up late and turning down breakfast actually made the decision for him.

Something's Grumbling Down There

Why are you always hungry? Sure, irresistible treats are on every corner nowadays, but that doesn't explain everything. After all, even though the world is getting fatter, there's plenty of people who say "no" to dessert, pass by the intoxicating aromas of a bakery without batting an eyelash, and generally don't overeat (these are also known as people you despise and suspect of having some supernatural powers). What's their secret? Aren't their stomachs growling every hour? Don't their mouths water when someone mentions the word "cupcake?" You may even ask yourself, based on your vacuum-like tendency to chow down, are you human or just a black hole for calories?

Believe it or not, being hungry is a big part of being human. Millions of feast and famine years equipped us with a staggering amount of regulatory mechanisms to do one simple thing: eat. And not just eat, but consume foods filled with what would keep our primitive ancestors alive during leaner times. I'm talking fat, sugar, and salt. Back then, these nutrients were as rare as seeing someone on Sunset Boulevard in a loincloth today (on second thought, perhaps that's not the best analogy).

Without our natural inclination to gorge on these fattening foods, humans might not have made it. That's right: the reason our species lasted long enough for you to read this page and for me to write it, had just as much to do with our ancestor's ability to stuff themselves silly, as it did with large, frontal lobes or keen eyesight. It turns out that we're hardwired to be hungry a lot of the time.

Another amazing facet of our appetite is its precise control over our body weight and keeping it remarkably consistent in spite of tremendous variation in caloric intake. You might visualize your weight shooting up like one of NASA's Atlas rockets, but when you consider that the average person eats 900,000 calories every year, yet their weight may only rise a pound or two annually, weight moves rather glacially.

Okay, so you're thinking, "Speak for yourself." But it's possible and here's why. In general, your body controls its weight by adjusting two internal thermostats: RMR and appetite. I've already shown you how the body tweaks RMR based on perceived survival adaptations. We now know fad dieting makes RMR free-fall and muscle cranks RMR up. Appetite works the same way, making you hungrier when you're losing and less so when you're gaining. However, when you compare appetite to RMR in terms of physiological complexity, RMR is child's play.

Blame it on the Taste Buds

Appetite involves dozens of seemingly disjointed bodily systems – the brain, digestive, endocrine, and circulatory systems all play a major role (in creating yet another major roll, but this time, of fat). The science of appetite, something long considered confined to the mouth, turns out to be one of the most complex and redundant bodily systems we've got, which makes sense if you think about the importance of eating and survival. In fact, the science of appetite is so complex that its hormonal tapestry resembles the IRS tax code. Only a handful of people fully understand it and no one's ever been able to locate it (because the location is not allowed on Google Maps).

Adding a creamy custard layer of complexity to an already tricky system is the recent discovery that individual preferences for macronutrients differ, which has serious implications for fat gain. When researchers put rats on diets, they find that some are carb-crazy, others can't get enough fat, and a smaller percentage prefer protein. In rats and humans, scientists have linked these inherent preferences in the mouth with obesity.

Sarah Leibowitz, Ph.D., a research professor at Rockefeller University, goes as far as to say that our inborn love for all things fattening may indicate a lifelong weight loss struggle to come. She firmly believes that our taste buds are an underrated contributor to obesity: "We think there's more to it than just metabolism. We are on the verge of linking that early taste with later eating behavior and weight gain."

Despite its complexity and ingrained influence, you can still outsmart your appetite. To do so you'll need a two-pronged attack. You see, even though appetite is a head-to-toe phenomenon, appetite quality control lies in your brain and stomach. Like trying to pop a greased balloon, laying down the law on one appetite center will just cause the other to rise in opposition. It's the dual nature of appetite that explains why diet approaches such as Volumetrics (which relies on eating high-volume foods that "trick" the stomach into stretching) don't seem to work in the long run. The brain realizes it's being fooled and adjusts its appetite accordingly. The same goes for low-calorie diets – fool me once and shame on you, and as George W. Bush so famously said, "You can't get fooled again."

Insatiable Cravings

Speaking of the gray matter, the area of the brain that's considered one of the oldest, the *hypothalamus*, which regulates such survival whoppers like acid/alkaline balance (aka: pH) and temperature, also plays a massive role in hunger. Just like keeping your body at a balmy 98.6°F (37°C) in the shade, most of your appetite happens behind the scenes. That's why so much of your impromptu decisions for lava cake and butter tarts are completely out of your conscious thought. Not to be outdone, the stomach is no longer seen as just a sack of flesh to deposit your recently chewed food. It's a very complex organ, producing hormones critical to making you feel either hungry or full (unfortunately, the vast majority of these make you feel hungry).

In reality, it's not the stomach or brain that pushes you toward another fistful of M&M's®. The true instigators of face-stuffing are a set of hormones that work together, in what neuroscientist, Satya Kalra, Ph.D., calls an "appetite-regulating orchestra." Most of these appetite hormones travel up and down an appetite-inducing superhighway, called the *vagus nerve* that connects the brain and stomach.

Here's an example of how they work. After a few hours of fasting, a stomach-produced hormone called *ghrelin* shoots up the vagus nerve, telling the brain to start thinking chocolate thoughts (then again, when doesn't it?) But it doesn't stop there – ghrelin also blocks a hormone called *Pro-opiomelanocortin or* POMC for short, which reduces appetite (yet another trick from Mother Nature to help us stick around on the planet). In a final act of hunger havoc, ghrelin stimulates the same center of the brain that controls cravings for addictive drugs like heroin and cocaine, making cravings nearly irresistible.

However, ghrelin is far from the only appetite hormone in your body's arsenal. An alphabet soup of hormones with names like *PYY* and *CCK* work day in and day out to make you crave, and not alphabet soup. In the brain, one of the most abundant neurotransmitters that rival even the well-known serotonin and dopamine is *neuropeptite Y.*

Neuropeptite Y (or NPY for short) is a protein that's found in the brain and along the entire nervous system. NPY has an impressive breadth of functions—from bone formation to stimulating intestinal movement, but one of its most important jobs is making us hungry. NPY has a sinister method of making you eat. When NPY kicks in (and after a decently-sized fast, it will), it doesn't just make you hungry for anything

– but specifically for high-carb and yes, lite foods. Worse yet, NPY activates fat storage enzymes to make sure those carbs are applied directly to your butt and thighs (gee thanks).

Brain Sex

Once NPY has done its dirty work, and you have fork and cake in hand, your brain takes things a step further to make sure you remember how awesome it feels to eat the sugary foods. From the first bite, the brain unloads a rush of dopamine and serotonin—two neurotransmitters that give you palatable pleasure and make darn sure you remember it. In fact, the brain signals that come from a sugar rush are almost indistinguishable from another well-known rush, an orgasm. Talk about self-pleasuring. Now you know where the moan that slips out after a bite of cheesecake comes from.

But modern day sugary foods play even more perverse tricks on our primitive brains. Studies with rats that were fed nothing but sweets containing HFCS illustrate how overpowering sweet foods can become. After a few weeks of a 24/7 sugar high, the rats became downright addicted and were maddeningly keeping their paw on a food-releasing pedal, twitching uncontrollably, and developing pneumonia from literally inhaling food. How does sugar turn us into such fiends?

Walter H. Kaye, MD, a University of California San Diego psychiatrist, claims sugary foods can act like drugs. Indeed, dopamine release is how many substances get people high. "Drugs hijack the food-reward pathway," says Kaye. Lite foods, which provide consistent exposure to highly-processed carbs and reduce inhibition, turn us into babbling, drooling, food-addicted, obese zombies. If that weren't enough, our stomach has its own bag of tricks to make sure you don't skip a meal without feeling the pain.

It's 2:00 p.m. and your stomach's growling so loudly that you're disturbing a co-worker three cubicles over. While this might make you think your stomach has a mouth, it should at least tell you that it's connected to the brain. Ghrelin, the gastric peptide that stops at nothing until your appetite spirals out of control, turns out to be one of the most important regulators of appetite. Since its discovery just a shade over a decade ago, appetite researchers have been looking at ghrelin as one of the few ways to biologically quantify appetite. In essence, they've found that ghrelin starts to creep up a few hours after a meal and continues to rise until you get around to eating your next repast.

Once ghrelin hits your brain, it orders NPY production—and we already know what a mess that can bring on. Scientists think ghrelin shares a good chunk of the burden for your ravenous appetite that occurs after shedding a few pounds. A study published in the *New England Journal of Medicine* found that ghrelin shoots up 25% after a "so-called" successful weight loss bout, no doubt your stomach's way of making you fat again.

Based on what I've told you so far, you might think these hormonal systems are completely out of your control. Not so. One of the most important steps you can take to losing serious wads of fat is to simply chill.

Here Come the Cookies and Ice Cream

Have you ever found yourself curled up on the couch with a pint of Ben and Jerry's® after getting dumped? Well, it's not just the comfort food phenomenon at work here. Stress plays a pivotal role in appetite. To understand how a reprimand from your boss can turn into a potato chip chow down, it's helpful to look at worry from your body's point of view.

When someone cuts you off on the highway that rush of horn-honking anger you feel is actually from a flood of *adrenaline* circulating through your veins. Your body thinks there's an imminent threat—from a lion perhaps—and gets your muscles and mind ready for go-time with a rush of hormones and chemicals, the most important two being adrenaline and *cortisol*.

Cortisol is an extremely important hormone in times of legitimate danger, but with our modern-day on-the-go stressful lifestyle, cortisol does much more harm than good. Cortisol's most important job is to release stored carbs in the liver—and from your valuable muscle tissue—so they can get used up for a quick bout of intense physical activity, like running from, or punching something dangerous (think: fight or flight). Unfortunately, our stressors are usually of the imagined variety, and the rushes of circulating carbs have nowhere to go except our waists. The liver processes the unused carbs and swiftly converts them to fat. Those newly-converted carbs are so close to the liver and the adrenals where the stress hormones originated from that they tend to get stored as belly fat. But your body isn't satisfied yet. It wants more carbs coming in so it can replenish its stores just in case there's another stressor hiding somewhere.

To accomplish that mission, it again turns to cortisol. This time, cortisol journeys up to the brain where it turns on NPY-creating cells. Just a few minutes after the road rage wears off (keep in mind that cortisol has a very long half-life, meaning even after you've calmed down, cortisol is still hanging around for many hours), the NPY starts to kick in, forcing your hands to turn the wheel toward 7-Eleven® for an extra-large frozen Snickers® and Super Slurpee®. Besides following NPY's marching orders, the carbs actually satiate the brain, melting away the stress temporarily with a cocktail of feel-good brain chemicals. That's until the next stressful situation comes along and starts the cycle all over again. (Why is that guy driving so close to me?)

What We Can Learn from a Bowl of Soup

As if we weren't tricking our bodies enough with stress-induced phony danger signals, the way food is presented to us also does a number on our appetites. Imagine that you walk by a sign on your way to work that reads, "Unlimited Free Soup." You're a soup fan, so you make sure to visit the restaurant on your way home. The maître d' informs you that the catch to the soup special is that before you walk out the door you have to fill out a form estimating how much you ate and how full you felt. In essence, this is what Cornell University researchers did in one of the most clever nutrition experiments of all time. What's so clever about handing out free soup to research subjects, you ask? The trick in this particular experiment was that the soup bowl was actually attached to a device under the table that subtly refilled it, with the soup-happy subjects being none the wiser. This study was so popular, creative, and enlightening that most nutrition researchers simply call it The Soup Bowl Study.

What did The Soup Bowl Study tell us, besides the fact that people should start checking to see if their bowls are rigged? Not surprisingly, people who ate from the refilling bowl ate more than their standard-bowl counterparts – 75% more, in fact. But what made the results of this study famous is it quantified the fact that a fair amount of our hunger, fullness, and portion estimation is based on what we see and not what we eat. Even though the refillable bowl subjects downed much more soup, their estimations of fullness and how much they ate were identical to those who had a standard bowl of soup. Study author Brian Wansink, Ph.D. (incidentally, the same guy who designed our M&M's® study from Chapter 2), said it best when he concluded, "People use their eyes to count calories and not their stomach." As we've learned, they should stop counting calories anyway.

Plastic Neurons

Our estimations get thrown off with liquids, too. Even professional bartenders with an average experience of six years get confused when guesstimating the amount of liquid in different sized glasses. Research from over 50 years ago shows we approximate the size of a container largely based on height, almost completely ignoring width. That's why we will always drink more from a short glass than a tall, skinny one. The lesson from The Soup Bowl Study and the one on drinking glasses expose two fatal flaws in our appetite control: 1) we're horrible at figuring out how much food is in front of us; and, 2) we eat it all just the same.

Over the last two decades, plates, glasses, and bowls have swelled in size. The plate Grandma served you Thanksgiving dinner on would look like the size of a rice cake today. These days, we eat more without realizing it or even sensing the fullness you'd expect from consuming significantly more food. At most restaurants, you can expect your plate to be an entire foot long, a three inch increase from 25 years ago. There's even a small plate movement whose sole mission is to cut down on the size of plates in restaurants and kitchens around the US or we could just eat in swanky five-star restaurants where the portions are served on the same size plates your Barbie dolls used to eat off (or perhaps those have changed, too).

Why bother going through the effort of trading in your Frisbee-sized dinner plate for a saucer? Do it because it works. Just because you have more hunger hormones than dollars in your wallet, or the fact that a refilling soup bowl drops your IQ 40 points doesn't mean you're doomed for a life of overeating, controlled entirely by your subconscious. I'm going to show you how to tap into your appetite control centers and make them work for you for a change. Or as neuroscientists have learned firsthand over these last ten years or so, neurons are plastic and they have an incredible ability to change. Therefore, we can re-educate our neurons – teach them new tricks – and the same applies to your appetite, because it has a reset button as well.

So how do we begin to "re-educate the neurons" so they start taking orders from us, and not the other way around? The first step is to quiet the hormonal traffic that's turned you into a 24/7 food vacuum. To do so, we need to be patient. It takes about three days for hormonal traffic to slow down, and another few weeks for it to retune to normalcy. It may be hard to hear, but your unruly appetite, which took years to develop, isn't going to go away overnight. However, the good news is it won't take that long to fix it either. You just need the right program (yes, you'll find it with *Dirty Diets*) and a touch of patience.

Like any kind of addict, you need to wean yourself away from the chemical-induced pleasures of sweet foods. Lite foods, which you know are sugar in clever packaging, are so popular in part because they give your brain the fix it craves, albeit quite temporary. That's right; you're a virtual sugar addict. I'm sorry to report that you'll have to go pretty much cold turkey here.

The macronutrient ratio I advocate will give you plenty of carbs from natural sources, but doesn't leave much room for reduced-fat cookies. To help you along, you can retrain the way your brain views sugary foods. University College of London researchers recently discovered that lowering your sugary addictions is easier than you might think. The scientists gave self-described chocolate junkies their fix at two different times: one right after a meal, and one on an empty stomach. The group that did their chocolate chomping immediately after dinner rated the chocolate as less tasty and they reported that it felt less of a pleasure rush. Those with food already in their system, didn't get a hormone signal from their brain to go bananas over the sweet-tasting chocolate.

This is one of the main reasons I advocate eating at least five small meals per day. By eating healthy, nutrient-rich foods every few hours, you take yourself out of the "danger zone" where foods like chocolate can get you high. And if you do indulge in a piece of dark chocolate (over 55% cocoa), your brain's pleasure signals will be seriously blunted. The macronutrient ratio that you're shooting for, as I've said, is around 40% fibrous carbs, 30% fat, and 30% protein and happens to be the same ratio that keeps your appetite under wraps. A study published in *Clinical Science* found that a meal with this ratio caused ghrelin to rapidly free-fall and kept it suppressed for longer than a higher-carb version. Ghrelin may be a gremlin, but it quickly vanishes after eating the right nutrients at regular intervals.

Stress is also an enormous craving villain, and getting that under control should also be one of your appetite-stopping priorities. Swedish researchers put the stress reduction theory to the test with some remarkable results. Instead of asking their overweight subjects to waste their time counting calories or measuring portions, they simply had them attend sessions where they let out a catharsis of emotions and discussed their frustrations with food. The average subject lost a very respectable 16 pounds in ten weeks, (unfortunately, the researchers didn't measure body composition). Perhaps they should have called it the Talk It Off Diet. Most importantly, they avoided the seemingly inevitable weight rebound. In jaw-dropping fashion, the subjects continued to lose weight at a time they "should" have regained it. Research has also confirmed that stress-reducing techniques like mindful breathing, yoga, listening to brain-frequency altering sounds called *binaural* frequencies, and emotional soul-searching are underappreciated, yet effective, ways of shedding fat.

Become a Trickster

There are also ways in which you can trick your eyes—to your advantage, of course—when looking at portion sizes. For example, a study found that trading in your 12-inch plates for a set two inches smaller cut down food intake by 22%. Because your eyes falsely perceive there to be more food, you get a fuller stomach on less grub. But what about healthy foods that you aren't that into like leafy greens? You can dupe your eyes here, as well. Serve your salad or steamed spinach in an enormous bowl and watch more of it end up in your mouth. The same deception that got you into this mess can get you out of it.

As you can see, shifting your appetite from an unmanageable monster into something you can control doesn't require rocket science. Even if you don't wear a lab coat (or can't even fit in one), you can take advantage of the appetite research I've presented for you here to feel hungry, but never famished, full, but never stuffed, and feel like you finally have one hand on the brake of a formerly runaway train.

Even if you become extraordinarily diligent by eating every 3 – 3 ½ hours on the button, giving your oversized plates and stout glasses to Goodwill, and meditating four times a day, your efforts will be largely wasted if you stay up late doing it. One of the hottest areas of metabolic research is laser-focused on a time when you're not eating at all, the one-third of your life you spend in bed—sleeping.

We'll cover that next.

CHAPTER 7 – You Snooze You Lose

"An' here I go again on my own. Goin' down the only road I've ever known. Like a drifter I was born to walk alone. An' I've made up my mind. I ain't wastin' no more time..."

The ear-splitting White Snake song blaring from the radio alarm clock jars Sue out of her peaceful slumber. She tries to open one eye and look at the time, but she's just too tired.

By the time she'd put the kids to bed for the last time, cleaned up the kitchen, and tossed the clothes into the dryer, even David Letterman was in bed. For the second night in a row, Sue could count on one hand the number of hours she had been able to lie in a blissful state of sleep. But today, she has to get up because this is when she swore she'd start working out before leaving for her job.

"If I don't get my butt out of this bed right this minute, I won't make it to the gym," she says, sitting up. But just as quickly, her thoughts turn to her favorite luxury in the morning. "First... coffee," she says with a yawn as she begins to move.

Squinting from the kitchen light, Sue staggers over to the coffee pot and pours her first cup of the day. "Even better than White Snake," she says. "But not by much." Sitting right next to the coffee pot are her workout clothes. She'd put them there the night before after everyone else was in bed, to make sure her resolve hung in there long enough to get her butt to the gym. A little guilt can go a long way. It was a parenting tip she had picked up from her mother.

Sue takes another sip of caffeine and stares at the Under Armour® hoodie and a pair of her husband's sweat pants and wishes once again they were cuter and a smaller size. "Nothing really fits anymore," she notes, adjusting her pajama bottoms.

Sue found out at her last physical that's she's 75 pounds overweight and she received a long lecture from her doctor about what lay ahead if she didn't start moving more. "Less candy and more salads," he said. "As long as he leaves my coffee alone, I'll be fine," thought Sue.

After a half-hearted kickboxing class where she imagined giving the co-worker in the next cubicle who insisted on reading her Tweets out loud a good swift kick and then a morning train ride crammed up against two guys in business suits who were rating their girlfriends, Sue arrived at work ready for her second jolt of coffee for the day.

Luckily, a Starbucks® just opened down the street from her office park, close enough for her to be able to grab coffee and get back within the allotted fifteen minute break.

"I'd like a 'Shot in the Dark,'" says Sue. "A Grande just isn't going to do it today."

"I-understand-completely," says the chipper barista. "I-enjoy-a-few-shots-of-espresso-myself-every-day."

Sue tries to focus her tired eyes a little more. Was it just her or was the barista talking so fast that all of his words ran together? "Shot-of-syrup?" he asked.

"Sure. And, I'm starving," Sue says, realizing she didn't eat anything yet. "I'll also take two of those blueberry thing-a-ma-jigs, you know, the ones with the sugar icing on them. Yeah, those."

She knows exactly how many steps it is until she hits the large trash can near the door to her building, so she takes extra big bites, swallowing most of the scones whole, barely taking the time to chew. She nears the trash can just as she swallows the last of the espresso and does a jump shot into the bag, feeling a momentary burst of energy. Okay, maybe this day doesn't suck after all.

The day stretches on into two meetings, five Tweets from Alice about her cats eating next to her at her kitchen table, and a call from accounting about too much overtime until the wall clock near Sue's cubicle finally hits three p.m.

"Hey Sue, listen to this one," says Alice peering over the makeshift barrier between their desks. "It's just a short one. The ocean is blue because it's a liquid sky."

Sue is exhausted already and her patience is running out, as she quickly snatches a bottle of a 2-Hour Energy Shot from her desk drawer. Mmmm, Mango Madness, her favorite.

"Ooooh, that stuff will kill you," Alice says very motherly.

Sue thinks about downing a case of the stuff just to get away from her co-worker. "You can Tweet about it," Sue says sarcastically.

"Good idea!" Alice says and then disappears from view.

Sue reads the label of her energy shot, wondering if something that packs such a quick wallop could actually be good for her.

"Not exactly sure what that is," she says, trying to pronounce some of the ingredients. "I definitely like the way it makes me feel. Even Alice is a little easier to take. Well, that might be an exaggeration."

Throughout the day, Sue downs the cocktail of chemicals without reservation. On her way to the train, she picks up caffeine fix number three, this time in the form of an extra-large black coffee from a street cart. A night of parenting, school projects, making dinner, cleaning up afterwards, doing bills, and more laundry awaits Sue at home.

"I'm not going to get much sleep tonight," she says to her husband, Ralph, when she gets home. He nods his tired head in agreement. Sue can feel the stress descend upon her like a heavy cloak. "Oh well, tomorrow's another day, thank God for coffee," she thinks and rubs her weary eyes.

And the cycle begins again.

Over one hundred years ago, poet Edgar Watson Howe remarked, "There is only one thing people like that is good for them; a good night's sleep."

Little did he know just how good sleep is for you, especially when it comes to your waistline.

Vitamin Z

No matter how you look at it, sleep deprivation makes you fat. Dozens of research studies dating back from decades ago confirm the sleep/weight connection. Scientists from Warwick Medical School in the United Kingdom found that severe sleep deprivation nearly doubles your risk of being obese. But it doesn't take all-nighters for this phenomenon to set in and take hold. Simply sleeping less than seven hours dramatically boosts your chances of being fat.

Any doubts about sleep's influence on weight were put to rest when a group of scientists collected data from a dozen or so studies, essentially giving them 1.1 million research subjects to study. Their findings? That anything less than eight hours makes you overweight, and less than six makes you obese. As a well-known research junkie, I'm always skeptical to make cause and effect connections unless there's strong research to support it. In the case of sleep and fatness, though, there's plenty of evidence.

You already know BMI doesn't tell the whole story. You may be thinking, "Maybe these sleep deprived folks are spending their waking hours on the treadmill." Sorry, no dice. People who sleep less tend to exercise less and the more sleep deprived you are, the larger your waist circumference – a crude, but accurate way to assess body fat. When it comes to sleep and fat loss, there are no shortcuts. You have to get your vitamin Z's.

Unfortunately, less and less of us are getting enough dream time. It's been estimated we sleep 25% less than our ancestors did even though our body has remained relatively unchanged. While the average amount of shuteye our ancestors in 1900 got was nine hours, most people currently check in at a paltry seven. The amount of people who are severely sleep deprived is exploding. Almost one-third of all North Americans now sleep less than six hours per night. Alarmingly, the vast majority of our new sleep habits cropped up over the last ten years. Our modern life is filled with text messages, energy shots, and brightly-lit computer screens that keep us up well after our bodies desire a soft bed and comfy pillow.

Evolutionary Signals

How can sleep, a state where you're doing practically nothing, have such a profound impact on weight? Shahrad Taheri, Ph.D., of the University of Birmingham remarks that, "Sleep is not (as commonly believed) a passive state; it is a highly active and complex state whose precise physiological functions have remained a mystery." While the physiology of sleep has become somewhat unraveled (largely due to the emerging area of "sleep science"), one of the most surprising discoveries is just how much sleep influences how much you weigh.

Emmanuel Mignot, MD, a sleep researcher at Stanford University, sums up the current state of this research area. "It's certainly not the only factor. It's not that sleeping two or three more hours will solve a weight problem. It's one of many factors, and a factor that no one has looked at very much. It's good that sleep loss is getting so much attention right now. It's amazing what we're discovering."

Or as, Dr. Patricia Prinz, research professor at the University of Washington, states, "There is a well-documented relationship between short sleep duration and high body mass index." Documented? Yes. Understood? Not so much. Although unconfirmed, many scientists believe depriving yourself of sleep sends evolutionary signals to the body saying, "Let's store some fat!"

On a side note, it is interesting to mention that researchers at Laval University in Quebec, Canada, have found that sleeping too long can also pose its own problems when it comes to your body fat. The study which evaluated sleeping patterns of two hundred and seventy-six adults (aged 21 to 64) over a six year period, found that those who slept between nine to ten hours had a 27 % increased risk of obesity. The optimal sleep duration—according to this study—was between seven to eight hours.

In hunter-gatherer times, food was more plentiful in the summer months when plants were at their peak ripeness and animals were out in the open, and not in hibernation. Coincidentally, the summer also has much shorter nights with less darkness, therefore fewer hours of sleep time. In today's world, your body may associate a shortened circadian (24-hour cycle) rhythm as a signal to store fat and eat everything in sight for the long winter months ahead. In other words, the body knew to take advantage of the available buffet while it could.

Sure enough, research shows that even a single night of subpar sleep makes you hungrier the next day. As "sleep debt" grows, so does your cravings for sugary foods. Research at the University of Chicago mandated a group of men limit their sleep in the laboratory to just four hours. The next day, their appetite and hunger levels shot up 25%. But it wasn't just hunger that a lack of sleep brought on; it was what they were hungry for. When asked what types of foods they were craving, the volunteers rated sweet and salty foods as most appealing – with fruits and veggies checking in as the least desirable. One of the study's authors crunched some numbers and estimated that if left alone to eat whatever they wanted, they'd down an extra 500 calories per day.

The Hormone Shift

Why does pulling an all-nighter do such a number on our appetite? Michelle May, MD, hypothesizes that, "When you're tired, you're less resilient to stress and other common emotional triggers for eating. When you eat to help you cope with emotions, you're more likely to choose comfort foods like chocolate, ice cream, or chips."

Dr. Patrick Strollo, MD, medical director for the University of Pittsburgh Sleep Medicine Center, has another theory. "Hormones change with sleep loss and deprivation. Sleep deprivation can affect appetite and also the type of food that one desires. When you're sleep-deprived, you generally don't crave carrot sticks." After reading about appetite hormones in the previous chapter, the fact that a slight fluctuation in hormone levels could do so much damage should come as no surprise.

In particular, a sleep-deprived state throws off two appetite controlling hormones: ghrelin, which you're already acquainted with, and leptin, a hormone whose impact on weight is somewhat controversial. When scientists first discovered leptin, they thought they had found the "Holy Grail of weight loss." Even though that's shown not to be the case (or else you'd probably already be on your sixth leptin injection), your leptin levels can make a serious dent in your appetite.

Unlike ghrelin, leptin is produced by fat cells – with each of the billions of fat cells in your body pumping out an equal amount of the stuff. Therefore, the more fat you've got on board, the more leptin is floating around inside of you. As a flip side of the coin to ghrelin, leptin is one of the few hormones in the body that actually suppresses appetite.

It's leptin's hunger-fighting property that originally had scientists all excited. However, one anomaly came up (and still does): if overweight people have more leptin, why are they still fat? It seems that over time, you can develop so-called leptin resistance. That's a situation where you need even more leptin for it to work properly. Also, because leptin is outgunned (remember, 90% of appetite hormones tell you to eat more food), it has a place in regulating appetite, but it doesn't tell the whole story. Just because leptin isn't the end all or be all of appetite, doesn't mean it isn't significant. For example, scientists think one of the reasons people get hunger pangs after losing a few pounds is from plummeting leptin levels.

Sleep, Obesity and Diabetes

In 2004, researchers put healthy people on a sleep-restricted schedule to see what effect it would have on their internal appetite thermostat. After a few days, leptin fell by nearly 20% and ghrelin shot through the roof, climbing 28% higher. To give you an idea of how dramatic that is, cutting your calories nearly in half, a situation where your body puts hunger on overdrive, decreases leptin by nearly the same amount. If that wasn't enough, a bad night's sleep also throws off our old friends NPY and cortisol. Subpar sleep doesn't just influence what you eat, but what your body does with the food after you've swallowed.

One of the most alarming effects of sleep deprivation is the striking rise in insulin resistance. Scientists have understood that sleep deprivation, obesity, and diabetes are usually found in tandem. However, because obesity is the prime risk factor for a sleep-impairing condition called obstructive sleep apnea (OSA), which also throws off insulin, there was a bit of a chicken or the egg phenomenon happening.

The same people who have diabetes tend to suffer from OSA; therefore it was hard to tell what was causing what. That was until a pair of studies finally untangled this confusing web. The first study curbed the sleep time of healthy weight young men to six hours a night. After about a week, they became so insulin resistant that if you were to look at their lab results, you'd think they were diabetic. Less sleep = more insulin = more fat.

If the raw amount of sleep time was all that mattered, then people with OSA, who tend to get plenty of sleep, wouldn't be at such high risk of getting diabetes. Over twelve million North Americans suffer from OSA – a disease where the airway becomes blocked during sleep, making it difficult to breathe. Although body fat percentage and OSA are strongly linked, OSA itself is more than enough to derail your body's natural regulation of insulin, glucose, and fat storage. That's because all sleep isn't created equal. When you sleep, you cycle in and out of four separate stages, the final and most important known as delta or "deep sleep."

The second revealing experiment took another group of healthy men, but instead of shaving off the hours of sleep, they monitored their sleep cycles and set off a noise every time they drifted into deep sleep – essentially simulating OSA. Overnight, these robust young men transformed into tired, irritable, and essentially diabetic versions of their former selves.

The best thing you can do to cure OSA is to lose fat. However, this is no easy fix as OSA also increases appetite, insulin, and ghrelin. To get an edge in this uphill battle, you may have considered turning to sleeping pills, which are one of the worst things you can feed your tired-self.

Just Say No to Sleep Drugs

"These drugs do things we do not understand," says Daniel Kripke, MD, a passionate critic of sleeping pills. Despite his proclamation, there's a lot we do understand about sleeping pills – especially their popularity. Americans now dole out $4.5 billion every year on sleeping drugs, and the amount of prescriptions handed out at doctor's offices has gone up over 70% in the last ten years or so. According to a *New York Times* article in 2012, Americans filled some 60 million prescriptions for sleeping pills in 2011 and that was up from 47 million five years earlier.

Popularity aside, there remains a question of whether these things work as they claim. Despite costing upwards of $3.50 per pill (in the case of Rozerem® otherwise known as ramelteon), very few studies have found that these pills actually lengthen the duration of deep sleep.

The National Institutes of Health recently found that a battery of "cutting edge" sleeping pills like Ambien®, Lunesta™, and Sonata® only boost sleep time by about ten minutes. When it comes to side effects, prescription sleep aids make you act like you've just come from another planet. Many regular users report driving without remembering, sex that they can't recall and conversations that never registered in their minds. In other words, amnesia. A paid mouthpiece for drug companies, Gary S. Richardson, MD, told the *New York Times* in chilling fashion, "If you forget how long you lay in bed tossing and turning, in some ways that's just as good as sleeping." Sorry Dr. Richardson, but wiping our memories a la *Sunshine of the Spotless Mind* is not my idea of refreshing sleep.

Addicted to Sleep

The one thing you won't forget from taking these meds is your addiction to them. A particular class of sleeping pills called benzodiazepines is especially habit forming. But that doesn't mean taking newer drugs are a safer bet. All sleeping pills hit your brain's addiction centers on two fronts: physiological and psychological. Sleeping pills are drugs, so there's a certain level of chemical dependency that inevitably occurs over time. The only way to get over this is to wean yourself off the drug.

Some people report a very different kind of addiction, called "rebound insomnia." Because you've trained your mind to associate sleeping pills as a prerequisite for sleep, anxiety sets in when you lie down without them. Fortunately, you don't have to be at the whim of addictive pills to sleep soundly. A handful of natural sleep aids oftentimes work much better and without the bizarre side effects and addictive qualities of prescription meds.

When evaluating natural sleep aids, you should look for a mechanism of action that is effective, yet safe. You'd be surprised to find that many so-called "natural" products are just harsh chemicals in disguise. Any natural formula for sleep enhancement should work by:

- Boosting melatonin or tryptophan levels in the brain

- Blocking the tryptophan-destroying enzyme IDO (indoleamine 2, 3-dioxygenase)

- Lowering high levels of circulating stress hormones

So Close...Yet So Far

You open your eyes. It's the middle of the night and you have to go... again. It's the third time your usually stoic bladder has awakened you up tonight for a bathroom run.

Even though your toilet is only down the hall, you feel magnetically glued to your comfy bed – making the bathroom seem miles away.

If this sounds familiar, then you may want to try water-soluble, pumpkin seed extract. Clinical trials have shown pumpkin seed extract to be one of the few natural overactive bladder supplements out there.

A double blind, placebo-controlled study found that water-soluble pumpkin seed extract improved excessive urination symptoms in 75% of the people taking it – talk about the great pumpkin. And if that isn't enough to get you interested, the famous syndicated medical columnist, Harvard trained Dr. Gifford Jones, also recently gave only water-soluble pumpkin seed extract two thumbs up when it comes to ultimate bladder control.

Unlike sleeping pills, which are synthetic, side-effect prone, and highly addictive sedatives, the following nutrients work with your body's natural sleep pathways. If you do your homework, you can sometimes find them in one or two – what I would call – ultimate sleep formulas:

L-lysine is one of the most research-backed natural sleep aids. Your body produces IDO, an enzyme that's on a non-stop seek and destroy mission for the sleepy amino acid tryptophan—the same chemical in turkey that makes you tired after Thanksgiving dinner. Lysine works as an IDO bodyguard, letting tiring tryptophan build up in the brain. Sure enough, scientists have linked lysine levels with better quality sleep.

Melatonin is responsible for (ideally) making you tired at night. Based on darkness and circadian rhythm, an area of the brain called the pineal gland pumps out melatonin as a subtle hint that it's time for some shut eye. However, many people don't produce enough melatonin – especially as you get older and when you subject yourself to bright lights too late at night, as in watching late night television, checking emails before bed, or keeping the lights at full brightness right up until bedtime. Research from The Lancet found that, "Melatonin deficiency may have an important role in the high frequency of insomnia..." and that popping a melatonin before bedtime significantly improved sleep quality.

Griffonia is a shrub extract with high levels of a natural form of 5-Hydroxytryptophan (5HTP). 5HTP is a form of tryptophan that's especially important for serotonin production – a "feel good" neurotransmitter that can induce relaxation and sleepiness.

If you want more tryptophan, why not go right to the source? Tryptophan is a necessary precursor for serotonin. Research suggests it goes one step further by improving natural melatonin production. A research review titled, "*Effects of L-tryptophan on sleepiness and on sleep*" concluded that taking one gram or more of tryptophan helps you fall asleep faster and may even improve sleep quality.

Theanine is the reason you can drink four cups of tea—which has more caffeine than your average espresso—and not get the jitters. Theanine is found in high concentrations in tea, and has the unique ability of "smoothing" out erratic brainwaves, as confirmed by EEG. Sure enough, Japanese research subjects that took 200mg of theanine before bed reported better sleep –findings confirmed by sleep monitors.

Ziziphus, also known as Jujube, may be the "first" sleep supplement. The Chinese have been taking Ziziphus for centuries –and for good reason. Modern-day scientists have pinpointed special compounds in Ziziphus, called sapponins, which bring on relaxation.

Valerian is an old school sleep aid. Hippocrates, the father of modern medicine, was a personal fan, and there are records of valerian root being prescribed to people with insomnia way back in the second century. Swiss researchers found that valerian shortened the time it took to get to sleep and made slumber more refreshing overall.

It may not get the press of an overhyped "super fruit" from South America, but tending to your sleep is one of the most important decisions you can make for fat loss. Don't hit the pillow just yet. If you're a man (or if you know one), make sure you stay up for the next chapter, where I show you how the male body and mind view fat gain and fat loss.

Don't worry ladies; you'll get your turn, too.

CHAPTER 8 – His Fat

Barry tries to suck in his stomach just enough to see why "little Barry" isn't doing his job down below. He thought this sort of thing wasn't supposed to happen until he was a few decades older.

"Not again," he mumbles too quietly for his wife, Donna, to hear him. He can't hold his gut in much longer and tries to let his breath out slowly so his belly won't look like a rapidly inflating blubber balloon.

Every night this week, his brain has engaged, but certain parts of his body keep refusing to deliver. At first, he thought he was just tired, but by the third night a little panic set in and now he's wondering if he's hit some middle-aged thing when he wasn't looking.

Barry is used to solving problems. At work he's known as the go-to-guy and he runs the checklist through his head trying to see where things have changed. Donna is still quite a looker so that isn't it. He no longer seems to have his old sexual appetite despite the sexy lingerie she tries to entice him with.

"It's okay," Donna says. "Really, it is, but I'm a little concerned that you've been more enthusiastic about overhauling the engine on your Jeep lately than getting my motor humming."

Barry isn't sure what to say and tries to smile as he looks down at what used to be his wife's best friend. He wants to cry, but he's pretty sure that will kill all memories of him as the man of the family.

"Maybe it's part of getting older," Barry suggests, hoping Donna disagrees.

"Just six months ago, you were good to go almost every night," she says, shaking her head. He can see she wants to cry, too.

Barry wants to kiss her just for saying that, but he doesn't want to give her any false hope.

"You didn't age that much in half a year. What's changed over the last six months?" she asks.

Barry sighs and scratches his head. "Well, I got that promotion in June, but that shouldn't have anything to do with it. I guess I'll make an appointment with Dr. Weinstein and start popping the little blue pills." He thinks he hears Donna let out a tired sigh, as well, but she smiles at him reassuringly. She looks worried, but he can't tell if it's more for his health or her lack of action.

Tired, bored, and sick of trying, Barry lies back in bed, reaches for the remote, and flips though the channels hoping for an *NCIS* marathon or a rerun of *The Sopranos*. James Gandolfini. "Now there was a real man," he thinks to himself as he rubs his round belly. He stops when he sees that the 11 o'clock news is on. The newscaster is talking about a research study linking belly fat to a low libido and erectile dysfunction (ED). Suddenly, an idea grows in his mind—the only thing to take shape that evening—and he sits straight up in bed full of excitement.

"So that's it!" Barry shouts out. "Did you hear that, Donna?" Barry calls out to his wife, who has now gone in search of chocolate. She's been eating more of the sweet treat after every failed attempt that week. "My beer belly is what's making me as limp as a cooked piece of spaghetti."

"That's more like a taco and guacamole belly than beer," Donna, says holding up the super-sized Milky Way® bar she found hidden in the back of the cupboard. Barry realizes he has to get back into the saddle as soon as possible or there's going to be a lot more of Donna to love.

Time to Man Up

Barry isn't the only person suffering from a growing belly and a shrinking sex life. Records from as far back as the Byzantine Empire, proposed that a large abdomen makes sex more difficult and that's not just because it gets in the way. Modern science can now confirm some very ancient wisdom.

Research published in *The Journal of Sexual Medicine* found a direct link between obesity and rates of erectile dysfunction using a large sample of men. Dr. Irwin Goldstein, the Director of Sexual Medicine at Alvarado Hospital in San Diego, summed up the significance of the results. "This is a landmark study in that it shows sexual health is clearly linked to overall health, and that improving one's general health provides a man the opportunity to improve his erectile function." I can't think of a better motivator than that.

The health problems that accompany obesity—hypertension, cardiovascular disease, and diabetes—wreak havoc on the delicate vascular system of the penis. Also, ironically, being fat can make you biologically less of a man and maybe even more of a woman – from a hormonal perspective, anyway. Men who are obese have significantly less testosterone—and often more estrogen—than their normal weight counterparts.

You can read even more about this great topic in my award-winning book, *Beer Belly Blues*, which outlines how men with a great deal of fat in their midsections also produce a large amount of an enzyme called *aromatase*, which converts testosterone into estrogen. The process wreaks havoc on a man's life – not to mention the women who are part of it. So, if you think a woman's weight loss plan will work for a man, think again. Men are unique in how they store, burn, and think about fat.

But just like Barry and Donna, there are simple things that a couple can do to help improve health and get back to tuning the marital engine.

American novelist, poet, short story writer, art critic, and literary critic, John Updike, once remarked, "Inhabiting a male *body* is like having a *bank account*; as long as it's healthy, you don't think much about it." Unfortunately, few men have a healthy body and yet they *still* don't tend to think much about it. Body size, body image, and body composition are remarkably different between the sexes.

It's no secret that men and women are different as any trip around the self-help section of a book store can prove. However, for some reason, I notice that many men think their approach to weight loss should be a carbon copy of most popular diets and 90% of those are targeted toward women.

The Metabolic Advantage

Do you really think you'll get the physique you want by downing tofu, hitting aerobics class, and stretching while watching *The View*? While the fundamentals of fat loss I discussed in the previous chapters apply to both men and women, when it comes to metabolism, you may be surprised at just how different the bodies and minds of the genders can be.

You may also be surprised to learn that there's a giant gap in weight loss science for men. While male-centered sex discrimination in medical research has been well publicized, when it comes to weight loss science, men aren't very likely to sign up as guinea pigs. Weight loss researchers who want to recruit both men and women are lucky if they wind up with 20% of the volunteers being male. Women are more amped for weight loss; therefore, there's much more research into female fat loss. Despite this, science still provides us with more than enough exploration to give us insight into male fat physiology.

The most noticeable example of a man's unique biology is his body fat storage sites. Fat men tend to have an apple shape, which means fat tends to get stored in the chest and abdomen. Scientists refer to this male propensity for central fat storage as an "android" shape. Sure enough, men tend to have larger waists than women even if they weigh the exact amount. Unfortunately, the same belly that's useful as a built-in beer can rest also significantly increases the risk for a host of chronic diseases.

If you happen to be of the male persuasion with an ever-expanding waist, don't feel like nature has it against you. Your body has a number of advantages when it comes to fat-burning. The first is body composition. All things considered, men have more muscle on board than women and by quite a bit. Pound for pound, males tend to carry 10-20% more muscle. You already know the dramatic metabolic edge that muscle provides, so consider yourself lucky. This extra muscle translates into metabolism rates that resemble men's favorite cars: Porches and Mustangs. In fact, a study done at the University of North Carolina found that men had an RMR *50% higher* than women. Some of the metabolic discrepancy can be attributed to men simply weighing more (as more weight generally means a higher RMR), but most of the RMR edge comes from muscle.

However, men still make up more of the soaring obesity rates than women. Statistics from the National Institutes of Health concluded that, "among women, there has been no change in obesity prevalence between 1999 and 2008." Men are getting fatter as a group while women are dealing with the same baselines.

Why are men losing the battle of the bulge despite having such a tremendous intrinsic advantage? One explanation is a guy's love affair with food. Pop culture may lead you to believe that swooning over chocolate cake is the exclusive territory of women, but you'd be wrong. (Not that I fall under this guise, of course.)

Australian researchers were surprised to find that men actually prefer food over sex (I can assure you, however, that *I* was not one of the study subjects). Despite eating more food and calories overall, men are much less likely to eat five servings of fresh fruits and vegetables, which are important allies in the quest for fat loss.

The Manly Brain

The thing that makes "his fat" so unique is the male brain. You don't have to read my good friend and colleague, Dr. John Gray's book, *Men are From Mars, Women Are from Venus* (HarperCollins 1992), to know a man's brain is quite different from a woman's. The same brain that can effortlessly memorize the line-up of baseball's All-Star game is horrible at evaluating whether the body is properly monitoring its own metabolism or not. Talk about denial.

According to the US National Center for Health Statistics, the likelihood of an overweight man incorrectly categorizing himself as "normal weight" is twice that of a comparatively-sized woman. Interestingly, as more and more men get fat, less and less of them seem to notice. About a decade ago, before the flames of the obesity epidemic took on so much heat, 41% of overweight men saw themselves at a healthy weight. The number of misguided souls has risen 10% in ten years. Now, every man in the neighborhood has the real life physique of a Homer Simpson, but thinks they look more like Ned Flanders' buff frame. D'oh!

A study done by a research group from the Netherlands illustrates the "*his* fat blinders phenomenon" exceptionally well. The researchers collected basic health information (body weight, waist circumference, cholesterol, etc.) from a group of about 2,000 men and then asked them what they thought about their health and weight. As expected, most of the men considered their weight "just right," even if the numbers said otherwise.

Therefore, as might be expected, many of the men weren't trying to move a muscle and lose the fat. They didn't think there was a good enough reason. Compared to women, men were about half as likely to say they were trying to lose weight. The authors described the situation bluntly, "…a number were doing nothing about their weight, although frankly they were obese." More specifically, 70% of the study group wasn't doing a thing about their extra layers of flab.

Why are men so blind to the fat that is staring back at them in the mirror? There's a variety of psychological issues at play such as social, biological, and psychological factors. While research abounds regarding obesity wrecking women's body image and quality of life, studies suggest this doesn't seem to occur nearly as much in men. The same group of Dutch men didn't think being fat made much of a difference to their quality of life.

Also, studies show that being fat is less stigmatizing for a man than it is for a woman. As surprising as it may seem, the research suggests men aren't dieting simply because they don't know or care that they're fat, or both.

Gender Specific Foods

Another factor that's related to a sense of false fat perception is something I like to call, "The Dumb Male Diet." The Dumb Male Diet is not a weight loss diet. It's a pop-culturally derived system that tells "real men" what they should want to eat. This mindset categorizes flab-provoking foods like ribs, sausage, and fried bacon as manly and they go well with gulping it all down with some—make that a lot of—beer to enhance your midsection. Some of the healthiest foods on the planet like fresh vegetables, yogurt, and beans get relegated to an off-limits "wimpy" category. A man's way of thinking is, "I didn't make it all the way to the top of the food chain just to eat vegetables."

You already know when it comes to food and fat loss, lite foods are the fast track to fatness – but you may not know how much they contribute to a jiggly male midsection. Research in *The American Journal of Clinical Nutrition* found that a high intake of refined grains and sugar resulted in growing waistlines in older men. The high glycemic index of those foods churns out insulin – the chief predecessor to your body's belly fat production.

You may think that eating 16 ounces of deep fried chicken wings in one sitting makes you more of a man, but you'd be wrong. It just makes more man. Fatty, processed, meats that serve as the cornerstone of The Dumb Male Diet are also a surefire way to grow your belly. Research shows that a high trans-fat intake, which is often indicative of eating platefuls of fried meat, as well as processed lite foods, is strongly linked to a larger waist.

"But the alarming part of all this is we seem to accept that foods should be gendered," says an article in *Sirens* Magazine. The science backs this up. When the two sexes are polled about their favorite dishes at fast food joints, men are twice as likely to order a Big Mac, but are half as apt to order a salad as female diners. The same study also found that men tend to order processed red meat dishes like hamburgers instead of healthier foods like leaner chicken. The Dumb Male Diet is very real and its hypnotic pull on an entire gender is what is making men fatter and a lot faster than women.

Dudes Diet Differently

I'm not saying that every fat guy on there is thinks he's God's gift to women or hasn't had his fair share of dieting letdowns. When I travel across North America with *Beer Belly Blues* or *The Ultimate Male Solution*, I meet plenty of hard-working guys who have tried everything to lose the extra fat they have on board. Sadly, men are fair game to the lite food deception, as well. However, being ignorant to fat has at least one positive. On the one hand, you're rolling the dice with your health and ignoring a heart attack warning practically tattooed on your own body. But, on the other hand, you're also avoiding becoming a *smaller fat person* because you don't succumb to the perils of yo-yo dieting.

At least that's what a study published in *The Journal of the American Dietetic Association* reported. When men do hunker down and try to drop some flabby layers, they tend to do it right. Men go for extreme diets, like low-fat or low-carb, less than half as often as women. The important difference is when men do take note of their bulging waist, they'd rather hit the gym than starve themselves. The study authors concluded that men "...[who] do want to lose the extra pounds tend to try to achieve this through exercise rather than dieting." It turns out that dudes diet differently, and so when they finally do notice they can't see their feet anymore, they're more likely to be successful at it.

Man Juice

That's the good news. But if you don't make the effort to burn fat, especially belly fat, which most men don't, then you can easily find yourself with testosterone levels lower than the 2008 stock market. As you may already know, testosterone is the primary male hormone. Way back as a fetus, it was the release of testosterone that flipped the switch that made a baby boy. As an adult, however, a bulging belly is like a trap door for the loss of testosterone production. In fact, men with a waist measurement of 40 inches or more typically produce 30% less testosterone than men with a waist size of 37 inches or less. Scientists don't fully understand why, but it seems that fat around the midsection sends signals to the rest of the body to shut down testosterone production. All this time, you thought your belly was a symbol of manliness, not that women are ready to claim it.

Why does testosterone matter? First, testosterone is an important determinant of a man's body composition. Luckily for the men who still dream of a chance at the Big Leagues, the testosterone floating around inside of them is a perfectly legal anabolic steroid. Anyone who watched a baseball game in the 1990s knows what steroids do: they pack on ludicrous amounts of muscle and make you strong-like-bull. However, because the testosterone your body produces is natural, there aren't some of the possible nasty side effects that come with the injected variety. That means, men aren't getting the advantages nature is trying to give them and unless they get their belly under control, building muscle is going to be an uphill battle, indeed.

Testosterone is also an underrated ally in the battle against fat. Exercise scientist, Christian Finn, described how fat cells are set up to flux. "Just like a car, your fat cells have a series of brakes and accelerators. The parts of a fat cell that accelerate the release of fat are called *beta-receptors*." One of testosterone's little-known jobs is to tell fat cells to make more beta-receptors. Clinical research has also found that testosterone is able to shut down fat storing enzymes such as *lipoprotein lipase* (or LPL, which was introduced in Chapter 4) that are necessary for the uptake of fat into the body's fat cells. When fat cells are exposed to testosterone in a test tube, the activity of LPL is dramatically reduced. Aside from this, testosterone stimulates fat-burning by increasing the number of certain receptors on the fat-cell membrane that release stored fat.

A good amount of men out there have no issues with testosterone, at least before the tender age of 30, but after that we can lose approximately 10% each decade. However, for many men, the Beer Belly Blues are a large part of their low testosterone equation. (The blues comes from studies showing that men with low testosterone are 271% more likely to show clinical signs of depression than men with higher testosterone levels.) The Beer Belly Blues is a common condition caused by testosterone levels taking a nosedive in middle-aged – and sometimes much younger – guys. Research suggests that testosterone therapy (natural, as in bioidentical hormones and nutrients that help raise testosterone and synthetic, as in properly administered injections) can reverse many of the most detrimental signs of the Beer Belly Blues, like increased belly fat, muscle atrophy, loss of strength, low energy, depression, and ED.

Note that there are many ways to tell if you are starting to experience the Beer Belly Blues. For instance, poor overall health, lack of energy, depression, high cholesterol, blood sugar problems, loss of muscle and strength, excess belly fat, low libido and a loss of erectile function are all signs of low testosterone. (For a more accurate assessment, visit *www.UltimateMaleSolution.com* and fill out the on-line ADAM—Androgen Deficiency in the Aging Male—Testosterone Questionnaire.)

Having said that, the best way to tell for sure is to visit a doctor who understands how to properly read a testosterone blood test. I don't say that to be a wise ass; I say it because most doctors just look at an age-adjusted laboratory reference range to tell if a man is suffering from low testosterone or not. The problem is that most of these reference ranges are way too low to begin with and so many-a-man has gone undiagnosed and is then left to suffer in silence.

Pump Me Up

If you do find yourself with a legit Beer Belly Blues diagnosis and are a bit skittish about taking prescriptions, you may want to consider some research backed testosterone boosting nutrient combinations like zinc and *Eurycoma longifolia jack* (Tongkat Ali) that can be found on *www.UltimateMaleSolution.com*, as well.

Whether a guy has the Beer Belly Blues or not, the safest and most effective way to get ample testosterone is to melt away the fat that's set up shop in the midsection. The only way to do that is to overhaul the way men eat and exercise. And speaking of exercise, there is one manly activity that *does* improve testosterone levels – strength training.

Pumping iron drives up testosterone in two ways. First, the weight load on the muscles is a direct stimulus for testosterone production, but the positive effects wear off soon after the workout. Consistent sessions of strength training help testosterone levels to steadily rise over time. Second, the addition of fuel to the body's metabolic engine from new muscle helps the entire system more effectively melt away belly fat—the super villain in this low testosterone story. Combined with a proper macronutrient ratio, the weights can start a chain reaction of more testosterone → less fat → more muscle → even more testosterone.

Now that the men are squared away, it's time to focus on all of the women readers. The next chapter is all about you – especially how to take advantage of the female body and mind to finally fight fat and win.

CHAPTER 9 – Her Fat

Jane gulped down hard when she looked at the email and then felt a tight knot in her stomach. The subject line read: *"House Warming Party – Bring Your Bathing Suit!"* The words seemed to jump out at her like an accusation. The familiar daisy chain of thoughts ran through her mind. Too fat, too lazy, wasted all of that time, shouldn't have eaten the Halloween candy, or could have joined that aerobics class...

There was a long list of woulda-coulda-shoulda's that all ended with Jane's dismal evaluation of herself.

Jane continued to read the email anyway hoping for some kind of loophole that would make it acceptable that she showed up in her usual uniform of long pants and a sweater set. Maybe there were babies who'd need watching. She could volunteer, stay with the small set, and earn points as the friend who gave up a good time to help others.

Still... she read on: *"Hey everyone, please come share in our joy! Jack and I finally closed on our dream house with the backyard and Olympic-sized swimming pool just calling out for friends and family!"*

"You've got a body like Beyoncé. Of course you'd buy a house with a pool," she said to the computer screen as though she were speaking directly to her friend, Kim.

"To celebrate, we're throwing a giant pool party bash at our new home!"

Jane sighed hard. "Walking around in a bathing suit with my thighs shaking every time I take a step is not my idea of a bash," Jane said to no one. "I wonder if you can wear a bathing suit under a long cover-up and just never take it off."

"We're going to have the new double grill on, so get ready to eat!"

Jane threw her hands up in surrender. "It's like the woman is trying to torture me. Just what I need... more temptations."

Jane thought about all the times she'd tried not to fill her plate at parties, but she would get so hungry that she'd wait for everyone else to get buried in a conversation and then she'd go sit off by herself wolfing down food and feeling guilty about it afterwards.

"The party is this Saturday at 1:00 p.m. The weatherman said it's going be sunny and hot, so bring your swim wear and be prepared to play

and relax pool side! We'll provide the rafts, food, and fun."

"I'll be praying for rain," Jane said, looking out the window at the clear blue sky. She wondered just how many days had she wasted sitting by this window?

"See you soon! Toodles! ☺ Kim and Jack"

"Easy for you to be so cheerful. You're not going to have rolls of flab bursting out of every edge of your bathing suit," Jane said to the computer, trying not to cry. "Why couldn't we meet up at the mall like normal people?"

"P.S. And don't think we'll fall for the, 'I forgot my bathing suit' line. We have a pool and we plan to use it! No judgments at the Smith residence. Promise!"

Jane knows she shouldn't let the image of herself get in the way of enjoying her good friends' celebration. She *is* happy for them and *does* look forward to catching up, but when Jane looks in the mirror, all she can see is the fat and the flaws. Every beautiful part of her seems to be invisible.

So, the idea of parading around half-naked is like wearing a sign in front of all of her friends that she's failed. The looming part is overpowering all other thoughts.

A week of nerves, eating almost nothing, and obsessing over how she looks from every angle finally passes. Saturday has arrived and Jane resolutely puts on her bathing suit, takes one long last look, and then covers herself up in Capri pants and a long-sleeved shirt.

At Kim and Jack's house, Jane feels that the walk to the backyard is as slow and painful as the time she tried to pull a cantaloupe out of the bottom of a pyramid at the grocery store and the entire pile came crashing down, rolling out in every direction. It seemed to take forever to recapture all of the bruised fruit and help the bag boys build a new display. Jane still wasn't sure why the manager felt the need to keep announcing there was a spill at the front of the store long after help had arrived. She remembers how awkward she felt bending over, wondering if everyone was comparing her round butt to a big, ripe melons.

She walked into the party expecting to hear plenty of splashes and raucous laughter. But no. Instead, there's a low hum of voices chatting. Jane is dumbfounded when she finally reaches the pool and standing before her is a crowd of people thoroughly covered up, nervously eyeing the pool with sweat standing out on their foreheads. No one is even going near the edge. Jane laughs inwardly wondering if everyone is worried Kim will make them go in first.

"I'm not alone," Jane says. "I love these people." Everyone at the party, except for the hostess, is thoroughly covered up in t-shirts and shorts. Jane isn't the only one skittish about her body. Even though the gathering is on a beautiful, hot summer day, not one of the men and women in the backyard are wearing only their bathing suit.

It certainly confirmed something Jane's mother swore was true, years ago: The most feared words in every middle-aged woman's vocabulary are, "Pool Party!"

Distorted Self-Images

When reading that story, did you picture Jane as a rotund, bloated, old lady or as a slim and lean, vibrant woman? Based on the words Jane chose to describe herself, you probably imagined her as way too pudgy and past her prime. However, Jane's friends didn't see her that way, and often said so. According to myriad research, it doesn't really matter how others perceive a woman's body because the body that is looking at you from the mirror is the only one that counts.

Remember, perception equals *personal* reality.

Sadly, a critical body image is extremely common in women. While men tend to wear rose-colored glasses when looking down at their flab, women view their body as it would appear in a fun house mirror – distorted and out of proportion. This leads many women, even healthy, fit ones, into the pitfalls of fad dieting.

Studies show that women are much more likely than men to go to extreme lengths for weight loss. It's been reported that laxative use, liposuction, and self-starvation are extremely common in the female population, and is almost nonexistent among males.

But it's not just extremes that draw women in – women cover all areas of the dieting spectrum. In fact, it's been said that, "To be female is to diet." There's more truth to that statement than most people would like to admit. At any given moment in time, and regardless of body fat, women are twice as likely to be "trying to lose weight" than overweight men. Weight Watchers® did a study a few years back, which found the average women has tried three diets *in the last year alone*, while another study found that women were four times more likely than men to try an extreme, low-fat diet. At any given moment, one-third of women can be found either starting a diet or finishing one. (Or breaking their diet as they pull out of the fast food drive-through with that highly-advertised two dollar triple cheeseburger they just had to have.)

Why do so many women diet? There's no doubt social pressures weigh women down more than a few extra pounds ever could. The media, especially those targeting women, are extremely beauty and body focused. Worse yet, the role models for an ideal female body are often represented by emaciated runway models wearing size zero clothing. Rationally, you may be disgusted when you see an airbrushed photo of featherweight women in your favorite magazine, but your subconscious absorbs the message that this is normal, or even ideal because, after all, she's in a magazine isn't she?

The discrepancy between real life bodies and the ones paraded around in Victoria's Secret catalogs (not that I'd know of course) is always growing, no pun intended. *Newsweek* reports that, "Twenty-five years ago, the average female model weighed eight percent less than the average American woman... Today, models weigh about 23 percent less than the average woman." The pressure to be thin overrides the brain's logical systems that tell you your body is fine as-is.

When asked to evaluate their current weight, like men, women miss the mark. However, unlike men, women tend to *overestimate* their weight. Twenty-three percent of women who are normal weight, based on BMI, still consider themselves as fat. While this statistic often gets lauded as evidence for distorted body image, I would argue that many women are right-on in this assessment, but for a different reason. Research shows that half of all women with a normal BMI are actually obese, based on body composition. A good chunk of that group, because they considered factors like how their clothes fit, is actually more in tune with their bodies than a flawed BMI formula.

But that's not to say their intuition is perfect or it justifies anyone beating themselves up about their weight by resorting to tactics that harm their health. However, it's an unfortunate reality that women remain overly-critical of their bodies. One study found that women think their hips are 16% wider and their waists are 25% larger than they actually measure. This wasn't a case of general estimation ineptitude because the same women had no issue estimating the size of a box.

Tinkering with Your Mind

Body image distortion underlies much of the motivation for dieting. When women are asked why they diet, 76% say it's to improve their appearance, *not* their health. Desperation for thinness drives many women to become hypnotically drawn to fad diets and lite foods.

In fact, if you're a woman, it's even more critical that you ditch crash dieting and lite foods for good. Studies suggest the dieting roller coaster does funky things to your body – especially your brain. Research done at the Institute of Food Research found that traditional, calorie-cutting, food-obsessed dieting actually chips away a few IQ points. When a group of women performed a battery of cognitive tests, those who were dieting performed the worst. The study's authors noted, "...slower reaction times and poorer immediate recall of words when they were dieting." Scientists think dieting may impair the female brain in two ways:

1. By starving it of nutrients; or,

2. As Nicola Jones, MD, of the University of Bristol put it, "...dieting depletes the cognitive resources available for non-dieting tasks."

Unfortunately, the psychological ramifications stemming from repeated dieting bouts are much more profound than performing a cognition test in some laboratory. Diet failures also take a large toll on the female psyche. A study done by the Dutch National Institute of Public Health and the Environment assessed the effects of repeated weight loss failures on the quality of life. Unlike the men they studied, the psychological ramifications of women's yo-yo dieting experiences remained long after the weight came back. The researchers concluded, "Only with history of frequent weight loss, and uniquely in women, was there a significant reduction in scores on mental health and limited emotional role functioning." Other studies confirm the fact that trying and failing on a number of diets creates emotional scars, which can leading to binge eating disorders and other types of emotional eating issues as discussed in Chapter 3.

Lite foods don't actually help you lose weight. That's enough of a reason for every woman reading this to put them down and stop buying them for good. They don't help you achieve your goals. In fact, studies show that for most women, the more they diet, the fatter they become. If you've lost more than ten pounds on six separate occasions, you're much more likely to become obese. Shockingly, five weight loss attempts over the last year more than doubles your obesity risk. The fatty rebound from fad diets practically guarantees that you lose weight, but still end up fatter than before (i.e. the Smaller Fat Person Syndrome).

The Metabolic Paradox

As touched on in the last chapter, and just in case you're a woman reading this chapter and decided to skip over the last one, women have often wondered why men seem to lose so much more "weight" on the same diets. Once again, the answer lies in what that weight consists of.

Men have a lot more muscle than women (30 – 40 pounds more on average), which allots a man a much greater metabolic advantage. Since muscle is the key metabolic engine of the body, men are able to burn an extra 30% in calories over and above women, even sitting on their hairy behinds (that is unless they shave said hairy behinds) doing nothing. This is why weight bearing activity or resistance training is so important to a woman's ability to burn fat in the long run.

Kooky for Cocoa and Cortisol

Fad diet obsession doesn't tell the entire story. The female appetite is decidedly unique. How else can you explain the fact that research shows 92% of self-reported "chocolate addicts" are women? Can you say "PMS?" After all, journalist Miranda Ingram once said, "It's not that chocolates are a substitute for love. Love is a substitute for chocolate. Chocolate is, let's face it, far more reliable than a man." I want to argue that fact, but it's really best to leave it alone.

What is it about chocolate that makes women go gaga? In general, the types of foods that women crave tend to be sweet, starchy, and with a touch of fat. Chocolate certainly fits the bill there. As you may expect, it's not the female brain as much as the hormones that create *chocoholics*. In general, women tend to have higher levels of NPY than men—a huge instigator of sugar cravings. Exacerbating this love for sweets is the fact that restricting foods, known to most women as simply dieting, boosts cortisol production. This one-two hormonal punch makes women much more likely to succumb to binge eating sessions.

But dieting isn't the only precursor to elevated cortisol levels in women. A study published by the University of California San Francisco with the descriptive title, *Stress May Add Bite to Appetite in Women: a laboratory study of stress-induced cortisol and eating behavior*, found that women are especially prone to stressful eating. When the researchers put women in a tense situation, and confirmed cortisol release via a blood test, they found that the women with the highest cortisol levels ate the most amount of food. They also tended to crave sweets. This increase in appetite continued for the days after the women had left the lab. Not only does stress bring on more cortisol for women, its dastardly role as an appetite-instigator sticks around for longer.

Hormones may partly explain why a recently study published in the *Proceedings of the National Academy of Sciences* found that women have a harder time turning down dessert. The researchers in this study polled a group of men and women about their favorite foods. After fasting overnight, the volunteers visited the lab and were surprised to find a buffet of their favorite foods right in front of their eyes (how mean is that?) The volunteers were then asked to try their best to shift the focus of their attention away from the food.

Even though both the men and women reported their thoughts were elsewhere, their brain scans told a different story. While the men's appetite centers were dormant (and the women are thinking, aren't all their brain centers?), the women's continued to fire on all cylinders. The head of the study, Gene-Jack Wang, MD, stated, "There is something going on in the female... the signal is so much different." (And I'm thinking, "Seriously, you went to medical school to learn *that*?")

Lovely Lady Lumps

Brain scans can shed light on certain aspects of the women's appetite control mechanisms, but there's something that's hard to detect by a machine: comfort. Studies show that when women seek out food for comfort, they tend to look past the nutrient composition and strongly consider how much effort it takes to eat it. While men assuage their stress with good ol' mac and cheese or a T-bone and taters, women prefer foods that are ready in a flash and don't need a lot of prep time.

Dr. Brian Wansink, a marketing professor who heads the Food and Brand Lab at the University of Illinois at Urbana-Champaign, guesses that the reasons for this stem from childhood associations. "Because adult females are not generally accustomed to having hot food prepared for them, and as children, saw the female as the primary food preparer, they tend to gain psychological comfort from less labor-intensive foods such as chocolate, candy, and ice cream."

Lite foods take advantage of the flaws in female appetite regulation. They're sugary, ready to eat, and, perhaps worst of all, tend to be chocolate flavored. Not to mention, they don't talk back or demand anything.

Oh, and those fat cells, fashioned out of the latest lite ice cream binge session, don't end up just anywhere. In most women, fat tends to accumulate in the same areas: attached to the butt, thighs, and hips. The figure that female fat sculpts is commonly called a pear shape, or what scientists call a *gynoid* body type. On the bright side, a pear shape puts you at lower risk for chronic diseases that are more likely to strike apple-shaped men. But as you probably know firsthand, the downside is the fat cells that end up in those "trouble spots" are persistent little bastards.

Alpha & Beta

The reason why you can spend hours on the treadmill while chewing on iceberg lettuce as a snack and *still* not fit into your jeans is because the fat cells that form the apple shape have fewer beta-receptors (the fat cell's accelerator), and many more alpha-receptors, which serve as the brake. Simply put, fat loss is physically harder for women than men.

Blame it on Mother Nature

For years, scientists have been trying to figure out why a women's body composition leans toward being on the fatter side despite eating less. Anthony O'Sullivan, Ph.D., says, "From an energy balance point of view, there is no explanation why women should be fatter than men, particularly since men consume more calories proportionately. In fact, women burn off more fat than men during exercise, but they don't lose as much body fat with exercise, suggesting women are more efficient fat storers at other times. The question is why does this paradox exist?"

The answer to Dr. O'Sullivan's question is surprisingly simple. The twist of fate that has bestowed women with the curse of fat storage efficiency is a hormone everyone associates with the female body: *estrogen*. That's right; the same hormone responsible for making you a woman is working its tail off to make you plump. A recent study out of the University of New South Wales was the first to break this story.

The scientists found that women store more fat after eating a meal, even a healthy one, than a similarly-sized man. Once the meal is over, estrogen travels around the body, turning off fat-burning enzymes and making sure the food you just ate gets stored, not burned.

But that alone doesn't explain the marked differences in the bodily shape of men and women. It turns out that estrogen works against you even between meals.

Evil Estrogens

When new fat cells are made, they ask the dominant hormone in the body where to go. When there's a lot of estrogen in the body, it routes the fat cells to the butt and thigh areas (Yippy). Worse yet, estrogen tags them with lots of alpha-receptors, and relatively few beta-receptors, giving them a longer-term lease than women would probably like. Also, when estrogen becomes overly-dominant, it displaces fat-burning and muscle-building hormones like progesterone and testosterone, which women need.

There's a huge evolutionary advantage in all of this. Mother Nature wants you to have loads of fat hanging around in case of pregnancy. Estrogen is the foreman—or in this case forewoman—of the operation ensuring that not one single calorie goes to waste. In fact, this is exactly what happens when a woman gets pregnant or starts birth control pills. Estrogen shoots up and fat cells respond by opening wide for new fatty payloads.

This may sound natural, but there are signs that the estrogen in today's women is anything but normal.

That's because we're now living in an age of estrogen, most of it not even produced by our bodies, throwing off normal hormonal checks and balance systems. In the last century, estrogen in our environment has skyrocketed. These unnatural forms of estrogen, called *xenoestrogens* (literally "foreign estrogen") may be part of the reason you store more fat than you burn.

John R. Lee, MD, notes how prevalent these xenoestrogens are in our modern world. "You would have to virtually live in a bubble to escape the excess estrogens we're exposed to through pesticides, plastics, industrial waste products, car exhaust, meat, soaps, and much of the carpeting, furniture, and paneling we live with indoors every day." And the kicker is, that even more of these problematic estrogens are being delivered transdermally (directly through the skin), by using expensive creams, shampoos, deodorants, etc., that have preservatives like methyl paraben in them.

The overall health implications of xenoestrogens aren't yet clear; however, numerous studies show they are extremely problematic where natural hormone chemistry is concerned. Considering our bodies weren't designed to handle them, it's definitely best to stay away from xenoestrogens with the proverbial ten-foot pole.

Another important area of estrogen exposure Dr. Lee doesn't mention is in our food. Even if you've taken a meal out of its xenoestrogen-based packaging and washed off xenoestrogen-lined pesticides, if the food is a soy product, the majority of the estrogen is still very much there. Foods like tofu and soybeans—aside from being genetically modified (unless they are organic) contain high levels of a form of estrogen called a *phytoestrogen*.

While likely more safe than xenoestrogens created at a power plant, there are signs that phytoestrogens can also raise estrogen to fat-creating levels. While the occasional tofu stir-fry or soy ice cream isn't going to kill you, going overboard with soy products may throw your hormonal balance for a real loop. In fact, there is so much negative research on soy that I personally never go near the stuff and would warn anyone else interested in staying as healthy (and lean) as possible to be very cautious as well.

Choose the Right Path

In reality, it's a bit misleading to use the word estrogen. Estrogen is actually a class of hormones and not one hormone all by itself. The body has two competing pathways that determine which type of estrogen becomes dominant in your body.

One pathway, which happens to become accelerated by xenoestrogen exposure, is a nasty form of estrogen, known as *16-OH estrogen*. John Foster, MD, sums up the current research on 16-OH estrogen when he says, "The 16-OH form is carcinogenic and causes diseases of tissues that are responsive to hormones, including disorders and cancers of breast, uterus, cervix, and prostate, and probably lung and colon." On the other end of the health spectrum is *2-OH estrogen*, a beneficial form of estrogen that actually counteracts the 16-OH form. Sure enough, when researchers look at breast cancer risk, they find that those with high levels of 2-OH estrogen have almost half the risk than those with sky-high levels of the 16-OH form.

Indoles to the Rescue

What can women do to get estrogen levels back in check? The first is to limit how often they come into contact with xenoestrogens. Because xenoestrogens raise overall estrogen levels and push the body toward making more 16-OH estrogen, a woman wants to stay as far away from these as the 21st century world will allow you to. But avoidance isn't the only tactic in your arsenal. Very special compounds called *Indoles* – nutrients that are found in cruciferous veggies like broccoli, kale, and spinach – are known as some of the most powerful weapons, when it comes to excess estrogen in the body.

One of the most researched and powerful of these indoles is called *Indole 3-carbinol* or *I3C*. Studies show that I3C hits phony estrogens hard. Research from the University of Nebraska Medical Center discovered that I3C works by improving the detoxification process in the liver, thereby helping your body filter out extra estrogen molecules. However, a few bites of broccoli at dinner won't do the trick. Studies show that you need to eat at least three servings of high indole containing plants per day to get a benefit. If the thought of downing three cups of cruciferous vegetables per day makes you gag (as it does me), then you're in luck because natural I3C is available in supplement form and seems to be just as effective.

That pretty much covers the primary biological hurdle that women have to face, but what about the downfalls that happen above the neck and between the ears? Body image issues, which were crafted from years of societal and person influences, aren't going to disappear overnight. On the bright side, there are steps you can take today to get your mind and body back on the same page.

1. First, strongly consider throwing away your trashy gossip magazines. (That's right, I said it.) Studies show that repeated exposure to body-focused media makes you more self-conscious about the way you look. While you may miss the rush you get from seeing the latest celeb gossip, you won't miss the renewed sense of confidence about your body.

2. Another important step is to change your eating environment. Because so much of the dieting industry puts undue focus on calories, many women develop a sense of subconscious guilt about eating *anything*. Instead of eating alone watching *Sex and the City* reruns, make plans to meet your friends or coworkers for dinner. Over time, this can change your food paradigms and you will learn to appreciate that food is part of your entire life and not just something with calories that you chew and swallow.

3. Poor body image has little to do with your body and everything to do with self-confidence anyway, so it's time to start

exercising. Besides the body composition and metabolism benefits I told you about already, studies show that exercising regularly, primarily with progressive resistance routines (i.e. weight training), can vastly improve the way you feel about yourself and your body. Exercise helps to align the image of your body in your head with reality.

Let's not forget the perils of lite foods – an entire industry preying on the weak spots in women's psyches. As publicized by Mireille Guiliano's book, *French Women Don't Get Fat*, (Random House, 2004) French women have an entirely different way of viewing food and tend to shun light foods (*"la nourriture léger"*). The best way to get lite foods out of your life may be to start enjoying the food you eat even more.

Many women turn to lite foods because they don't have the guilt tied to them that other foods carry. Guiliano notes that in North America, "There's so much guilt and sin associated with food." Realizing that lite foods are the only foods you should *actually* feel guilty about eating will go a long way toward a new, healthier relationship with food.

Whether you're a man or a woman, if you have children, then you need to stay tuned for the next chapter. I'm going to show you how, by changing *your* lifestyle, you may literally save your child's life.

CHAPTER 10 – Not So Mini-Me

"What are we going to do about it?" The words stumble out of Bill's mouth, accompanied by flying bits of barbecued flavored potato chips.

"What *can* we do about it?" Heather replies, feeling hopeless and frustrated, as she ducks the food shower. She's been married to Bill for a long time and knows better than to sit too close or ever come between Bill and his snacks. Heather's had nightmares where Bill's head turned into a snapping alligator just as she was reaching for the last donut. She shudders at the memory.

Plopped on the couch in front of the TV, they are discussing little Matthew's recent report card between commercial breaks. But this report card has nothing to do with how Matthew is doing in geometry. Like many schools around the country, Matthew's school has begun to give out report cards grading a child's weight.

Much to his parents' horror, Matthew received a resounding "F," for fat, for the third period in a row. The school nurse scribbled in the comments section that his weight is "causing him to have early signs of diabetes," even though he just turned nine.

Matthew looks just like his parents. The apple fell from the parental tree and stayed right next to its big, fat trunk. The entire family is obese and getting fatter by the month.

Bill brushes salt and food dust off his hands as he rubs them together. "On the news the other day, they said watching too much TV can make kids fat. Maybe we should take the TV out of his room?" He's trying to think of an easy answer or something that won't take much energy or time. Maybe Heather can carry the TV out of Matthew's room. They could put it in Bill's bathroom.

"That'll never work," Heather says too quickly. "He'll freak out if we did that. Besides, how would he get to sleep without the background noise?" She knows just who would have to handle all of that and she's already got a good idea where the extra TV would end up. No siree, Bill is not getting his way, she thinks.

"What if we started giving him water or juice instead of all those cans of soda he drinks?" Bill finishes the last swig of an extra-large Big Gulp® and belches long and proud. "The kid's addicted to that stuff. Besides, if we take it out of the house, what would we drink?"

For good measure, he adds another burp to the end of his question. He's awfully proud of his talent of talking and burping simultaneously, something he learned at the college frat house and continued to hone into his adult years. His best talent is burping the entire alphabet. Bill taught it to Matthew last summer, but the poor kid can only get to the letter K. So far.

The conversation halts abruptly as Matthew waddles his way into the room. The only sound is that of the TV cartoon tiger in the background trying to sell an orange cheese snack.

"How was your day, dear?" Heather asks.

Matthew's bottom lip quivers and looks like he's close to tears.

Earlier that day, a group of kids from his class had grabbed Matthew's fitness report card out of his hand and read it aloud to everyone within earshot. Matthew was humiliated and ended up sitting by himself at lunch, surrounded by noisy tables full of kids enjoying themselves.

Matthew takes a good, long look at his parents and understands there's no rescue coming from these people, especially when *Wheel of Fortune* has just come on.

"It was fine, I guess," he finally says to his mother, but she's already wrapped up in the first puzzle of Before and After. Heather seems to have forgotten she ever asked Matthew a question.

Matthew clumps along and heads to his room after nabbing a snack from the kitchen. With a Coke in one hand and the bag of peanut-fried chips in the other, he falls over on his bed to flip through the channels of the TV until he falls asleep, bleary-eyed in front of John Stewart.

Somewhere between *Wheel of Fortune* and the late news, Bill finally notices the report card again, which has fallen between his fat thigh and his wife's wide expanse.

Anger and irritation soon zips through him. "Hey! Shouldn't his school be teaching him this stuff in health class or something? I mean, isn't that why I'm paying taxes?"

Heather nods her three chins vigorously in agreement and sets the empty Reese's wrapper on her bedside table. "One thing *we do* know, it's not *our* fault," she says.

Bill practically chokes on a soda bubble as he agrees with his wife.

The Responsibility Factor

This is where it all starts. Fat parents grow fat kids like it's a new kind of farming system. The kids become fat adults and eventually fat parents themselves, keeping up the fat cycle.

As you know, the chances of a fat adult getting down to an appropriate size are slim, no joke. To keep your children healthy for life, you need to develop a program at an early age when they are most receptive to forming habits that will stay with them into adulthood. Like you're hardwiring them to eat well and keep moving.

It's also time to take responsibility for your kid's fatness. Remember, children don't buy the groceries, parents do. Whether your version of your own little Matthew is a tad fat or just right, now's the time to be proactive about your child's obesity. It all starts with you.

If you thought the obesity stats I showed you in Chapter 2 were disturbing, and then wait until you see how quickly our children have become ticking time bombs for diseases like heart attacks, stroke, and most pressing of all, diabetes. Unfortunately, the obesity epidemic hasn't spared any age group. At the same time that adults were blowing up like a lard balloon, their children were bulging out right behind them. Like adults, the number of obese children has soared in the last 25 years or so. In fact, the rate of childhood obesity is growing much more rapidly than adult obesity. The number of obese kids has tripled (yes, tripled!) since the late 1970s and now one in five children are overweight or obese.

Because kids are supposed to be growing vertically (and not just horizontally like adults), health experts use a slightly different measurement for assessing whether a kid is classified as "obese" or not. They do use BMI, but instead of interpreting the raw number, they compare it to other kids of the same age, a measurement called BMI for age. For children, BMI for age is more accurate than run-of-the-mill BMI, but because it doesn't assess body composition, it has the same flaws as the BMI we know and love – or hate).

A Kid's Genes

Oh, and you can't blame this on your inherited genes, either. Like adult obesity, this issue cropped up in the last 30 years – not nearly enough time for genetics to change one iota. However, as epigenetics shows us, the biological systems genes control is under the direct influence of the environment in which those genes live.

Unfortunately, I'm not talking about baby fat that your kid will "grow out of." The longer a child is classified as obese, the more likely he or she will be obese their entire life. Indeed, 75% of obese teens end up as obese adults – yikes!

While obesity's emotional scars are certainly detrimental for an overweight kid, it's nothing compared to the internal damage that is happening inside their growing body. Diseases that were once considered part of the aging process are now commonly cropping up in kids before their 10th birthday. Nothing illustrates this phenomenon better than the renaming of Type 1 diabetes, formally known as *juvenile diabetes*. Because the signs of type 1 diabetes first appeared in children and type 2 diabetes wasn't something that developed until adulthood, the word "juvenile" worked well as an accurate age-based divider between the two.

Sadly, as more and more children become stricken with type 2 diabetes, the term juvenile could apply to them as well. While in the 1970s and 1980s the terms "juvenile diabetes" and "type 1 diabetes" were used interchangeably, today you'd be hard-pressed to find a medical journal that still uses the term. This isn't a simple matter of semantics for clarification – the change in terminology represents an alarming trend.

From 1982 to 1994, a short 12-year period, diabetes in kids shot up an astonishing 1,000%. The situation is so dire that experts predict 40% of children born in the year 2000 will wind up with diabetes. Worse yet, the side effects of diabetes—cardiovascular disease, amputations, blindness, and nerve damage—are happening at younger and younger ages.

Elderly Kids

Today's overweight generation of kids are also aging faster. Dr. Geetha Raghuveer, MD, from the University of Missouri Kansas City School of Medicine states, "There's a saying that 'you're as old as your arteries,' meaning the state of your arteries is more important than your actual age in the evolution of heart disease and stroke." If that's the case, then modern-day children are older than ever.

Research presented at a 2008 American Heart Association meeting found that a surprising number of overweight children have what appear to be 35-year-old arteries (and just imagine what an obese 35 year-old's arteries resemble) with abnormal plaque to match. Children as young as nine are being diagnosed with *atherosclerosis*—clinically significant and dangerous hardening and thickening of the arteries. Most disturbing of all, many experts predict this may be the last generation that has a shorter lifespan than their parents.

How did we let our nation's youth get so unhealthy? You'd think, the factors that create fat kids are unique, but they're not. Our children are really Mini-Mes. In other words, their biochemistry is a shrunken down version of ours and what applies to our ability to use fat as energy also applies to theirs. So why then do so many programs designed for adults fall flat when they're tested on kids? It could have a lot to do with how influential the younger generation really is.

So-Duh

Soda consumption happens to be one of the most accurate risk factors for childhood obesity. In fact, if you were to look at only two factors for predicting a child's weight, soda consumption would probably be the most telling (with TV-watching not far behind).

Why is soda so devilish? First, it contains loads of high fructose corn syrup (HFCS) – the same stuff that makes insulin shoot up like a hot air balloon. Also, soda contains loads of caffeine, which scientists think can make kids physically addicted over time. Also, there's evidence which suggests the constant acidic assault from soda upsets internal pH, wrecks teeth, and makes diabetes more likely. As bad as that sounds, it's not the soda itself that's wreaking havoc; it's how much of it kids chug day in and day out. A study conducted by the Centers for Disease Control found that soda was the number one source of calories in the US (and especially so for children). The average teenager chugs 24 ounces of sugary soda a day – the equivalent of about 20 teaspoons of HFCF and 290 calories.

Previous New York State Health Commissioner, Richard Daines, noted that The Bronx is New York City's borough with the worst obesity rates and has the highest intake of sugar-filled beverages. Daines knew this was no coincidence. "Sugar-sweetened beverages are underpriced and oversized. They are universally available and relentlessly marketed."

The Unnatural, Natural Sugar

Unlike whole natural fruit (not fruit juice) that contains fibre, high-fructose corn syrup has been documented in human studies to raise both blood sugar and insulin, easily placing the body into a fat storage mode and setting the stage for obesity and type 2 diabetes. This is due to the way fructose (in the processed form as opposed to fructose consumed in fruit) is metabolized. Unlike glucose—which is easily converted to the most abundant form of bodily energy – *adenosine triphosphate* (ATP), fructose is broken down rapidly in the liver, ultimately engulfing the metabolic systems, and, in turn, creating fat formation.

Numerous published studies using rodent models show that rats fed fructose develop insulin resistance in a relatively short period of time (just a few weeks). In fact, my good friend, and co-author of *Bio-Age: 10 Steps to a Younger You*, NASA neuroscientist Dr. Michael Schmidt, notes these effects are so predictable that many scientists now use fructose to induce these conditions in animals so they can study drugs that might correct them.

So exactly how much harm is soda doing to kids' bodies? Plenty. Research published in the *International Journal of Obesity* found that for every soda a child drank down per day, their likelihood of being obese increased by 60%.

Plugged In and Paying for It

The food that kids are washing their soda down with isn't anything to put on a bumper sticker either. While fresh fruit and vegetable consumption is almost non-existent in today's kids (especially teens), about 75% of youth don't eat even one citrus fruit or green leafy vegetable serving per week.

Displacing healthy foods from the diet are fast food and soft drinks. Nearly every child in North American drinks soda every day and 75% of kids in 7th to 12th grade eat at a fast food joint every week. The implications are very real. One study found that simply having a fast food restaurant near a school increased the risk of obesity of the entire school. Largely due to factors outside of their control (after all, they're just kids) kids' diets have gone from bad to horrible in the last 25 years – and they're paying the price for it.

When today's kids aren't eating (or more accurately, when they *are* eating), they're plugged into something. Research by the Canadian mental health organization, the Kaiser Foundation, found that almost eight hours of a typical day for today's 8-18 year old is spent using an electronic device. I'm not pulling the old, "in my day we used to go out and get fresh air" speech on you. After all, I'm not that old, (well at least that's what I keep telling myself). However, there are consequences to being plugged in during half of your waking hours. As you may have seen in the news, the amount of time kids spend using electronics, whether it be a TV, game console, or a computer, is associated with being fat.

The Fat Box

By far, the worst electronic device for kids is television. The average child watches more than 20 hours per week. Its remarkable influence on modern kids' fat levels makes the nickname "idiot box" a misnomer. TV should now be known as "the fat box." The associations between kids' TV watching and their weight, like the fact that watching four or more hours of TV in a given day increases obesity risk by 20%, is well known.

However, researchers are surprised to find that the calories *not* burned by a child sitting on his tush don't account for the extra fat. For example, a study published in *The American Journal of Clinical Nutrition* found that for every hour of TV watched per day, the child's body fat (not just weight) tended to be 2.2 pounds higher. An hour of TV watching, while by no means a calorie torching activity, still shouldn't create an extra two pounds of flab – especially on a growing kid.

When researchers dig deeper, they find that TV messes with not just calories *going out*, but calories *coming in* to the body. Research by scientists at Harvard's School of Public Health found that TV watching has a very real impact on eating habits. For every hour of TV watched per day, intake of fresh fruit and vegetables dropped by a serving per week. As the authors note, one serving per week quickly adds up to a meaningful change. "Essentially, a young person who watched three hours per day of television at baseline and increased his/her television viewing by one hour per day had, on average, 2.25 fewer servings of fruits and vegetables per week, or greater than 110 servings per year than those who did not watch television."

Why would watching back-to-back episodes of *SpongeBob SquarePants* make a kid turn down a serving of carrots? The issue isn't TV, or even the programs themselves, but the commercials that play between them.

Marketing Madness

Right off the bat, let's establish just how pervasive ads are on TV. Every year, kids under 11 see 2,000 commercials, which is the equivalent of almost ten entire days. While you may reminisce about Saturday morning cartoon commercials that advertised your favorite GI Joe, you may also be surprised to find that when it comes to advertising to kids, toys are out and food is in. Over half of all TV ads targeted to kids are for some sort of food.

Food marketers know—all too well—that television advertising has a massive influence on the foods and beverages children (ages 2-11) prefer to consume and how much those children will scream and lobby to get their parents to make those purchases for them. The sad part about this reality is that over two-thirds (69%) and more than $4.2 billion per year of all food advertising targeted toward our toddlers is for processed food.

Have you ever seen any ads for broccoli? Oh no, it's an onslaught of cookies, crackers, and faux fruit snacks. In fact, 50% of all ads that run during children's TV programs are for some sort of sugar-based food product like cereal or candy. To build instant rapport with child viewers, many savvy advertisers have paired the child's favorite characters, like Dora the Explorer™, with the product they're pushing, blurring the line between the program itself and the advertisement.

What's most interesting is the TV commercials are also influencing what kids perceive as healthy. I don't expect most eight-year-olds to know that the scoops of sugar contained inside their favorite cereal makes them fat or puts them at a higher predisposition for diabetes. Food advertisements are certainly aware of that and aim ads set out to shape kids' core concepts on health and nutrition.

University of Minnesota researchers recently sat down to document the health messages coming at today's TV-watching youth. They found that 49% of the ads implied the food was "nutritious" and nine out of ten sugar cereal ads claimed their food was part of a "complete" breakfast (what part exactly is that, the sugar part?)

Either through clever marketing, repetition, or a combination of the two, the ads work. When researchers document what foods tend to be overeaten the most, they find a consistent parallel: the same foods that get the most airtime.

To Serve and Protect

As a parent, you have a duty to protect your kids from obesity and its affects. Just like you dash out the front door to give your child his or her bike helmet when they forget, or double-check to make sure they're buckled up before you put your foot to the gas, your child's well-being starts and ends with you.

If you're in the camp that claims, "Little Johnny is just a bit chubby, he will grow out of it" or "my Little Erika is big boned," it's time for a reality check. One study found that 43% of parents with obese kids think their kid's weight is "about right." Admitting that your child is obese doesn't reflect anything about them as a person; it just means they need help. While public health measures, like cutting the soda from schools, may make a dent, the most important ally your child has is always going to be you.

Obviously, one of the most important first steps you can take is to strictly limit TV time (I can see it now - kids all over North America banding together to boycott this book). Not only is less television good for your child's body, but it benefits their minds, as well. And make no mistake; putting a cap on TV watching is more effective at fighting fat than throwing away junk food. One study out of the University of Liverpool, England, found that simply decreasing TV time, without making the kids exercise or eat vegetables, significantly reduced BMI. The importance of shutting off the TV cannot be overstated.

Children, especially younger ones, look up to their parents more than any other person on Earth. In fact, many kids see their parents as all-knowing deities that understand the secrets of this giant, confusing world. That's why your fat inevitably rubs off on them. One obese parent in the house triples the chances of the child winding up obese; two obese parents make it a practical guarantee. In the long run, there's no such thing as, "do as I say, not as I do." Lead by example (by losing fat and building muscle using the principles in *Dirty Diets*) and watch your child follow you.

Because TV ads have completely warped kids' minds, making them want some of the least nutritious food on the planet, it is imperative you take control over the shopping cart. Don't give the kids 100% free rein over good choices as most parents do. Scientists recently polled over 18,000 children and found that four out of five of them make all of their own food choices. Not good. I'm not suggesting you be some sort of food dictator, doling out food as you see fit, either. Have your child involved in every step of the food process, from shopping, to cooking, to serving. Of course, you have the final say, but their participation will softly reestablish them as part of, and not completely ignorant of the decision making process.

Be careful not to use your newfound perch on the pedestal to dump a dieting mindset upon your impressionable overweight child. Emphasizing calories, fiber, and sugar to a kid is only going to make them more self-conscious about their weight and may raise the risk of eating disorders forming. Worse yet, forcing a diet on a kid doesn't work. Studies show kids that diet when they're young are more likely to end up as obese adults because early diets turn them into early adopters of lite foods. Instead, begin to instill good food *values*.

Food values are factors unrelated to specific nutrients. Show your kids by example that eating natural, unprocessed foods are good for their bodies and that sitting and eating food without the blaring distraction of a TV makes it more enjoyable. Also, try tweaking the way you use food with your kids. Consider taking a page from the French. One study found that French parents tend to very closely monitor their child's food intake and weight. French parents are also less likely than their North American counterparts to use food as a reward or comfort tool, avoiding detrimental patterns that tend to stick with the child for life. Actions and words like these make the biggest difference as evidenced by research on family mealtime and kids' eating patterns.

The Family Unit

University of Delaware researchers set out to see if eating together as a family had any impact on how kids ate. They found that kids who ate with their family just five times per week were 20% less likely to under-consume vegetables and fruit. This effect was multiplied if the child ate with their family six times per week (as another incentive, other studies show that eating as a family also reduces the risk of drug use and teen pregnancy). While our hectic lives or living situations (divorced parents sharing custody of the kids) may make this arrangement challenging, you may be surprised by how much time you and your child have on hand when you cut out a fair amount of TV/computer time from the schedule.

Regular exercise is also a must for children in order to keep them lean and healthy. But besides the obvious metabolism-boosting benefits of getting your kid to play on the monkey bars more often, did you know Junior can also improve his grades? It's true!

A study by the American College of Sports Medicine (ACSM) found that children who engaged in regular physical activity more often have better grades than their sedentary computer-game playing counterparts. The study compared the students' physical activity—both in and outside school—with their grades in subjects like science, English, mathematics, and world studies. Lead author, Dawn Podulka Coe, Ph.D., said, "Physical education and activity during the school day may reduce boredom and help keep kids' attention in the classroom... the students who performed better academically in this study were the most active, meaning those who participated in a sport or other vigorous activity at least three times a week."

Fortunately, the skills and values that sports teach and instill last a lifetime. It's been shown that kids who play sports are not only leaner as children, but as adults, as well. The value that comes from exercise isn't confined to a treadmill or stationary bike. It's one that lasts a lifetime.

In an era where finger pointing is the norm, to find the root cause of your child's fat, just look in the mirror and then point. When it comes to your children's health, the fat and bad habits could stop with you.

DIRTY DIETS

PART II

CHAPTER 11 – Carb Crazed Confusion

"Excuse me," Stan says, trying to get the flight attendant's attention without drawing any more stares from others. "Excuse me," he says again, this time just a little louder.

She finally turns and looks down at Stan. "Yes, sir? What seems to be the problem?"

A red-faced Stan sits there holding the two ends of the seat belt with a few inches of space where they should be meeting. "It's not working."

"I have just the thing," the flight attendant says, as several nearby passengers take a good, long glance at the inadequate seat belt and Stan's round belly jutting out over his lap.

The attendant quickly returns with a seat belt extender. "Brand new," she says, with a reassuring smile. "We've had to get several new ones lately."

Thank goodness they've stopped serving meals on flights, he thinks as he attaches the belt extender. He learned the hard way on another flight that the tray didn't have enough clearance space and came to rest at a slight angle atop his recent flab.

Of course, just as he was trying to let down the tray and take his Dr. Pepper from the flight attendant, the plane hit a bubble of turbulence and the soda made a nice arc of sticky, brown spray all over his seat mate. The woman next to him had already been huffing and letting out long sighs letting Stan knew she wasn't happy that he took up so much of the arm rest and a little bit of her seat, as well.

He tried not to look at the brown splotch in her lap for the rest of the flight, but if he forgot for a moment, her loud "tsk" reminded him. He kept his tray in the upright position on every flight after that.

Unfortunately, Stan has to travel constantly for his job, which has hollowed out his self-esteem like it was a chocolate Easter bunny. All of that time on the road in unfamiliar places for only a few days at a time has also made it more difficult for him to eat healthy or exercise and over time his weight has crept upwards.

Until recently, it was just the predictable middle-aged spread. Then, something happened and in the last few years Stan's weight and girth seem to have grown like one of those crescent rolls from that cute little cartoon chef that giggles every time his belly's tickled.

Stan never had a weight problem when he was younger. He had no childhood obesity and he wasn't raised on a diet of fast food or cookies. It was a pretty typical menu with moderation in everything. Stan liked to think that was the theme for his life in general. Nothing too extreme. So, what has changed, he wondered.

When Stan's flight landed and he returned home, he had a long talk with his wife, Paula, who has also surpassed pleasingly plump and is heading into "can't get up a flight of stairs" territory. Even their kids are looking a little like they're wearing permanent flotation devices with a nice ring around the middle.

The family sat down together and Stan brought to the table the same deductive reasoning he uses when evaluating corporate bottom lines, only this time they needed their personal bottom line to shrink.

Stan and Paula quickly discovered that a few years ago something changed after they had decided to become more health conscious in their busy two-income, kids-on-the-go schedules. They started substituting some of their more fattening food choices with "lite" versions that had less fat and fewer calories. The kids loved the way they tasted, the products were convenient, and said they were healthy right on the box. "If you can't trust the government, who can you trust?" thought Stan.

But, over time Stan found himself craving something sweet late at night and the portion size got harder to keep under control. Soon, the waistline of everyone in the family was growing and they were buying more and more fat-free processed food trying to stem the fat war. Something was wrong, though. They were clearly losing.

Stan went and grabbed a frozen lite dinner out of the freezer and looked at the ingredients. The third item listed was corn syrup and the carbohydrate count was well north of 45 grams, but the fat calories were low, as usual.

He scratched his head and looked at his wife pensively. "I wonder if all of this diet food has anything to do with our newfound sizes?"

Paula just shrugged.

Same Engine, Wrong Fuel

If you ever have a chance to visit the Museum of Natural History in New York City, dart past the ominous bones of the T-Rex and wade your way through a few hundred stuffed birds, until you find yourself face-to-face with a replica of your ancestors – the cavemen (and to be politically correct – cavewomen). One exhibit displays members of an ancient family drawing on the wall of a cave while a man in the forefront tends to a primitive fire.

What does this have to do with carbs, you ask? Oh, just about everything.

Imagine yourself dropped in front of the image I just described, except this time insert a loaf of 13-grain bread. Or a granola bar. Or a reduced-fat box of Wheat Thins®. Carb sources like these, which are inescapable today, were absolutely unheard of just a few thousand years ago. While technological advancements in the last few centuries have been cranking on a maddeningly fast, all-cylinders pace, our ancient DNA hasn't even begun to catch up.

In fact, the hands that hold the book (or snazzy ereader) you're reading right now are the same hands that would have been wrapped around a spear. The eyes that dart left to right across the page would have darted across the savanna, looking for a meal. Put another way, your body hasn't changed since humans first burst onto the scene 17 million years ago – even if our diets have. So, you see, the machine is still the same, but the fuel you're putting in it isn't.

How did we get here? How did our carbs, which were once picked from a plant, get doled out in plastic containers with the word "lite" plastered on them?

The Grain Train

Believe it or not, it all started with the invention of fire. For the first time, foods that were otherwise impossible or difficult to chew could now be heated and eaten (like plants with hard coverings). Then, at about 9,000 BC (a blink of the eye in the life of human history), the ancient Egyptians started to do something with plants that hunter-gatherers never did – grow them. There's anthropological evidence that the Egyptians grew and harvested wild versions of wheat and barley (not even close to the hybrid versions we eat today). The Romans quickly followed suit and successful cultivation of wheat has even been attributed to the swift expanse of the Roman Empire.

Soon to follow was the "agricultural revolution" where farming methods were refined and tweaked, crops were picked for optimal yield, not nutrition (and still are—with even less nutritive value), and grains became a mainstay of the diet for much of the civilized world. Foods that a caveman wouldn't recognize – like bread and pasta – were now a staple food in almost every corner of the earth.

But grains took a turn for the worse with the advent of electricity and steam power. A grain like wheat requires an incredible amount of pounding and grinding to extract the nutritive portion. Even with tools, there was still a man or woman banging like hell on the grain until it became edible, which limited its use. Electricity not only made refinement more efficient, but it made it more effective, as well. Parts of the grain, which lead to spoilage but also contained the highest quality nutrition, like the bran and germ, were wiped away with the push of a button and a sweep of a steal roller. Thus came the introduction of refined grains. That's when shelf life became more important than human life.

Saving Money and Taking Lives

Even then, grains weren't a mainstay of most people's diets because they needed to be processed and packaged, which made them too expensive for most. But the food industry recognized a golden opportunity to make a lot of bread (pun intended), invented cheaper manufacturing, and we gladly followed with currency in hand.

Compared to protein and fats, grains are dirt-cheap. The four grains that compose almost 50% of the world's calories: wheat, corn, rice, and barley, have been scientifically modified through selective breeding (aka: hybrids) to be effortlessly grown. As you know, raw flour isn't making anyone filthy rich. But with a few twists, colors, dyes, and a shiny package, a nearly worthless clump of wheat and corn can be transformed into a marked-up dessert, bread, or a lite food.

Grain's ability to line the pocket of food company execs helped their popularity explode in the 20th century, and they are now more pervasive than ever. The USDA found that the average American grain consumption has shot up 45% since 1970.

It's a question I hear all the time, "Aren't grains, especially whole grains, good for me?" As much as it pains me to say this, the type of grains that we eat (highly refined) and the amounts we eat (2,000 pounds per year), they certainly *aren't* good for us.

For many, grain bashing is tantamount to treason. As Melissa Smith states in her aptly titled book, *Going Against the Grain* (Contemporary Books), "In a society where wheat is eaten at every meal, pasta is promoted as a health food, and the heart of the continent is endearingly referred to as 'the breadbasket,' it can seem almost sacrilegious (or unconstitutional) to speak out against grains." Personally, some of my fondest childhood memories are of my mom baking a fresh loaf of bread or muffins. However, grains, especially refined ones, don't necessarily have the "goodness" that food companies would like you to believe.

The Heart of the Matter

What's so bad about chowing down on grains day in and day out? To answer that, let's look broadly at the effect that refined grains have had on society as a whole. In the early 20th century, when refined grains were making their mark, diseases related to insulin, like cardiovascular disease and diabetes were unheard of – literally.

President Dwight D. Eisenhower's personal physician was quoted as saying he had never even heard of heart disease after graduating from medical school in 1911. By the mid-1940s (the same time-refined grains became widespread) it was the number one cause of death in the US. In a very short period of time, refined grains made the industrialized world fat and sick – and this madness continues to this day.

But if I'm telling you that you should be eating approximately 40% of your diet in carb form, how can you possibly do that without cereal in the morning, bread at lunch, and pasta for dinner? Easy. Anthropologists estimate that upwards of 40% of the caveman diet was in carb form, but not a single ounce of it came from grains. The vast majority of carbs cavemen enjoyed were in the form of roots, shoots, tubers, and leaves.

Since we've limited our carb sources to a handful of plants (less than 0.1% of all edible plants to be specific), many people nowadays can't even name many of the plants our bodies needed to evolve, like roots, shoots, and tubers. In essence, roots, shoots, and tubers perform the same basic function for us that they do in the plant – storing energy. Like your fat cells, plants have devised ways to keep excess energy on board as a rainy day fund, the same way a battery stores energy in cells. A sweet potato or a yam (as opposed to a regular potato, which is a tuber, but not nearly as healthy as we have been led to believe) is the perfect example of a tuber because it is energy dense and fibrous.

However, most tubers that cavemen ate still had much fewer carbs, a lower GI, and more fiber than our modern potato. They were carb sources packed with antioxidants, vitamins, and minerals – something we would now consider a "super food" – but were commonplace in the caveman diet.

Another plant that cavemen couldn't get enough of was leaves. Some nutritional scientists think that the average caveman ate six pounds (the equivalent of two phonebooks) of leaves every day. While it's not necessarily ideal to chomp on leaves like rabbits (as you have greater access to other foods like lean meats and healthy fats than cavemen did), it shows just how far we've deviated from the carbs our bodies prefer – not to mention what makes us thrive.

Ever so Seedy

Where do grains fit into this plant picture? Grains fall under the category of seed, specifically a grass seed. University of Colorado professor and frequent guest of my *Transforming Health with Brad King* podcast, Loren Cordain, Ph.D., refers to grains as "civilization's doubled-edged sword" because they've contributed to the formation of cities and scientific progress, but have eroded our health in the process. He points out the historic basis (or lack thereof) of refined grain consumption. "There is little or no evolutionary precedent in our species for grass seed consumption." Yet, that is exactly what we're eating.

What's the harm in eating seeds? Like humans, plants have evolved a number of methods to keep potential dangers at bay. Humans have traditionally dodged danger by running away from it or outwitting it. A plant, being tethered to the ground, is afforded no such luxury. As a means of protection to its most vital part, the seed, the plant has devised ways to make the seeds less desirable to predators. In fact, the natural form of most grains have a number of protective layers that make it difficult or painful to chew, hence the processing required to make it edible.

However, no amount of processing can remove all of the detrimental effects from excessive seed consumption, the most noted of which is essential fat deficiencies. While you may think that omega-3's are only found in fish, they are actually common in natural plant foods, as well. Cavemen, even if they never saw an ocean in their entire life, still got a fair share of omega-3's from tubers, fruits, and leaves. Unfortunately, seeds are extremely high in omega-6 fatty acids – creating fatty acid imbalance that a myriad of research shows increases inflammation and induces insulin resistance.

The Rule of Three Years

Also, the defenses of the seed still remain – even after being bludgeoned to a pulp and baked into white bread. All grains contain something called *antinutrients*. Antinutrients, a strange term that sounds like something people eat in Superman's Bizarro world, is actually a nice word for toxins.

Studies show that antinutrients tend to block absorption of important vitamins and minerals, and even disrupt enzymes in the body – the plant's way of teaching you not to mess with its kids. When eaten in small amounts, and within the framework of a nutrient-rich diet, antinutrients from limited grain consumption shouldn't do any harm. That's why I preach eating limited amounts of whole grains as part of your 40% carbohydrate intake. But if you overdo it – as most North Americans do – you'll wind up with excessive omega-6 fat intake and antinutrients damaging your vulnerable cells.

The hazard from eating too many refined grains isn't just theory. Thomas L. Cleave, MD, was a noted surgeon who traveled the world in the early 1900s, documenting the diets of ancient cultures that were still untouched by modern influence. He coined a phrase called, "The Rule of 20 Years."

Twenty years after refined grains and sugar were introduced, diabetes and obesity set into our culture. But with refined grains more readily available than ever, it takes much less time for health problems and obesity to crop up than in the past. Research published in *The Journal of Epidemiology* reviewed Japanese immigrants who recently moved to the US. Within three years, those who assimilated most into the Western diet became fatter and tended to get diabetes in much higher rates than those who stuck to their Japanese way of life. Perhaps the proper term in North America should be: "The Rule of Three Years."

And if these Japanese people were to try to lose those pounds by dieting based on the faulty recommendations of most North American "experts" – and replace their nuts, monounsaturated oils, and other healthy fats with carbs, they'd be even worse off. Low-fat, high-carb diets prime your body for fat storage. As you know, eating more carbs than our primitive bodies are accustomed to promotes insulin production. Insulin targets a crucial enzyme called *lipoprotein lipase*, abbreviated as *LPL*. LPL's job is to fish for fat floating around in the blood, and reel it in so it can be stored as fat. Like most enzymes, LPL can be switched on and off as the body needs it. LPL either punches in its timecard or takes the day off based on how much insulin is present. If insulin levels are high, like on a low-fat diet, LPL works overtime. But the amount of carbs don't tell the entire story – the form they're in is just as important.

Looks Count

What should most of your carbs look like to avoid a fat fate? The majority of your diet should come from organic vegetables—especially arugula, Bok Choy, broccoli, Brussels sprouts, cabbage, cauliflower, kale, kohlrabi, mustard greens, and watercress—and fresh fruit (or frozen when fresh isn't available)—especially berries. Vegetables and fruits (which are roots, shoots, and tubers) are a fantastic form of carbs because they have a low glycemic index, are fibrous, and are bursting with nutrients. Berries are particularly loaded with antioxidants and most closely resemble fruits your relative from a few hundred generations ago would have eaten.

What happens when someone switches their carbs to roots, shoots, tubers, leaves, and fruits? They rapidly lose weight, eat more fiber, and become more insulin sensitive. At least that's what happened in a study put together by scientists at the University of Lund. What impressed me most about this research weren't the results from the diet itself (although they were fantastic), but how it blew away a diet that's widely considered one of the healthiest: the Mediterranean diet.

Nutrition is wrought with controversy, but if there's one thing almost every nutrition scientist can agree on it's that the Mediterranean diet is the best diet out there. But what the scientists found in the above mentioned study was a diet that has its carb roots based in pasta, cheese, and white bread is only healthy when compared to the Western eating pattern, and it wilts when compared to a diet rich in the types of carbs our bodies evolved to eat.

In fact, while the overweight subjects placed on the Mediterranean diet found themselves with only a slight improvement in insulin sensitivity, those that ate carbs based on Paleolithic availably could brag about cells that were 26% more sensitive to insulin – meaning less insulin had to be produced. It's important to note that the diet was not low-carb: they ate 40% (there's that number again) of carbs – a moderate amount. It was the form that made all the difference.

The Soda Bloat

Speaking of form, the farthest deviation from a natural food, and one I imagine a caveman would assume poisonous, is liquid sugar – popularly referred to as soda pop. As stated in the previous chapter, soda is the number one source of calories throughout North America. Liquid sugar does a number on the body's fat utilization and appetite regulating systems. As you might expect from a sugary food (or drink in this case), the glycemic index is through the roof.

Drinking liquid sugar, either in the form of soda, "fruit" drinks, and even 100% juice, causes rapid insulin release –pressing the "on" button for LPL and fat storage. Because people tend to sip on soda, rather than down the entire container in one sitting, you're essentially giving your body a constant sugary onslaught – which is quickly converted into fat. Not only that, but research published in *The International Journal of Obesity* found that people who tend to drink, and not eat, their calories are hungrier and eat more than people who chew their food. Sipping on your carbs, instead of chewing on them in the form of fruits and veggies, shuts down fat-burning.

Fiber: The Missing Key

Coca-Cola® and Pepsi® have added vitamins to their products in order to fool people into thinking that sugary soda is somehow healthy, but they have yet to add a nutrient that's often the missing link in today's diet: fiber. Since so much of the food supply is processed to death before it ends up in our mouths, they tend to be completely devoid of fiber. Studies show that most North Americans get less than half of the recommended 25-30 grams of fiber per day, which is a serious blow to overall health.

What makes fiber so great? Isn't it just "roughage?" Far from it. Your fiber intake has tremendous applications for fat loss (or gain). Researchers from Indiana University discovered that one of the closest dietary links to a high body fat percentage was how much fiber one ate in a day. Those who ate the most fiber had the leanest body composition and those who ate the least had the most fat on board. It may not be the sexiest nutrient out there, but fiber burns fat.

How does fiber do its magic? One of the least appreciated tricks up fiber's sleeve is that it keeps ravenous appetites at bay. University of California Davis scientists recently fed a group of men and women a breakfast with differing levels of fiber. Those that ate the highest fiber meal felt the most satiated and stayed fuller longer than those who dined on a low-fiber meal. Because of its volume, fiber fills up your small intestine, which sends a signal to the brain telling it that it's (and you are) full.

Even more significant is the fact that fiber controls the rate at which sugars enter the bloodstream – ultimately controlling the insulin response. This is extremely important because sugar that suddenly appears in the blood is quickly rerouted into fat stores, via insulin. On the other hand, when you eat a meal with fiber, sugar enters your body like an IV drip – and insulin never gets elevated enough to promote fat storage. In the long run, this means more of your meals get burned off and avoids a fat storage fate. However, no amount of fiber will be able to stop the games that high fructose corn syrup plays with your insulin metabolism.

The Frankenstein of Sugar

High fructose corn syrup (HFCS), something that just a few decades ago was an ingredient rarely used in food, is now omnipresent. Because sugar tariffs in the US are so high, and corn farms are subsidized, HFCS use has taken off. The average North American now eats 71 pounds of HFCF every year. Needless to say HFCS is something completely man-made, isn't found anywhere in nature, and isn't a food that our bodies have ever dealt with before. Fructose, the primary ingredient in HFCS is a sugar that is relatively rare in the wild. When you eat it, fructose does some wild things to your fat storage systems as you'll soon see. Our bodies aren't handling the fructose tidal wave very well, which is why dozens of studies have linked HFCS intake with obesity and diabetes.

In rats, scientists have a bit more leeway with what they can test since it's not exactly ethical to ask a person to drink four liters of Coca-Cola® before dinnertime. Feeding rats HFCS results in more weight gain than rats that eat normal table sugar (sucrose) –even if they both eat the same amount of calories. How is this possible? It has everything to do with how HFCS interacts with you liver and your body's insulin sensitivity controls.

When HFCS enters your blood stream, it actually makes you temporarily insulin resistant – compelling your pancreas to shoot out more insulin. The elevated insulin levels in the blood alone are enough to shift you into fat storage mode, but HFCS takes things one step further. A study published in the journal, *Cell Metabolism* concluded that HFCS is more easily converted to fat in the liver than other sugar types. HFCS turns on a gene found in the liver that's responsible for storing fat. In essence HFCS orders your liver saying, "Turn me into fat!"

Oh, and don't be tricked by a recent PR campaign by HFCS producers. HFCS is as evil as experts say it is. Princeton University scientist and HFCS expert, Bart Hoebel, warns that you shouldn't believe the hype saying HFCS isn't that bad for you. "Some people have claimed that high-fructose corn syrup is no different than other sweeteners when it comes to weight gain and obesity, but our results make it clear that this just isn't true."

Since HFCS is added to so many different foods, you have to be a real label sleuth to spot it. Popular foods that tend to have the most are: soda, juice, commercial yogurt, condiments, ice cream, bread, (and especially) lite foods. In reality, these are foods that you should be avoiding anyway. If you stick to my eating plan where carbs come from unprocessed sources, HFCS shouldn't be an issue. And if you think you can assuage your sweet tooth with "natural" and "healthy" sweeteners like Agave, think again.

Agave nectar, one of the fastest growing alternative sweeteners on the market, is not what you think it is, either. While the Agave nectar labels conjure up images of an ancient tribe squeezing the juice out of a medicinal plant, the reality is much less exotic. It turns out that crafty manufactures are processing the heck out of the starch in Agave, turning it into almost pure fructose. While the typical drop of HFCS has 55% fructose, Agave has upwards of 98%. Needless to say, eating something that is almost 100% fructose is as unnatural as living on the moon

Simply put, the "truth" about carbohydrates is that they aren't the devil they're made out to be. Just as important as eating a set amount of carbs is the form they come in. Forty percent of carbs in the form of bell peppers, beets, and sweet potatoes is treated a lot differently by your body than the same amount of Pepsi®, Skittles®, and Wonder® bread – nuff said!

CHAPTER 12 – Fat Phobia

Sarah and Casey have been best friends since junior high school and have done everything together from cheerleading to softball to their first job at the local grocery store. But now that they're approaching their thirties, they're not as active as they once were in terms of sports and exercise. They're more concerned about their careers, finances, and responsibilities than paying attention to the extra pounds they've both put on since graduation. They both know that needs to change.

"You know, I read that you should eat a lot more fish in your diet," Sarah says to Casey as they sit together for a Saturday lunch. "It helps you get healthier and lose weight."

Casey screws her face up in a winced expression. "I hate fish."

Sarah lowers her brows. "How can you hate fish? We ate tuna all the time in the school cafeteria." She picks up the menu the waitress had left and starts looking at the lunch choices.

Casey does the same and frowns again. "Well, tuna comes in a can and you slather it in mayo." She knows she needs to lose weight as she is definitely feeling the extra twenty pounds she's been unable to shed since her daughter was born last year.

"I'm talking decent seafood," Sarah says. "It's supposed to be more nutritious and it provides that good type of fat they're always talking about on television."

"How is any fat good?" Casey asks.

Sarah shrugs and points at the menu. "They have all sorts of fish dishes here: flounder, salmon, tilapia, lobster, and shrimp."

Another grimace from Casey. "I hate shrimp. And don't even get me started on lobster. Nasty bottom feeders."

Sarah slams her menu to the table. "Well, I'm going to be healthier and eat more fish. And you need to do it, too."

"Fine," Casey says, mimicking the menu slap.

The waitress arrives and asks what they'll be having. Sarah's anxious to work some good seafood into her diet. All of the experts say it's what's best. She'll eat fish and lose those pesky, flabby pounds around her middle.

"I'll have the fried fish with French fries and extra tartar sauce."

Casey looks up. "I'll have the salmon Caesar salad. May I have extra dressing with that? Oh, and lots of parmesan cheese."

The waitress leaves and the friends smile at each other.

"We'll be losing weight in no time," Casey says and the two girls clink their glasses of soda together.

See Food

While you don't want to deep fry or drown your fish dish, you definitely want to work the choice of seafood into the mix of meal time. However, next time you order the fish of the day, you might want to consider thanking it before you dig in. Why? Because those special fats within the fish are responsible for the structure and function of that incredible machine inside your noggin called the human brain.

A few million years ago, Neanderthals ruled the land. With a relatively intelligent brain and the body of an ape, these precursors to Homo sapiens had no match. That is, until humans showed up.

For decades, anthropologists (scientists that study human development) wondered how humans were able to suddenly and swiftly appear on the fossil record – seemingly out of nowhere. Contrary to popular belief, human beings aren't the end result of a linear evolutionary progression. There are scattered findings of human-like offshoots that never quite made it. These are believed to be our former (unsuccessful) competitors. So the question is why did other early advanced apes die out when Homo sapiens seemed to thrive?

Fish Heads

When anthropologists investigate skeletal records of that crucial period, they find that fat had everything to do with what makes humans human: our big, giant brains.

Anthropologists have come to a near consensus that human life began on the southern tip of what is now South Africa. The diets of the tribes that lived on the coast was, as you might have guessed, concentrated with seafood.

The special type of fatty acids in seafood gave early Homo sapiens a unique advantage that none of the competitors had access to in the form of a group of fatty acids known as: omega-3's. In fact, researchers from

Washington University discovered that modern humans consumed at least half of their protein from seafood (giving them massive amounts of omega-3's in the process). For the first time, the brain had access to a wonderful fat that allowed more plastic neurons for learning and more rapid neuron signaling for faster information processing.

The new super brain created smarter and more intelligent babies and adults. Susan Cunnane, Ph.D., points out that, "You don't need a big brain to collect mussels and clams, but living on them gives you the excess energy and nutrients that can be directed toward brain growth."

The early humans who lived near water sources and ate seafood experienced much greater brain development, while those who ate only omega-6 fats petered out. The *Australopithecines*, a primate species closely related to humans, lived inland and survived on a diet made up of game meat – which is relatively low in overall fat, but high in omega-6 fat. Unfortunately for them (but good for us), their brains stayed about the size of an orange for more than 2 million years – allowing us to take the reins

Starving for Fat

Millions of years later, Homo sapiens rule the world with essentially the same brain makeup of ancient times. The brain now, as it was then, is made up of almost 70% of a particular type of omega-3 called *docosahexaenoic acid* or DHA for short.

If you eat like the typical North American, you probably eat like a Neanderthal – even if you mind your manners at the dinner table. One part fat phobia, one part seed-based carbs, and a dash of processed lite foods have created a genetically-inspired and hormonally-driven recipe for unhealthy levels of fat for many – and I don't mean eating too much fat. In fact, it's fair to say we don't eat nearly enough fat, especially the monounsaturated variety. Also, omega-3 deficiency is rampant. A Harvard Medical School study estimated that 96,000 people die annually from not getting the omega-3's that they need, which is far more than those who perish from eating excessive amounts of fat.

If all this talk of omega this and omega that has left you scratching your head, let me explain to you how different fats are divvied up. You'll find that like carbs, fats aren't inherently good or bad for you, rather it's the form they come in that is of paramount importance.

The Name's Bond – Double Bond

From your body's perspective, there are two types of fats: *essential* and *nonessential*. Like the name suggests, essential fats are those your body can't make and ones which you need to eat to survive. On the other hand, nonessential fats aren't necessarily healthy or unhealthy, but if you went long enough without them, your body would be able to piece them together with the scraps from the other fats in your diet.

Another piece of the fat name game is this whole omega business. To understand the critical difference between omega-3's and omega-6's, it helps to look at a fatty acid as one giant chain. Some links in the chain are reinforced with what's known as a double bond. The number that follows from the "omega" notes how many links from the beginning of the chain that double bond happens to be. So an omega-3 means that the double bond is three links away from the end and an omega-6 has a double bond six links away. On the surface, this seems like a minute point gleaned from a hefty biochemistry textbook, but as you'll see, that tiny double bond has massive implications for your health.

Although there are dozens of fats out there (technically *fatty acids),* the most popular of which are *saturated*, *trans*, *monounsaturated*, *polyunsaturated* among others, only two types are essential: *linoleic* and *linolenic* acid. These pairs of fats are found mostly in plant foods.

You're probably wondering: "If I can get these fats from plants, what makes the omega-3's in seafood so great?" That answer lies in what your body does to linoleic and linolenic acid after you eat it. The body actually doesn't think these essential fats are anything special – and it much prefers the more beneficial and biologically-active omega-3 fats EPA and DHA – which are essential to heart and brain function.

Because humans evolved with omega-3's everywhere they looked, we never created an efficient way to turn linoleic and linolenic acid into DHA and EPA with any boastful efficiency. It's been estimated that on a good day, your body can turn at most 5% of the linoleic and linolenic acid you eat into EPA and DHA. On the other hand, when you eat lots of seafood, you're essentially cutting out the middleman and giving your body straight-up EPA and DHA, which is exactly what it craves. And sadly, this is exactly what most people are missing out on.

Most of the blame for a world full of fat deficient people is the low-fat farce perpetuated by scientists, the government, and the *so-called* health "experts" around the world. As discussed in Chapter 1, fat-phobia stemmed not from a legitimate health threat, but from shaky science and a hypnotized nation looking for a quick fix.

Low Fat Fallacies

If there was a face for the low-fat craze, it would have to be Dean Ornish, MD. In the early 1990s, Dr. Ornish became famous after he published a number of studies that showed that a produce-rich, low-fat diet, along with exercise and stress reduction, reversed coronary artery plaque buildup in those who recently had a heart attack.

Since then, he's been reaping millions from those results. He advocates a vegetarian or vegan diet that's extremely low-fat even by fat-phobic standards (i.e. approximately 10% of calories from fat). Based on his authority —and many of his followers— thousands of people have become fat-phobic only to find their health worsen because of it. As a vocal mouthpiece for fat-phobia, he, and other physicians like him, lit the powder keg for the explosion of low-fat and no-fat foods that now runs rampant in our food supply.

As we've seen on a grand scale: nations get fatter as they eat less fat. Despite having a stack of research papers supposedly supporting their results, the low-fat diet benefits that low-fat zealots tout aren't all they're cracked up to be. When these early low-fat studies were done, the "control" group they used (if you could call it that) for most of the research was a typical, horrendous-for-you Western diet. Of course, a diet rich in plant foods would outperform one based on fast food and processed crap. But instead of seeing the low-fat diet for what it was – a lesser of two evils – the low-fat advocates were convinced there was something special about staying away from fat and worse yet, lumping all fats into the same category of evilness.

Fortunately, more and more scientists are jumping ship from the low-fat bandwagon and are finally putting low-fat diets to the test. And when they do, time and time again, low-fat diets fall flat when matched up against a fibrous-carb, moderate protein, and high monounsaturated fat diets.

The seminal study that demonstrates the myth of low-fat diets is known as the Women's Health Initiative. In this enormously detailed and expensive research study, scientists investigated the effects of a low-fat diet in almost 50,000 women over the course of a decade. A mountain of data later, the researchers found that a low-fat diet didn't decrease the risk of diseases we've been led to believe a low-fat diet is supposed to prevent: obesity, heart disease, stroke or cancer.

No facet of a low-fat diet was clearer than its effect on body fat. Eleftheria Maratos-Flier, Ph.D., of the Joslin Diabetes Center in Boston said, "They (low-fat diets) have the paradoxical effect of making people gain weight." She's not the only one; many other nutrition experts are with me in calling out low-fat diets for what they are: an almost surefire way to becoming a Smaller Fat Person.

One of the nutrition researchers I respect is Walter Willet MD, Ph.D., of Harvard School of Public Health. When I'm on the fence about a nutritional issue, I dig deep to find out what other nutrition experts— including Dr. Willet—have discovered about the subject. It turns out that Dr. Willet and many others like him agreed with my take on unfounded low-fat hysteria. In his commentary of the results of the Women's Health Initiative, Dr. Willet said, "It was a mistake, and this study really confirms that it was the wrong direction to go for nutritional advice. It did do harm. It was a lost opportunity. People were given the idea that it was only fat calories that counted. This should be the nail in the coffin for low-fat diets."

As you can see, after years of low-fat lies, the tide is turning. But I do disagree with one point Dr. Willet made. There's still one more nail in the low-fat coffin left: saturated fat.

Saturated Lies

In early February 2010, the nutrition world was aghast when the results from a study published in *The American Journal of Clinical Nutrition* hit the presses. In this research, a review of 21 other studies looked at the connection between saturated fat and heart disease. The authors found *zero* links between saturated fat in the diet and heart disease risk. What? This flies in the face of practically every public health message for the last decade. It turns out that saturated fat isn't the evil nutrient it's been made out to be. Say what?

This is something that internationally renowned nutritionist and lipids biochemist, Mary Enig, MD, has been shouting from the rooftops for years. Dr. Enig has admitted she is "on the fringe" of medical consensus, especially how it relates to fat. But with the mounting evidence in favor of eating moderate amounts of saturated fat, she now finds herself smack dab at the forefront. Her top-notch research paper,

The Skinny on Fats, thoroughly lays out the evidence on saturated fat and health. If you've been buying into the anti-saturated fat propaganda, then you'll probably be surprised with the studies she mentions. One section of her paper, titled, *"The Benefits of Saturated Fats,"* is enough to make most dieticians' jaws drop.

But she's 100% right. There are benefits to eating saturated fat. Unfortunately, they get drowned out by a cacophony of anti-saturated fat nonsense. The outer layers of our trillions of cells, which are incredibly important in all aspects of human health, are more than 50% saturated fat. A diet rich in saturated fat also help boost the amount of EPA and DHA that your body generates from essential fats – making that measly 5% conversion rate bump up a bit – and every bit helps. But a more practical issue is the fact that saturated fats *don't* increase your risk of heart disease and may even *reduce* your risk of it.

The Cholesterol Delusion

The reason saturated fat got such a bad rap in the first place is due to the fact that it raises cholesterol levels which are considered to make you a walking heart attack waiting to happen. What fat-phobic experts failed to mention was that saturated fat also raises *good* cholesterol, also known as *high-density lipoprotein* or HDL. HDL performs a number of crucial roles in the body, not the least of which is clearing out cholesterol buildup in the arteries. Or as Gary Taubes, the mega bestselling author of *Good Calories – Bad Calories*, wrote in the *New York Times*, "If you work out the numbers, you come to the surreal conclusion that you can eat lard straight from the can and conceivably reduce your risk of heart disease."

Like the mad dash to push fat as low as possible, people have been doing the same with blood cholesterol, despite the fact that half of heart attack victims have *low* or *normal* cholesterol levels. And those with lower than normal HDL levels have been suffering the internal consequences. HDL is needed to produce hormones necessary for life (like the muscle building testosterone) and even regulates the immune system. But HDL plays an especially crucial role in your brain, as it's an important part of healthy brain cells that allows them to work more effectively. HDL is also called upon to produce the "feel-good" neurotransmitter serotonin. It's HDL's brain-boosting role that explains results like those recently published in The *Journal of Neuroscience Research* that linked low HDL with poor memory and cognition.

HDL isn't just your brain's best buddy; cholesterol serves to guard your entire body from harm. Dr. Enig explains, "Just as a large police force is needed in a locality where crime occurs frequently, so cholesterol is needed in a poorly nourished body to protect the individual from a tendency toward heart disease and cancer. Blaming coronary heart disease on cholesterol is like blaming the police for murder and theft in a high crime area."

Beware Lipitor® and Other Statins

Lipitor® is the most profitable drug ever made. And why not? With a sizeable population "suffering from" high cholesterol and a medical field apt to hand them out like candy, it's not surprising that pharmaceutical companies like Pfizer have made a killing from the class of drugs referred to as statins – in more ways than one.

Lipitor®, and other statins like it are downright dangerous. Many of the side effects from taking Lipitor®, like cognitive decline and nerve damage, get swept under the rug.

Even scarier is the fact that many clinical trials using Lipitor® have found that it doesn't actually help save lives! For example, a study published in the *American Journal of Cardiology* found that Lipitor® didn't lower the risk of death in a group of nearly 10,000 people – but *did* harm their quality of life via dangerous side effects.

The evidence is crystal clear: statins like Lipitor® are far from benign and often come with serious side-effects that could possibly cause damage to your liver, nervous system, and brain.

But that's exactly what we're doing when we go to great lengths to lower cholesterol to ward off heart disease and end up at a higher risk of not just heart disease, but violent deaths as well.

Yes, you read that right. Researchers at the University of California found that low cholesterol levels upped the risk of dying violently. They found that those whose cholesterol levels were below 150mg/dl had an 80% greater chance of dying from homicide, suicide, or a deadly accident. These researchers poured over 163 studies and found that the association between low cholesterol and a violent demise held up. Worst of all, using cholesterol-lowering meds like Lipitor® also increased the risk of death by violence. Scientists aren't sure why low cholesterol levels cause the Grim Reaper to draw a bull's eye on your back, but they think it has to do with cell membrane defects in the brain when it doesn't get the cholesterol it needs. The avoid-cholesterol-at-all-cost-attitude has caused many a so-called health nut to shun one of the healthiest foods on Earth – the egg.

Egg in the Face

Perhaps you've been splurging on the $7.99 carton of egg whites for your morning breakfast routine because you know the yolk is jam-packed full of the all-evil cholesterol (don't even get me started on the fact that those cartoned eggs have been pasteurized to the point of becoming biochemically unrecognizable to your body – but that's an entirely different topic altogether).

What you probably don't realize is that cholesterol in your diet has little to nothing to do with the cholesterol in your blood. On the other hand, the healthy fats found in the egg yolk (including the saturated kind) can actually improve your cholesterol profile considerably. Subjects in a study published in the *Journal of Nutrition* were fed three-whole eggs per day (equal to 640 milligrams of dietary cholesterol) or the same amount of a cholesterol-free substitute. The group eating the real eggs showed an elevated level of "good" cholesterol (HDLs), without an associated increase in the level of "bad" cholesterol (LDLs and triglycerides). One of the reasons eggs are so healthy is that when produced from green (not grain) feed—aka grass, they have an impressive omega-3 to omega-6 ratio.

Be it from eggs, fish, or nuts, more omega-3's and less omega-6's is exactly what most people need. Because of our easy access to the original all-you-can-eat seafood buffet from the sea, humans evolved eating equal parts omega-3's to omega-6's. However, once grains burst onto the scene, the pendulum started to swing toward more omega-6's – many, many more. Our omega-6 ratio took on Godzilla-like proportions after farmers figured out that feeding grain to animals was cheaper than feeding them omega-3 rich grass. As Michael Pollen says, *You are what you eat eats.*

It's actually gotten to the point where omega-3 deficiency is commonplace. Most North Americans eat an omega-6 to omega-3 ratio of 20:1 (meaning for every 1 gram of omega-3's you eat, you down 20 grams of omega-6's). We're just starting to realize the implications of such a lopsided fat intake. Researchers have consistently found that those with the highest omega-6 intake tended to be at the higher risk for heart disease, osteoporosis, cancer, and yes, even obesity – all three of which have links to inflammation.

Getting Fatter with Inflammation

Aside from your achy back, sore shoulders, throbbing knees, and excruciating hip pain, where else is the inflammation coming from? Increasingly, researchers are pointing to our fat cells as prime production sites for pro-inflammatory messengers (called cytokines). To quote one commentator, "Indeed, fat cells behave a lot like immune cells, spewing out inflammatory cytokines, particularly as you gain weight."

Much of this research has focused on obesity, and the results are indicating that there is a direct relationship between the amount of these pro-inflammatory messengers in circulation and the amount of excess body fat that we are able to pack on.

Inflamed Fat Cells

Inflammation is a hot topic in the health field right now, and for good reason, because high levels of inflammation are thought to be the precursor to almost every chronic disease known to man. Special immune cells in your body, known as *prostaglandins*, regulate this potentially deadly process. Like a yin and yang, the body has two separate classes of prostaglandins to counteract each other, series 2 and series 3. In general, the more series 2 prostaglandins that are floating around, the more inflammation you have going on. Series 3 does the opposite; it quenches the flames of inflammation.

The raw material your body draws on for prostaglandin production is the fats that you eat. And because prostaglandins have a particularly high turnover (meaning they need to be replaced all the time), your body is constantly drawing from the fats in your diet to produce new ones.

The type of prostaglandins your body creates is directly proportional to the types of fats that you eat. So if you eat lots of omega-6's from grains and grain fed meat, your body has no choice but to pump up the inflammatory response. On the other hand, if you eat a diet rich in monounsaturated fats, seafood, fruits, and vegetables, inflammation gets turned down a notch.

Burning Fat with Fat

For inflammation's sake alone, you should base the fats in your diet around monounsaturated fats and then omega-3 fats. But switching to a diet rich in monounsaturated fat is a great way to burn off fat, as well. Research published in the *British Journal of Nutrition* found that a group of overweight men who added monounsaturated fats to their diet burned off an impressive five pounds of fat in just four weeks. Also, omega-3 rich fish oil has also been shown in clinical research to help burn off fat and keep muscle on board during weight loss.

However, the reality is that getting enough omega-3's is a challenge in today's food supply. Because food (including fish) is grown based on yield and not on omega-3 content, you'd be hard-pressed to get enough omega-3's without taking a supplement. But don't walk blindly into your local health food store and grab the first bottle with the word "fish" on it. Most fish oil supplements are poorly manufactured and may have high levels of contaminants. That's why you want to opt for those that have been molecularly distilled, meaning they've gone through an extensive purification process.

Before I bring this chapter to a close, let me leave you with my list of most recommended fat choices:

- Extra virgin olive oil
- Fish, but especially fatty fish farmed from cold waters like salmon, mackerel, and pollock
- Shellfish
- Nuts, especially walnuts, almonds, macadamia nuts, and pistachios
- Avocados
- Flaxseeds
- Fish oil and krill oil supplements
- Natural nut butters
- Eggs, ideally from grass-fed chickens
- Grass-fed, free-range animals like beef, bison, and venison

CHAPTER 13 – Ultimate Protein

A hungry caveman deftly peers around a tree and crouches low so he's not seen.

He has spotted his lunch.

No, it's not the golden arches that pop into his vision as they won't be invented for millennia. Instead, he sees, hears, and smells a plump and healthy a single deer stealing a drink from the nearby brook.

Quietly, the caveman stands tall, his back to the tree to stay covered. The meat from this animal will feed his family for several days and the skin will be most useful for clothing and covering. Nothing goes to waste.

He licks his lip and readies his spear. Deftly, he lifts his muscled arm, winds up, and fires the weapon toward his target.

Thwapt, thwapt, thwapt...

The deer stops lapping water and straightens up. He lifts an ear to catch a strange movement. But he knows what it is. There's no doubt as the whooshing sound of the spear piercing the air catches his full attention.

In the tense moments before the spear's inevitable trajectory reaches him, the deer's day flashes before his eyes. He'd started off the day eating a breakfast of berries from a nearby bush topped off with a few mouthfuls of fresh grass from the nearby meadow. After running and playing with his mates until his muscles could work no more, he took a brisk walk to look for another patch of the green stuff –and promptly dug in.

A few minutes later, the sound of the babbling brook caught his attention and he decided to take a sip.

Then... well, you already know what happens next.

The Dietary Foundation

An agribusiness owner with an MBA takes a trip from his office to a nearby "farm" to check on his product – beef cows.

After passing through the steel doors of the livestock house, rows and rows of cows as far as the eye can see enter the businessman's field of vision. The cows are in corrals so tight they can't even turn around (technically known as a "confined animal feeding operation"). On the bright side, they are getting as much food as they can eat – in the form of highly-refined grain-based feed (almost all carbs with little to no fat). As the businessman heads out, satisfied with the smooth running of the factory, he notices an employee injecting one of the cows with a giant syringe of antibiotics. More antibiotics are one of the crucial elements of the new policy he wrote up a few weeks before. He's happy to see it being put into action.

Protein. It's the one nutrient the diet industry hasn't been able to demonize just yet. Not surprising considering the overwhelming evidence that eating enough protein is one of the most important steps you can take for your health and body composition. That's why cavemen spent so much of their time fashioning weapons and hunting. They knew that without protein they were done for.

The word protein is derived from the Greek term *proteios*, meaning primary or vital. Protein is vital in the survival sense, as it forms the basis for much of your cell's structure, enzymes, and DNA. But when it comes to fat loss, protein is just as vital. Many public health experts think the displacement of protein in favor of processed grains was as much a cause of the obesity epidemic as people going low-fat (don't forget, cattle aren't exactly fattened up by being fed lard – instead almost all the fattening fuel is carb-source). In a way, the low-fat phenomenon has hit protein intake just as hard.

Because the most abundant source of protein in the human diet—meat—also contains fat, many low-fat eaters avoid protein in a misguided attempt to eschew fat in any way, shape, or form. Despite making upwards of 50% of an ancient human's diet, protein-rich animal products were sent to the top of the upside-down USDA Food Guide Pyramid. Lower-fat chicken and poultry went from dinner time rarity to meal staple. High-fat meats like pork and beef were quickly denounced as heart attack fodder. With the only "acceptable" meat in the North American diet being poultry, protein suddenly became a hard to find nutrient. And when you could get your hands on a lean meat, it was likely raised in unhealthy conditions and in unnatural confinement.

All Protein is Not Created Equal

Like carbs and fats, protein form—and not just the total intake—is the X factor. While there are differences between plant and animal sources of protein, the stark contrast in form I'm referring to here is between the meat our bodies evolved with and the meat you order off of your local steakhouse menu today.

In many ways, the lives of farm animals followed the same unhealthy trajectory as the humans that ate them. Animals that spent a good chunk of their day running, jumping, and foraging for their next meal, building muscle in the process, are now kept from moving much at all. This helps line the farmer's pockets as it results in a larger yield, but it's a classic case of quantity over quality. The result of this sedentary lifestyle is unnatural amounts of fat storage (sound familiar?) That's not to mention the potential harm from hormone and antibiotic "therapy" that farm animals receive every single day (at least in the US).

In the same way that both a glass of Coke and a freshly picked carrot are each carbohydrates, factory farm-raised meat and wild game meat are both protein – with their respective effects on health being polar opposites.

But the most striking difference between game meat and modern-day farmed meat are their diets. While you may think fish are the only animal that can brag about containing omega-3 fats, you'd be wrong. Remember the old cliché: you are what you eat? Well it applies to all living things. Chickens, cows, and even pigs that eat a diet packed with omega-3's from plants, insects, and grass contain multitudes more omega-3's than those fed grains. In fact, it's been estimated that the average ratio of omega-6 to omega-3 in wild animals resemble lean fish.

To test this theory, North Dakota State researchers fed bison one of two diets: a grass-based diet and a typical grain-heavy diet. Not only was the omega-3 vs. omega-6 content strikingly different between the two (the grain eaters had a 20:1 omega-6 to omega-3 ratio while those that chewed grass were 4:1), but the grass-feeders resulted in a much higher monounsaturated fat composition (the most abundant dietary fat according to human biochemistry). Other studies have shown that grass-fed animals have much higher levels of crucial nutrients like vitamin C, vitamin E, vitamin A (beta-carotene), and even protein than those forced to eat the animal feed equivalent of Special K®.

RDA = Ridiculous Dietary Advice

It's fair to say that the current RDA for protein is a joke. Developed a half century ago based on faulty assumptions, eating the recommended 0.8 grams of protein per kilogram of bodyweight would have you literally peeing your precious muscle away. Studies that developed the current RDA were based entirely on something called nitrogen balance. Because protein is made up primarily of nitrogen, scientists thought they were able to determine adequate protein intake simply by measuring your protein intake and contrasting it with the nitrogen you excreted. While a crude measure of whether someone's losing muscle, it's a far cry from accuracy. Note that the RDA doesn't take into consideration: body composition, muscle gain or loss, chronic disease risk, appetite, strength, or quality of life. Just the amount of nitrogen in your pee.

It's no wonder that nutrition scientists are calling for a new protein RDA. Someone who weighs 70 kilograms (about 150pounds) and follows the RDA would be eating a paltry 56 grams of protein for their entire day – the equivalent of a single nine ounce steak. And if that same person was overweight and weighed in at 90 kilograms (about 200 pounds), he/she would only be consuming about 70 grams of protein per day.

Now this may be enough to survive on, but not nearly enough to thrive on. Rather than wait for the bureaucracy to make a move, you're better off taking the reins and begin to reap the benefits of a protein intake that's at least 30% of your total calories.

Why should you ignore the so-called experts and bump up your protein intake? Because when you do, you'll find yourself weighing less, with more muscle, a weaker appetite, and with a more active metabolism than before. Here's why:

Dozens of studies show that a diet with limited carbs and plenty of protein, results in more long-term weight loss. Fortunately, the weight loss that protein promotes is mostly fat. A study published in *The Journal of Nutrition* found that a protein intake nearly double the RDA resulted in only slightly more weight loss but nearly double the amount of fat loss. Another team of scientists recruited nearly 20,000 people and noted that those that ate the most protein had the lowest body fat percentage.

Research done at the University of Cincinnati echoed these results. What's important to note about this study is they a) followed the volunteers for a full six months – a timeframe where most diets peter out; and, b) they let them eat as many calories as they wanted. Despite that, the researchers discovered a higher protein diet caused *two and a half times* the amount of fat loss (ten total pounds) than a low-fat diet.

Priming the Engines

One of the tricks up protein's sleeve is that it naturally revs up metabolism. Protein is considered a "thermogenic" nutrient, meaning that it causes you to use more energy after eating it. While most of metabolism's (resting metabolic rate, or RMR) impact is from resting physiology and physical activity, there's about 10% that goes into chewing, digesting, and absorbing food. Viewed another way, 10% of everything you eat is ultimately burned off simply by you eating it. Wouldn't it be great if you could push that figure upwards? Well, with protein, you can.

Scientists in the Netherlands gathered volunteers to live inside a chamber that accurately measures energy expenditure for an entire day. One group was fed a high carb diet while the other was given copious amounts of protein. They learned that protein's influence on metabolism is nothing to sneeze at – 25% of the protein ingested was burned off simply from the extra effort of digestion.

A review in *The American Journal of Clinical Nutrition* looked at a dozen studies on protein and RMR. They concluded that, "In each of these investigations, the higher protein meal exerted a significantly higher thermic effect than the higher fat or higher carbohydrate meals." One of the studies they reviewed found that eating more protein upped total metabolism by 4%. At first blush 4% may not seem like much, but over time, this tiny boost reaps massive rewards.

Let's say you burn off 2,400 calories per day, which is a reasonable amount for people who are over-fat and not particularly active. A 4% metabolism boost causes nearly 100 extra calories to be burned off per day, even if you did nothing else but eat more protein. If we follow the tried and true measure that 3,500 calories equals one pound of fat, you'd be losing ten pounds of pure fat every year. And, if you remember from way back in the introduction, most people gain weight slowly and incrementally, ten pounds of fatvery year accumulating over time. Of course, I'm not here to tell you to count the months on your calendar and wait for your fat to melt away. Protein's fat-burning effects don't stop with your metabolic rate.

Torching the Fat

Another one of protein's wonderful abilities is that it bumps up your body's fat-burning furnace. Remember LPL, that devilish enzyme responsible for grabbing circulating fat and cramming it into fat cells? Well, it turns out that insulin, stimulated by a high carb diet, is what puts LPL to work in the first place. But like any process in your body, fat-burning has two sides to its coin.

While LPL works night and day to build fat stores, its bitter enemy, *hormone sensitive lipase* (HSL) swoops in to save the day. HSL is a fat-torching enzyme that becomes active when insulin levels are low (the word "hormone" in the name represents insulin's job in deactivating it). High HSL levels allow fat to be used up as energy, and not stored as body fat. After eating a lite food, the insulin spike that's created turns on LPL and shuts down HSL activity, making the concentrations in your body like an imbalances see saw.

But when you eat a high protein diet, HSL ramps up and LPL takes a siesta. Because protein hardly stimulates insulin, LPL has no boss ordering it to get to work while HSL swiftly begins its fat-burning job. Research published in the journal *Nutrition and Metabolism* found that a high protein diet boosted HSL gene expression and enzyme activity.

So far, I've told you the ways protein targets fat cells for destruction. However, protein has a number of indirect, yet still very effective ways, of melting away fat cells, the most important of which is bringing more muscle on board. It's no secret that muscle is the most important determinant of overall metabolic rate that's within your control. When you think of muscle, the word that should come to mind is "protein." That's because, if you were to take a pinch of muscle and put it under a microscope, you'd see nothing but protein. Muscle is protein and protein is muscle. If you skimp on protein, by eating too many lite foods or succumbing to fad diets, then you'll quickly find yourself with muscles that shrink like a cheap T-shirt in a hot dryer. And over time, less muscle creates a puttering and stalling metabolism.

From your body's perspective, muscle is an expensive liability. In terms of energy cost, muscle is a 10,000 BTU heater while fat is a flickering light bulb. Your body is fine with keeping a certain amount of muscle on board, but it won't manufacture new muscle unless you give it the raw parts—amino acids from protein—it needs. A constant supply of protein simply makes your body's muscle assembly factory more effective.

Unlike carbs and fat, which can be easily stored, your body has no such luxury with protein. But when given a consistent stream of protein at regular intervals between five and six times per day, new muscle can be produced almost effortlessly. The moral of this story is that your body, as it's primarily interested in conserving energy, will only build muscle—and keep it—as you lose weight, if you pay it back with bushels of protein.

Going Above and Beyond

When scientists take the extra time and effort to measure body composition in people trying to lose weight, they always seem to find that sufficient protein consumption prevents muscle loss. One recent study found that feeding would-be weight losers nearly double the protein RDA (1.5 gram/kilogram), allowed them to hold onto twice as much precious muscle as those who stuck to the outdated RDA's. A review of high protein diets on body composition concluded that, "Randomized, controlled trials continue to show comparable, if not superior, effects of high-protein diets compared with lower protein diets on weight loss, preservation of lean body mass, and improvement in several cardiovascular risk factors for up to 12 months."

It's not much of a debate; you need to eat enough protein to maintain metabolism by supporting lean body mass and the only way to achieve this is to go above and beyond the protein RDA.

Eating more protein, and packing on muscle, pays tremendous metabolism dividends. German scientists recruited 250 men and women to see what made the most significant impact on metabolism. They measured weight, body fat, abdominal fat, and muscle mass, and then compared them to the individual's metabolic rate. The significant differences between metabolisms could be almost completely attributable to muscle mass. The more they had, the higher their metabolic rate.

This is why I emphasize fat loss over weight loss – transforming into a smaller fat person hits the kill switch on your metabolic rate every time.

In Chapter 6, I talked about appetite, and how challenging it is to get raging hunger pangs under control. Fortunately, protein is a potent elixir for an all-consuming (no pun intended) appetite.

In fact, it is protein's natural satiating effects that have convinced me that calorie counting is a complete waste of time and energy. Take a look at a study in the *American Journal of Clinical Nutrition*. The researchers took a group of overweight subjects and put them on a low-fat diet for a few weeks and then switched them to a moderate protein diet (30% of their calories from protein). Almost all of the subjects reported that they felt less hungry on the moderate protein diet. But what makes the results of this study so exciting is what they did next. While in the first phase of the study, the volunteers were asked to monitor their calories; in the second phase, they could eat as much as they wanted. The trick being that they had to eat well above the RDA for protein.

Protein kept them so full that they ate 400 less calories per day. Most importantly, fat melted off of them to the tune of eight pounds. of pure unadulterated fat per volunteer on average. In a response to these impressive results, Arne Astrup, Ph.D., of the Center for Advanced Food Studies in Denmark, hit pretty close to the mark when she concluded, "It is preferable to replace sugars from soft drinks with protein from low-fat milk, high-fat meat, and dairy products with the lean versions, and possibly white bread and pasta with lean meat without reducing the intakes of fruit, vegetables, and whole grain products." These are the basic tenets of the *Dirty Diets* Program – no calorie counting, replacing refined grains with high-protein foods, and loading up on fruits and veggies (however, I do advise limiting the consumption of most dairy products, especially milk.) But what is it about swapping out your lite frozen dinner for a grass-fed steak that keeps you fuller longer?

Keeping Hunger in Check

Protein has the unique ability to interact with your hunger hormones, making the bad ones drop and the good ones rise. While protein positively affects leptin, CCK, and appetite regulating areas of the brain, nowhere is protein's appetite fighting power more profoundly felt than on ghrelin levels. As you may recall, ghrelin is the gremlin that shoots up when you haven't eaten in a while making you ravenous. Protein acts as a team of sumo wrestlers on a rising elevator, holding down ghrelin's from ascent.

Scientists recently tested the theory that a high protein breakfast can keep people satiated longer than a typical North American high carb breakfast. After feeding volunteers the most important meal of the day, one high-carb and one high in protein, they measured ghrelin levels in the blood. The protein-rich breakfast not only made ghrelin levels plummet, but the protein kept ghrelin levels pacified for hours. More specifically, three hours after breakfast which is generally the danger zone for mindless snacking. During this time, ghrelin levels were twice as low in the protein group as the carb group. Our switch from bacon and eggs to low-fat cereal has done nothing but push our desire to consume more calories later in the day.

Interestingly enough, there's a large group that believes those bacon and eggs should be served raw. If you've taken a trip to California in the last ten years then you've probably heard of the raw food diet. However, this is more of a movement than simply a diet. Followers of this tout evolutionary evidence for eating raw foods, especially those high in protein.

Their theory says no other mammal on Earth put fire to food. In the same way, we weren't meant to snack on 100 calorie packs in the wild and we sure as heck weren't cooking our food until very recently on the human evolution timeline. The cooking our ancient ancestors did—namely hovering a piece of meat over a flickering flame for a few minutes—is a far cry from the stir frying, grilling, and broiling that's so common today. Or as Einstein once uttered, "Humans are the only species smart enough to cook their food but dumb enough to eat it." Touché!

Protein 101

What's so dumb about cooking our food? Before I get to that, it's time to do a (very) brief bit of Protein 101. Proteins themselves are made up of smaller molecules, known as amino acids. In reality, your body could care less about proteins, it wants the amino acids.

Like fats, your body has certain amino acids that it can't manufacture internally and needs to import via your diet. Even so, individual amino acids are rarely found in the wild, and your body has evolved to eat protein in its natural form. That natural form being folded protein in intricate, three-dimensional molecular configurations.

Protein in nature isn't a linear string of amino acids, like beads on a necklace. It's more akin to the work of a black belt origami maker; folded and twisted up, over, and around itself, and it's these very distinct three-dimensional shapes that hold the keys to our molecular locks. When the shapes of these protein molecules are destroyed, the keys are no longer able to fit into our molecular locks and all sorts of mayhem ensues. This is also why pharmaceutical drugs carry so many side-effects. Because their shapes are man-made (as opposed to organically nature-made), they do not fit the molecular locks of our body's trillions of cells. The delicate framework of protein is destroyed with high temperature cooking, a process known as denaturing. The best visualization of this process is a translucent egg turning white on the pan. The tight protein folds spread out from the heat, making it opaque.

Beware the Barbecue

I am well aware that almost everyone loves the smell and taste of barbecued foods – especially meat. Having said that, I need to caution you—especially if you are diabetic or obese (or both)—on cooking your food via this method, as the potential risks far outweigh the benefits (incredibly pleasurable food). Preparing food (especially meats) by barbecuing them on open flames and excess smoke create various cancer-causing and diabetes promoting toxins called *glycotoxins*.

Glycotoxins, as well as another dangerous toxin referred to as *heterocyclic amines* (HCAs), which are formed when you char your foods, are extremely serious problems and should be avoided at all costs.

This is why it is always best to consume foods that have been cooked at temperatures less than 250°F (121°C). So try your best to reduce foods cooked via frying, broiling, hot-oven roasting, and especially barbecuing and try to embrace foods cooked via braising, stewing, poaching, steaming, and slow cooking (i.e. using a Crock–Pot® cooker).

When a protein is denatured, the availability of the amino acids in your body takes a hit. At very high heat levels, above 200 degrees Fahrenheit or so, amino acids themselves breakdown. While I'm not an advocate of a 100% raw food diet (although I am a massive supporter of raw-food diets for dogs and cats), there's truth to the fact that we process and cook the daylights out of our food, changing the composition beyond anything our bodies have ever dealt with before.

In a more practical sense, when cooking foods like meat and fish, the best preparation method is slow and low. Frying can bring foods to upwards of 800 degrees Fahrenheit, denaturing (unfolding) most of the protein in the food. Surprisingly, those Texas grill fanatics who cook ribs and steaks for eight hours at low-temperatures have the right idea. It is always best to consume vegetables, fruits, and nuts in their raw form.

You Are What You Absorb

No discussion of protein would be complete without touching on an oftentimes overlooked topic – *bioavailability*. When you check out a nutrition facts label and you see 25 grams of protein, you probably think your body is going to get 25 grams of protein to work with.

Unfortunately, protein isn't as black and white as the label itself. The amount of protein your body makes use of is remarkably dependent on the source and the state that source is presented in.

Many of my vegetarian friends are incessantly asked, "What do you do about protein?" Truth be told, most vegetarians, and even many vegans, get more than enough protein. It's not protein in pure amounts that's the issue; it's the protein *quality*. Certain protein sources—specifically meat and other animal products—are absorbed and used exceptionally well by the human body. Others, like peas, beans, nuts, and produce don't fare nearly as well. Luckily, many nutrition scientists have made a career out of quantifying these differences, known as protein bioavailability.

You don't need to memorize the bioavailability numbers of each and every protein source to reap the benefits of more protein ending up as muscle. If you stick to animal products like eggs, fish, grass fed chicken, and beef you'll be getting more bang for your protein buck.

Rice to the Occasion

Just because animal-based protein sources—more often than not—fare much higher in terms of protein bioavailability than plant-based protein sources, this does not mean you have to live your life as a blood-thirsty carnivore to ensure quality protein. Certain plants offer top-notch protein as well, especially with newer extraction technologies. While most plant protein sources suffer from subpar bioavailability, one exception stands above the pack. To be clear, soy – while claiming high bioavailability – is *not* an ideal protein source. Its phytoestrogen content is sky-high and well over 90% of it is genetically modified. Instead, let's look at one relatively unknown vegetarian protein sources that deserve special attention.

First, there's organic, sprouted, and fermented brown rice protein. While brown rice itself isn't the highest-protein food in the world, its protein extract has some unique and remarkable properties. You may have noticed the words "sprouted" and "fermented" in the title and scratched your head. Sprouting represents the process of soaking the grain in order to neutralize antinutrients like phytates, and fermenting creates a much higher nutrients and protein yield.

This might seem like a minor detail, but it makes a tremendous difference in the protein you end up with. For centuries, the Japanese traditionally soaked and fermented their rice before cooking. It turns out the fermentation process greatly improves the bioavailability of rice protein. Because the amino acid profile of brown rice is remarkably close to whey protein and breast milk, you want as much as you can squeeze out of every grain of rice.

But what I really like about organic sprouted brown rice protein, and what sets it apart from most other plant proteins, is its high concentration of a special amino acid, GABA. Studies suggest that GABA helps combat chronic stress and inflammation naturally.

The Alpha King

If there's a king of protein bioavailability, it'd be whey protein. In fact, when scientists first devised the bioavailability chart, they awarded egg protein with the pinnacle score of 100 out of 100. Years later, when they noticed bodybuilders clinging to their gigantic bottles of whey protein, the researchers took note. When they ran whey through their test, they found that not only did whey outperform egg protein, but it trounced it by a whopping 50%. What significance does this have for you? Not to be corny, but with the right kind of whey protein (yes, not all whey is created equal either) you can expect "whey" more muscle and "whey" less fat.

To test this theory, a group of Boston scientists enrolled a bunch of cops whose long arms of the law were a little too flabby. The researchers put the officers on a weight loss regimen that tested the effects of whey protein. As is typical of this kind of research, whey made no difference in the amount of weight lost. But what made these results so "arresting" (I know it's bad, but I couldn't resist) is that whey protein nearly doubled the amount of fat loss and allowed the officers to increase total muscle mass even as they lost weight, which is usually very hard to accomplish.

Whey works not only because your body loves to absorb and use its perfect amino acid profile, but because it contains a special compound called *alpha-lactalbumin*, which, according to human studies, helps you burn more body fat, reduce excess stress hormones, allows for better sleep, and turns on your body's muscle building machinery. It doesn't get much better than that.

The Right Whey(s)

When I was given the task of formulating what was to be the best whey protein available, I chose—for the very first time—to elevate the alpha fraction of the protein to the same levels it appears in Mother's breast milk (33%). If you're going to benefit from whey's unique protein structure, and you aren't interested in the fat, sugars or casein components, then look for a High-Alpha Whey Protein *isolate* (containing 33% alpha-lactalbumin). If you aren't worried about a bit of fat, some natural sugars and some casein, then look for 100% grass-fed Whey Protein Concentrate.

That explains the new muscle the cops were sporting under their uniforms, but what about the disappearing fat? Part of the story is our classic more muscle equals faster metabolism and less fat formula. It turns out that whey protein can also keep rowdy insulin levels at bay.

University of Toronto researchers recently fed hungry participants one of the most common North American meals, and one that's notorious for spiking insulin levels: pizza. One group chowed down on their pizza dinner alone while another received a helping of whey protein. Those with the whey appetizer had much lower insulin levels than those who ate the pizza by itself. According to the researchers, "We concluded that the ingestion of whey protein prior to a meal resulted in lower post-meal BG (blood glucose) and insulin and reduced the amount of insulin required for the post-meal glucose response."

So that you're not alone in your protein journey, here's a partial list of recommended protein choices (including options for vegetarians):

- Grass fed chicken and turkey

- Grass fed (and finished) beef

- Grass fed (and finished) buffalo or bison

- Ostrich

- Fish of all kinds, especially cold-water fish like salmon and mackerel (make sure they are wild sourced and not from Japan)

- Whey protein (high-alpha isolate or grass-fed concentrate)

- Natural, unflavored Greek or goat yogurt

- Organic sprouted brown rice protein

- Help protein

- Organic free-range eggs

- Miso

- Tempeh

- Moringa protein

- Organic nuts and nut butters (especially almond and cashew)

- Lentils

- Beans

> **The Ultimate Recipe**
>
> Even though using a properly-formulated whey protein at meals is an easy and effective way to help control insulin levels, I would instead recommend constructing an actual shake – once or twice daily – using whey (or organic, sprouted, and fermented brown rice) protein as the foundation of its own meal. You can easily accomplish this by using a liquid base like water, almond milk, or coconut milk and mixing it with fresh fibrous vegetables (like kale and carrots) or fruit (especially berries) and a scoop or two of a high-quality stevia sweetened whey protein. Make sure to add the quality protein last just until mixed and don't forget to turn the blender speed down once the protein is added (especially with high-quality high-alpha whey). This is to ensure you don't denature the protein with the thermic agitating response of the blender.
>
> I have been using a strategy like the one above for over ten years with my followers and it has never failed me or them in helping to burn more fat, keep more muscle and feel more alive.
>
> Don't worry, as I will give you a much more detailed understanding of how to eat and put together fat-burning shakes at the end of this book. What, you didn't think I was going to leave you stranded did you?

In Conclusion

That's a wrap on our discussion of macronutrients. Before hitting the first page of this section, fat probably sent a chill down your spine, carbs made you cringe, and protein had you scratching your head. But the take away message from these three chapters is that these nutrients aren't "bad" in any sense of the word.

Their effects on your body hinges on the amount and form you eat them in. Once you have that covered, you're almost 100% of the way toward a low-fat frame. I'm not letting you off that easy, though. I haven't even touched on the crucial, and myth-laden, topic of exercise.

But that's all about to change.

CHAPTER 14 – All Talk and No Action

Christopher is one of *those* guys.

On the surface, he's overly confident, intimidatingly good looking, and very popular with all of his friends and co-workers. At first glance, women swoon and want to get to know him and maybe date him.

But then, they get a closer look.

Christopher doesn't have the edge he once did in his younger days. He's on the uphill side of fifty, although his Facebook age says he's "35." He's not the fit, young stud he once was, so that's why he's eliminated all carbs from his diet. Sure, he Tweets every day about going to the gym and exercising, but when he's there, he has a hard time keeping up with the routine his trainer set up and mostly spends the time preening in the mirrors or flirting to the membership gal. He likes to brag about the repetitions he does on this, that, or the other piece of workout equipment, but truth be known, he racks up more cell phone pictures at the gym than calories burned.

In his younger days, Christopher could get away with being all talk and no exercise action. Nowadays, though, his middle is getting a little thicker and his once-fashionable designer jeans hug him in all the wrong places. In fact, most all of his clothes are tighter and not because bulging of muscles. He's spent a fortune on his wardrobe, so he just crams himself into the clothes knowing he can just work it off whenever he needs to. Besides, tight clothes are in... aren't they?

Just the other weekend, he and his friends went to the water park and he overheard two of the girls snickering about the spare tire around his waist. As he sat at the picnic table vacuum-eating his third funnel cake, chased by an extra-tall energy drink, he heard one girl say, "Christopher has really let himself go."

The other girl replies, "I thought he'd look hot without a shirt, but I just want him to put it back on."

The first girl says, "Look at his back fat, though. His eating habits are catching up with him."

Her friend says, "But his status always says he's at the gym."

The girl snorts. "Image what he'd look like if he *didn't* work out."

Christopher shakes off the criticism from that day. They're just bitter because he's never asked either of them out before. They're trying to hurt his feelings. He knows he's still fit and trim. Heck, he's even thinking of training for a marathon. That'll get him a lot of attention on his Twitter page.

He picks up his gym bag and his keys and heads out to the garage. "They're just jealous of me."

This thought keeps him going as he weaves through traffic and then sits in line at Burger King® for twelve minutes to get the two-for-five chicken sandwich special. And fries. It's no big deal, he thinks as he wolfs down the first sandwich in three bites. He'll work it off at the gym, no worries.

And then he'll Tweet about it.

Exercise – No Longer an Option

Before I get into exercising for maximum fat loss, let's establish some common ground on the subject that everyone can agree on.

First, I'm sure many of you still believe that jogging is the pinnacle of fitness and health. Due to the unfathomable popularity of treadmills and the sheer number of joggers that zip by you in your neighborhood, jogging and running for long periods must be the best way to burn fat and build strength. Not to mention the fact that doctors since the 1970s have been advising their overweight patients to run around to get fit. Unfortunately, fitness isn't obtained by running around mindlessly like an overworked lab rat.

Studies show that excessive aerobic training can actually be harmful, especially when muscle becomes a scarce resource as you age. Too much aerobic training actually causes muscles to atrophy and only burns fat during the first few sessions. After that, your body ultimately adjusts to such a predictable routine and jogging may do nothing but make you a smaller fat person.

Ditto for walking. Like running, walking has been touted as some sort of magical fountain of youth. But relying on walking as your sole form of exercise is like bringing a squirt gun to the O.K. Corral—especially when you consider that the two chief causes and symptoms of aging are: low strength and loss of muscle. Sure, walking should be part of any fit lifestyle, but if it is your only form of exercise, you can expect your legs to be carrying around a skimpy, plump body for the better part of your life.

Allan Geliebter, Ph.D., and his colleagues at Columbia University, recently put the tried-and-true wisdom that steady state aerobic exercise like jogging and diet helps people lose appreciable weight and fat to the test. Over the course of eight weeks, those that dieted and did aerobics three times per week lost the same amount of fat and weight as those that simply cut calories. In other words, they wasted their time.

Exercise for Chicks

While we're at it, let's put a big checkmark next to the statement that, "Pumping iron is for men only and women's strength training should comprise of 'girl push ups' and possibly crunches." Instead, women's muscle should be built with the "butt blaster" stepping on the elliptical trainer and by haphazardly lifting two pound weights over your head while riding the exercise bike. The women that buy into this widely-held belief must yearn to have a slow metabolism, flabby frame, and subpar confidence levels (and may indeed need a butt blaster thing-a-ma-jiggy).

Strength training should be the cornerstone of any woman's exercise plan. Indeed, thinking women should be relegated to the cardio room is as outdated as the notion that they belong in the kitchen.

Both sexes need to expand their exercise boundaries outside of the hypnotizing buzz coming from the cardio room and into the grunts and clanging steel of the strength training area. When University of Pennsylvania scientists investigated the effects of strength training on body composition in 164 women for two years, they found that hitting the weights just twice a week resulted in a mind blowing 26 times *less* body fat than those who relied on aerobic cardio alone.

Finally, it's a near consensus that to be fit, you have to commit at least two hours of your day to exercise. In fact, the USDA guidelines recommend at least 90 minutes of physical activity every single day.

Get In, Get Out, and Get On with Your Life

Contrary to popular belief, slow and steady does *not* win the race when it comes to fat loss. I don't know about you, but I loathe spending hours of my cherished free time in a stuffy and sometimes offensively smelly gym. Luckily, the notion that your results are proportional to time spent exercising can be considered dead and gone. It may sound too good to be true, but you can get more results in much less time. That is, if you exercise the right way.

Do I have your attention now?

Exercising the "right way" means chucking 60 minute walking or jogging sessions in the proverbial trash can. Instead, adopt an entirely new and more effective cardio approach, known as interval training. Interval training is an exercise strategy—lasting anywhere from four to thirty minutes, which incorporates short periods (i.e. 20-30 seconds) of intense resistance exercise (i.e. weight training) with cool-down recovery periods (30 seconds to one and a half minutes). It's basically a higher-intensity form of cardio done in a fraction of the time that is usually wasted on most cardio workouts. Dozens of studies have proven that interval training burns more fat in less time.

Take this study that compared interval training with old-school cardio for 15-weeks. One group did 20 minutes of interval training three times per week. The other group spent 40 minutes three times per week on steady-state cardio work. Even though the interval training group spent half as much time exercising, they lost six pounds of fat, while the steady-state group actually *gained* fat. In other words, even though it eats up more time, steady-state cardio created a group of smaller fat people.

Join the Resistance

Please don't think that my kind words for resistance training are simply exaggerated. Jan Helgerud, Ph.D., from the Norwegian University of Science and Technology, states that, "High-intensity interval training is twice as effective as normal exercise. This is like finding a new pill that works twice as well... we should immediately throw out the old way of exercising."

That's exactly what I propose we do.

However, just as important as ditching outdated exercise notions is to add something better. That "better" is Biocize™. Biocize™ is a term I invented while writing one of my previous books, *Bio-Age*, in order to outline research-based exercise protocols that are the most metabolically sound. In a nutshell, Biocize™ friendly exercise programs give you accelerated results in significantly less time. Biocize™ friendly exercise programs also help create an in internal metabolic environment that fights off inflammation – the underlying cause of all chronic disease.

How? It does it by tapping into the synergistic effects of resistance training and interval training while pushing your body toward becoming a 24/7 fat-burning machine.

The cornerstone of Biocizing is providing your muscles the stimulus to become more activated. A sufficient (approximately 30%) dietary protein intake ensures that you will hold onto your valuable metabolically-active muscle tissue during weight loss (as opposed to losing almost equal amounts of fat and muscle as seen on so many unbalanced programs). However, if you exercise with resistance (i.e. elastic bands and/or weights), you can expect your muscles (and metabolism) to rev up. The best part is this happens even as stubborn fat melts away.

Researchers from the University of Maryland recently found that women who did regular resistance training not only lost weight, but they were able to build muscle while the number on the scale took a nosedive – music to any woman's ears. Best of all, resistance training laser-targets nasty, stubborn, and testosterone-killing abdominal fat. Spanish scientists found that just four weeks of weight lifting cut away 10% of deep (visceral) fat from overweight men's bellies.

Snooze and Lose

As you might expect, those that hit the weights found themselves with a higher metabolic rate than before. In fact, for every kilogram of muscle you tack on, you can expect 20 more calories effortlessly burned off every day. One study found that resistance training for 16 weeks upped metabolic rate by an impressive 7.7%. This effect continues even as you sleep. Studies show that intense exercise can boost sleeping metabolic rate (SMR) by nearly 20%.

Lactic Acid – Your New Fat-Burning Buddy

Resistance training works on a number of levels to make you leaner, healthier, and more energetic than a mere jog around the block could ever hope to do. A large part of resistance training's benefits stem from *lactic acid* production. As you work your muscles beyond what they're used to, oxygen demands begin to exceed what is available – known as an anaerobic ("without oxygen") environment. In response, your body creates a substance called lactic acid to keep your muscles flexing. Besides letting you get a few extra reps in, lactic acid also sends beneficial signals throughout the body. I bet that all this time, you thought lactic acid was a bad thing that just caused you pain.

While you won't be burning as many calories *during* resistance training as you would riding the elliptical for 45 minutes and reading back issues of the gym's *People* and *Us* magazines, the *total* amount of calories you'll burn from the workout will be much greater. The lactic acid buildup from resistance training has been shown to stimulate testosterone and growth hormone production; a pair of crucial hormones that push the body toward new muscle growth for both women and men. Not only that, but these two hormones stimulate the repair and growth of muscle cells that got beaten up during your resistance session; thereby boosting your metabolism even more. Note that this metabolism bump is not due to simply having more muscle. It starts after your very first workout and is your body's ways of recouping from muscle fatigue.

Vanishing Flesh

Resistance training is the best insurance policy for lifelong fat loss, which is something Geico® and Allstate® can't touch. Once you hit 30 years of age, and especially after menopause for women and andropause for men, a process called *sarcopenia* kicks in. Sarcopenia is the scientific term for what almost everyone has noticed firsthand – as one gets older they tend to trade muscle for fat. Believe it or not, it's estimated after your 30th birthday, you can expect to lose approximately five pounds of muscle every decade thereafter. Scientists debate the biological reasons for this, but it's becoming clearer that the issue has nothing to do with the date-of-birth on your driver's license and everything to do with your lifestyle as you get older.

Studies show that as people age, they tend to sit more and move less, which is an automatic recipe for fat gain and muscle loss. Fortunately, studies show that you can gain muscle at any age. Research subjects aged 90 years and above have been able to drastically increase strength—with only a few weeks of proper resistance exercise. In the most literal sense, you're never too old to start.

Exercise and Insulin

I hope the benefits of resistance training and Biocizing have you doing bicep curls with this book, but if not, here's one more reason to hit the weights: insulin.

A study from the *Journal of Clinical Endocrinology & Metabolism* found that even healthy women with lean body compositions were more insulin-sensitive after a strength training bout. And, unless you've skipped over the first chapters, you know that higher insulin sensitivity equates to less body fat accumulation. Other studies have shown that resistance training lowers insulin levels both right after the workout, as well as for hours and even days later. You can lift weights until you're blue in the face, but unless you add cardio to your exercise regimen, you'll be limiting your body's fat-burning abilities.

Perhaps, even after reading the myth-busting opening to this chapter, you might be a bit skeptical that you can really get more fat-burning results from less time. In reality, it sounds like something you'd hear shouted from the mouth of this week's late night infomercial diet guru. But wait, there's more.

Sprint to the Finnish

That being said, the numbers don't lie. When you look at the numbers, interval training, although not nearly as popular as steady state cardio, is the real deal. Interval training torches more body and belly fat, builds more muscle, and boosts metabolism higher than continuous cardio.

It really doesn't take much for the benefits of interval training to kick in. For example, research in the *Journal of Applied Physiology* tested the fat-burning effects of interval training on a group of young women. After only seven total 20-minute workouts over the course of two weeks, their ability to burn fat shot up by 36%. They also showed improvements in muscle function and lung capacity after just three sessions.

You may wonder how interval training is able to burn off so much more fat. The secret is that it revs up your metabolism during the workout, but it keeps the foot on the accelerator for hours after you've left the gym. Scientists from the University of Glasgow in the United Kingdom recruited a group of obese men into their study and had them do high intensity sprints on an exercise bike. Again, this was only for a two-week period, comprised of just six sessions. After the workouts, their total metabolism and total fat oxidation (amount of fat burnt) increased significantly. And even though the subjects weren't told to do a thing about their eating habits, those that sprinted lost appreciable amounts of belly fat from the half-dozen sessions.

It Gets Better

Like strength training, intervals stress and strain your muscles, lungs, and heart in a beneficial way. Because you're working beyond your body's ability to keep up, thereby creating an anaerobic environment, it has a lot of catching up to do afterwards. The muscle repair, lactic acid cleaning crew, and nutrient delivery puts serious energy demands on the body. In fact you can expect your metabolism to be humming for upwards of 18 hours *after* your workout ends. That is, unless you down a sugary and protein-devoid vitamin water or sports drink within 15-30 minutes after your workout. The sudden flux of sugar, as always, stimulates insulin, shuts down fat-burning centers, and ramps up fat storing. Instead, wait to eat a protein-rich meal about a half an hour post-workout.

Fat-burning and metabolism boosting is fantastic, but interval training has an extremely wide breadth of metabolic benefits. For example, a 2005 study comparing interval training and continuous cardio for an entire year found interval training bumped up the *good* HDL cholesterol by a whopping 25%, while the HDL levels of those that peddled—bored out of their minds—on an exercise bike didn't budge. Also, while any sort of physical activity will deter excessively high insulin levels, interval training was shown in this study to outperform steady state cardio in terms of insulin sensitivity and glucose levels.

Finally, one last factor that makes this unique cardio so remarkable is that it actually *builds* muscle. You only need to look at a picture of a marathon runner and a sprinter side by side to see the stark contrast of body types that these two training styles bring on. Sprinters are notorious for being muscular, lean, and strong while marathon runners are thin, weak, and frail. A good chunk of this difference can be attributed to the hormonal changes that interval training creates.

Scientists at the National Strength and Conditioning Association tested the hormonal effects of interval training on well-trained athletes whose muscle building (anabolic) hormones were already thought to be near max capacity. Even so, a single sprinting session increased growth hormone and testosterone, and reduced cortisol, creating an internal environment ripe for muscle growth. Simply put, the body composition changes that interval training brings on isn't just from fat-burning, it's from muscle growth as well.

How can you incorporate Biocize™ exercise routines into your life?

Before worrying about gym memberships, shoes, or weights, it's best to give your mind a warm-up before you head into your first workout. Research shows that how you view your new active lifestyle will make or break your success. If you go into it expecting to fail, truth-be-told, you most assuredly will. And, if the thought of your next workout brings on a flood of emotions like disgust, boredom, and dread, then you can put money on the fact that you'll never make it. That's why I don't advocate just tolerating your workout, but actually enjoying it.

The Mind Has It

Due to the incredibly high failure rate of traditional exercise plans— half of couch potatoes who start exercising wind up back on the cushions after six months—there's been intense research to find ways of getting people to stick to them. Fortunately, there are quite a few golden nuggets of wisdom that have been discovered from this practical-oriented branch of exercise science.

Did they find that a shiny new machine, a squeaky clean gym, or a boot camp workout run by retired drill sergeants work the best? Not even close. One of the factors most tied to exercise intensity and duration is a positive mindset. Research published in the journal *Preventive Medicine* followed 500 obese adults over the course of a year. Those that stayed positive, remained confident, and believed they could overcome barriers exercised significantly more and experienced greater benefits, than the "non-believers."

One of the most sensible ways to gain confidence is by setting and knocking off goals. Don't worry, I'm not going to go all Tony Robbins on you and demand you release "the giant within," but there's truth to the fact that setting and accomplishing short-term, actionable, and realistic goals helps people adhere to exercise. Your objectives should have two facets: *outcome* and *behavioral*. For example, instead of having the goal, "I'll lose two inches in my midsection by June 25th," add in a path to get there. "I'll do interval training at the gym three times per week" is a perfect complement.

I don't think I need to remind you at this stage of the game that weight loss measured in pounds should never be a goal. The confidence gained from accomplishing self-set goals acts as a snowball effect – growing in size (while you shrink) as you accomplish more and more.

You can multiply goal-setting's effects by eliciting support from friends and family. Studies show that simply sharing your new lifestyle with others helps you stick to it. The weight of social accountability weighs heavier than the fat in your midsection –pushing you past pain periods and moments of weakness. Also, working out with a partner gives you more of the most important facet of any exercise program – enjoyment – than going at it alone.

Exercise itself is a powerful way to boost confidence and relieve depressive symptoms that derail exercise plans. Duke University researchers concluded that a few sessions of exercise per week were comparable to prescription antidepressants for the treatment of clinical depression. Happily, you don't need to run to get an endorphin-laden "runner's high." Short bouts of exercise no more than 30-minutes long have the same mood boosting effect. Also, research shows that those who do interval training don't get bored – which is all too common with steady state cardio plans.

Biocize™ Tips

Even if you're pumped and excited about Biocizing™, it won't mean much if you're going at it the wrong way. Here are some helpful tips to maximize your results:

1. When you do resistance training, keep your body guessing. Your body is quick to adapt to anything you throw at it. Session #1 may have you limping with soreness the next day, but by session #5 or #6 of the same routine, your body will have long acclimated. Be sure to mix up rep amount, rest time, and exercises regularly.

2. Start interval training slowly and work your way up. If you've been raised on the old "walking for two hours is best" frame of mind, all-out interval training will hit you like a sack of bricks. The best way to ease yourself into things is to start with 3three to five minute intervals that are slightly higher than you're used to, with three to five minute walking-based rest periods. As your fitness capacity improves, decrease both the active and rest periods but up the intensity. Your goal is to be able to hit 80-90% of your maximum possible effort for 30 -60 seconds. But don't expect to get there on day one.

3. Exercise outside the box. Lifting weights and running on a treadmill aren't the only ways to get your fat-burning fix.

Martial arts, boxing, dancing, team sports, and individual activities like handball and tennis are fantastic ways to throw your body into a new level of fat torching and keep things interesting for you as well.

To get results, you have to work hard. Lactic acid doesn't set in from sitting on your butt and peddling indiscriminately on a stationary bike. To benefit from exercise, you need to give it your undivided attention and effort while you're there. While 90 minute bore-sessions may have conditioned you into a habit of thinking about work during exercise, with only 20-30 minutes total, you need to make the most of that time. When you do, you'll reap rewards from your workouts that you never thought possible.

CHAPTER 15 – Just What the Doctor Ordered

"Two hundred and fifteen pounds? Are you kidding me? I haven't lost a pound this month!" Ryan growls as he steps off his bathroom scale.

In despair, he opens up his medicine cabinet, overflowing with enough prescription drugs to put a strung-out rock star to shame. But Ryan isn't sick with a terminal illness like cancer... he's just fat.

As he mulls the stacks of half-empty pill bottles, his mind flashes back to about a year ago. After trying one fad diet after the other, out of sheer desperation, Ryan decided to visit his doctor for a solution. After Ryan poured his heart out, chronicling his decade-long uphill battle with his weight and body image, almost in tears, his doctor robotically spewed out something about eating less and exercising more.

"Really, is that the best you could come up with?" thought Ryan.

Not to be deterred, Ryan said he's already tried that dozens of times.

Realizing he had to do something more than his typical "eat less exercise more" speech, his trusty physician asks, "Have you heard of *Orlistat*?"

Thus began a year long journey of trying to lose weight by taking yet another medication, albeit one that is endorsed by his own doctor, which means it's got to work.

What he didn't realize was that aside from all the side-effects—most common of which are oily spotting on underwear, flatulence, urgent bowel movements, fatty or oily stools, increased number of bowel movements, abdominal pain and/or discomfort, and the inability to control bowl movements (now how nice does that one sound?)—he only lost a couple of pounds the entire year. His epiphany that his year of turning to medications for a lifestyle problem gave him nothing but stack of medical bills and side effects finally pushes him over the edge.

Ryan shows up at his local pharmacy and lets out a long sigh.

"May I help you sir?" asks the overly friendly clerk.

"Yes," Ryan says handing over a small bag. "Here are my drugs... I just realized I won't need them anymore."

In Search of the Cure

In the early 19th century, a now-famous advertisement for the most cutting edge weight loss drug of its time, a tapeworm, first made its appearance. Showing a thin woman about to go hog wild on a pile of food, the ad text reads, "Fat. The enemy that is shortening your life – banished. How? With sanitized tapeworms. Jar packed. 'Friends for a fair form.'" The idea that purposely swallowing something to block the absorption of your food may disgust you, unless you've ever received a prescription for an obesity drug from your doctor.

Sadly, while modern medicine has made stunning advances in many areas, drastically extending the world's life span in the process, one nut they haven't been able to crack is obesity. Although considered a "disease" by the medical establishment, as you know yourself, being fat isn't like catching polio. Unlike a virus or bacterial infection, the factors that go into obesity are a mile long. Hopefully you've learned thus far that "curing" this disease isn't straightforward or intuitive either. If it was, we wouldn't have an $80 billion diet industry and experts touting 30 year old myths as "cutting edge science." Despite this, the medical community continues to lump obesity together with other common diseases, thus approaching it with the same set of tools.

This flawed logic underpins the failure of every single obesity drug ever manufactured. Jason Halford, Ph.D., from the University of Liverpool, explains, "Anti-obesity drugs haven't successfully tackled the wider issues of obesity because they've been focused predominantly on weight loss. Obesity is the result of many motivational factors that have evolved to encourage us to eat, not the least our susceptibility to the attractions of food and the pleasures of eating energy rich foods – factors which are, of course, all too effectively exploited by food manufacturers." In other words, medical approaches to obesity are doomed to fail as they lack the "big picture" mentality required to tackle this complex issue.

The Big Three

But that hasn't stopped physicians from trying. In general, doctors use three approaches to deal with an overweight patient:

1. *cutting the calories* (starvation method),

2. *sucking it out* (liposuction), *or*

3. *tying it off* (Bariatric surgery).

Let's take a look at these one by one.

First, cutting calories. On the bright side of things, more and more doctors are broaching the topic of obesity to patients that are otherwise well. Sadly, most prefer to ignore the issue altogether. The National Institutes of Health (NIH) claims that the "majority of primary care professionals do not talk with their patients about weight." This is unfortunate, as studies show that doctors who take just five minutes of their time to discuss weight with their patients have a significant impact on their patient's motivation to drop the pounds.

Unfortunately, research investigating what goes on during doctors' appointments found that the discussion of diet typically lasts only 42 seconds. Another study found that you won't have much luck getting any golden nuggets from your doctor (besides perhaps the most magical one of all: "You really need to lose weight.") if you're brave enough to broach the subject. You're four times less likely to get any advice from your doctor if you're the one to bring up a weight problem.

On the other hand, the advice doctors dole out during these brief heart-to-hearts isn't anything you could hang your hat on, so maybe it's not all bad that doctors rush through their dietary advice. In fact, in nearly three-quarters of all doctors' offices, not one staff member has been trained in how to deal with obesity, including the physician. This lack of knowledge shows that the advice doled out by doctors leans heavily on calorie counting and portions (oh so old school). These are two subjects I've avoided in this book for one simple reason: *they don't work*. All a calorie-cutting discussion can hope to accomplish is to put an undue focus on a factor that makes almost no difference – perhaps pushing them toward lite foods.

If they weren't able to starve you out of your fat, sucking it out is the next logical choice. You may think liposuction is something only for the rich Hollywood snobs. You'd be wrong. Liposuction is still one of the most common cosmetic surgical procedures in the US. While it does suck away fat cells, the body quickly adapts, creating new fat cells in their place or enlarging the ones that are already there. That's not to mention the fatal risks associated with lipo.

Once you regain the fat that the lipo hose sucked out, it's back to the doctor's office. This time, it's to get your stomach tied up through a set of procedures known as bariatric surgery. Every day, well over 400 people go under the knife to get their stomach clamped, tied, or rerouted – all in an effort to make overeating physically impossible.

I already touched upon the mental implications of bariatric surgery in Chapter 3, a perfect example of purely medical obesity treatments missing the mark. But there are plenty of physical issues to go along with it. Nearly 40% of all people who get this surgery experience side effects within the first six months, including "dumping syndrome," a condition in which undigested contents of your stomach are transported or "dumped" into your small intestine too quickly, which obviously causes a lot of gastrointestinal distress in the process, hernia, infections, and even death. Bariatric surgery, oftentimes seen as a quick fix, is anything but. Nearly one-quarter of all bariatric surgery patients regain almost all their original weight back. How? James Ostroff, MD, has learned firsthand that patients "figure out how to eat around the operation." In other words, because the brain has remained untouched by the knife, it continues to order the body to overeat anyway it can.

Get Them Hooked

Of course, doctors have another weapon in their arsenal. In fact, it's their favorite: drugs. Like a construction worker hammers and a sprinter runs, doctors prescribe. It's simply what they do.

To understand why doctors rely so heavily on a flawed and dangerous treatment, it helps to learn about medical school training. Medical school can be broken down into two parts: *pathophysiology*, which is how diseases come about; and, *medical treatments*, how to use prescription drugs or surgery to treat a disease. By and large, most diseases in our society fit perfectly into this model. However, obesity is not one of them. No drug can counteract the body image issues you've had since you were a teenager, the void in your life that food fills, a diet laden with processed carbs, or your lack of motivation in exercising the right way.

And by and large that's what we're seeing in clinical trials of obesity drugs. Although there are a few drugs that are commonly prescribed for the "treatment" of obesity, the three most recommended are: Orlistat (brand names Xenical® and Alli®), Acarbose (brand name Precose®) and Phentermine-topiramate (brand name Qsymia®).

These drugs account for more than a billion and a half dollars in sales every year. This translates to nearly $100 per month out-of-pocket for the user. Truth be told, "off-label" use for amphetamines and other non-approved drugs is widespread, as well, meaning that even more people are popping pills to pop their inflated gut.

Targeting Children

Speaking of off-label, one of the growing targets for obesity drug use is in kids. I already showed you the bone-chilling numbers on childhood obesity in Chapter 10, and doctors are taking note. Unfortunately, many of them are putting children on drugs that are meant for adult use. British scientists found that anti-obesity drug use in kids shot up 15-fold since 1999, raising ethical and safety concerns that would have been unheard of just a few years ago.

With numbers like these, you'd probably expect the drugs to have a stack of research papers in their favor. Not exactly. In 2007, the National Institutes of Health funded a study that looked at 30 of the highest quality obesity drug research studies. What did they find? "The average amount of weight lost is modest, lower than the 5-10% placebo subtracted target recommended by current guidelines, and most patients will remain considerably obese or overweight even with drug treatment." In other words, not only will you stay "considerably" obese after taking these costly and dangerous drugs, but you'd be better off taking a placebo.

In an editorial response to this disappointing data, one of the few physicians who have seen the light, Gareth Williams, Ph.D. and professor of medicine at the University of Liverpool, wrote a scathing editorial in the *British Medical Journal*. He warns, "Selling anti-obesity drugs over-the-counter will perpetuate the myth that obesity can be fixed simply by popping a pill and could further undermine the efforts to promote healthy living, which is the only long term escape from obesity." Unfortunately, his insightful words fell on deaf ears as prescription Orlistat became over the counter Alli® a few months later.

The Anal Leakage Drug

Orlistat is the most popular weight loss drug, and held this title even before it became the only over the counter weight loss drug approved by the FDA. Orlistat works by blocking the absorption of fat – upwards of 30% of the fat you eat will go completely unabsorbed.

How does it work? Orlistat takes advantage of the fact that, despite what you may think, absorbing fat is no cakewalk for your body. Your body is made up of 70% water and as you may recall from junior high school biology class that water and fat don't mix. Millions of evolutionary adaptations have circumvented this issue, and the human body has an extremely effective system for absorbing fat. But this system lacks redundancy – if one link in the chain breaks, things go haywire. One of the most critical chains in this process is the enzyme lipase.

When your pancreas isn't cranking out insulin, it's making digestive enzymes like lipase. Lipase's job is to break down fat molecules into tiny versions of their former selves. In small molecule form, called globules, absorbing fat is a breeze for your body. But when you take a dose of Orlistat before your meal, it blocks this enzyme from doing its job – meaning much of the fat you eat winds up excreted. This may sound like a "miracle" drug, but as we've seen, Orlistat falls flat when the rubber hits the road. Not only in terms of weight loss, but fat loss, as well.

One study published in the *International Journal of Obesity* concluded that, "There were no significant differences between Orlistat and placebo groups as to any of the body composition variables (fat free mass, fat mass, fat mass percentage) at baseline or after one-year treatment." Results like these make the risk of side effects even less worth it.

Orlistat *is not* something you want to take before your next date or dinner party (especially if your next date *is* a dinner party). As mentioned, gastrointestinal side effects are extremely common. One study found that 90% of people taking Orlistat had fatty stools, incontinence, stomach upset, or excessive flatulence. Because the drug blocks fat, which your body needs to absorb the fat-soluble vitamins A, D, E, and K, some people develop nutrient deficiencies unless they heavily supplement. The FDA has recently flagged Orlistat as a drug "under investigation" for reports of liver failure. Orlistat isn't nearly as benign or effective as the drug companies would have you think.

The Who-Let-One-Go Drug

If obesity drugs were an SAT analogy, it would look like this: Acarbose is to carbs as Orlistat is to fat. Acarbose, a drug originally designed for diabetics, has a similar mode of action as Orlistat. Instead of impeding fat enzymes, it blocks digestive enzymes for carb absorption. In fact, it actually blocks two carb-digesting enzymes the pancreas produces: *alpha-amylase* and the small intestine dwelling *alpha-glucosidase.* Because complex carbs in the diet are too large to be absorbed effectively—hence the enzymes which are necessary to break them down—Acarbose keeps carbs from getting cut down to size.

In theory, this sounds almost perfect. As I've shown you, by and large, refined carbs have been the catalyst for the obesity epidemic. Acarbose makes it so you can literally have your cake and eat it too (but not digest it). Unfortunately, Acarbose doesn't equate to much fat loss in the real world. Turkish researchers put two groups of overweight women on low calorie diets for three months. One group received prescription doses of Acarbose while the other downed placebos. After comparing changes in BMI, fat mass, cholesterol, and insulin sensitivity, the researchers found, "...no difference between the two groups."

Like its fat-blocking cousin, Acarbose comes with its own list of side effects. Unabsorbed carbs became food for the flora in your small intestine. That means serious flatulence and diarrhea. There's also a risk of stomach upset and liver damage – although these are relatively rare.

The I Can't Sleep or Poop Drug

Phentermine-topiramate (brand name: Qsymia®), another popular obesity med (which is actually a mix of two drugs: phentermine, which is known to suppress appetite and topiramate, which is used traditionally to treat seizures and migraine headaches, but has a side-effect of weight loss) works differently than the first two medications I've discussed thus far. While Orlistat and Acarbose spring into action after you eat, Phentermine-topiramate works to *stop* you from feeling hungry in the first place and seems to help people who are suffering from depression (and on anti-depressant meds) to lose weight. As guessed, this drug is also riddled with side-effects, including; mood changes and possible suicidal thoughts or actions, tingling of hands and feet, dizziness, taste alterations (particularly with carbonated beverages), trouble sleeping, constipation, and dry mouth.

Natural Light at the End of the Tunnel

Fortunately, you don't need your health insurance card to give your fat loss efforts a serious boost. A handful of natural supplements do much of the same absorption-blocking action, appetite reducing, without the list of nasty side effects.

Be warned, though. While literally hundreds of "fat burners" line supplement shelves at your local health or drug store, only a select few fit the bill of efficacy and safety. Best news of all? These supplements work the same way – perhaps even better and with no side-effects – as the prescription drugs, and you're about to find out what they are now.

Block the Fat—Naturally

For decades, scientists have linked green tea intake with lean bodies. Only recently have they dug deeper into this phenomenon to determine how green tea works. It turns out that all of green tea's remarkable breadth's of benefits—from cavity prevention to metabolism boosting—are due to a class of compounds found within the tea known as *polyphenols.* While you could get enough polyphenols by drinking about eight cups of tea per day, unless you wanted to spend half of your workday running to and from the bathroom (no this does not constitute as exercise), this was far from practical.

Eventually, scientists extracted these beneficial polyphenols and *wham...* green tea extracts were born. Their rate of absorption skyrocketed far past what could be achieved by drinking the brewed stuff. When this green tea extract was given to would-be weight losers, the amount of weight lost was more than double that of those that of those who simply cut calories. More importantly, a fairly accurate sign of total fat, waist circumference, decreased 14% in the group taking green tea extract.

While a metabolism boost likely explained some of this rapid fat burn, there's certainly more to the story. According to scientists at the University of Connecticut, green tea works just like Orlistat – blocking the absorption of fat by interfering with lipases in the gut.

> **EGCG – The Super Polyphenol**
>
> Most polyphenols in green tea go by the names; catechin, epicatechin, epicatechin gallate, and epigallocatechin gallate or EGCG). EGCG is believed to be the most significant flavonoid in terms of revving up the body's metabolism. This is why properly formulated fat-burners use extracts of EGCG as high as 90%. There is a relatively small amount of EGCG in most green teas, as the approximate concentration of total flavonoids in the dried green tea leaves is anywhere from 8-12%. This means you need to drink a lot of green tea to receive the same amount of actual EGCG found in two to three capsules of an all-natural metabolic booster.

I don't want to start down a track that will bring out old remnants of fat phobia which might be lurking in the dark recesses of your mind, but there's some truth to the fact that too much of any macronutrient will induce body fat storage. This indeed, includes fat. While excess fat intake is an issue for some, most of the extra fat you're carrying likely originated from carbohydrates.

Sugar and Fat Loss

The life expectancy of North Americans has been on a steady rise over the past few decades, but now a distressing fact confronts us. If you've heard reports that the increase in life expectancy is predicted to steadily decline, you'd better take heed, because it's true. A report by *The New England Journal of Medicine* states the increase in future life expectancy is going to be shunted to a very large extent due to obesity. The same report also goes on to state—what you now know—that obesity is the culprit behind major ailments like diabetes, heart disease, and even cancer.

Even though you are now somewhat familiar with carbohydrates' role in stimulating our old nemeses, insulin, many people are still unfamiliar with blood sugar and how this all equates to increased body fat. Well, before I go any further, make no bones about it; one of the most prominent causes of obesity is elevated blood sugar levels.

What is Optimal for Blood Sugar Anyway?

On any given day, a typical – fasting (two hours after eating) – blood sugar reading for most North Americans is in the range of 100 mg/dL (5.5 mmol/L or,). And if you asked almost any physician whether there is any problem with this value, he or she would say absolutely not! Yet, according to a great deal of research, fasting blood sugar levels exceeding 85 mg/dL (4.7 mmol/L) are associated with more obesity, overall disease and even premature aging.

The main problem is that soon after a meal containing high-glycemic carbohydrates is eaten, blood sugar levels can easily spike upwards of 40 points or more (140 mg/dL/7.8 mmol/L), creating an environment that is completely geared toward accumulated body fat, insulin resistance, heart disease and early death.

As a side note, a person is only diagnosed as diabetic if his or her fasting blood sugar level is higher than 125 mg/dL after abstaining from food for at least eight hours.

This is one of the main reasons it is imperative to both fat-burning and overall health and vitality to maintain blood sugar levels lower than 85 mg/dL (4.7 mmol/L). And in case you haven't figured it out yet, we humans find it very difficult to stay away from carbs, which is why natural carb blockers are the obvious next step in controlling post-meal blood sugar spikes and helping us lose excess fat.

It is common knowledge that carbohydrates eventually break down into sugar (glucose), just at different intervals. As discussed, the ones that break down too quickly are the high-glycemic ones and those that take their sweet time are the lower or low glycemic ones (hence, much better for you). Whenever carbs break down into sugar too quickly (as in most starches), your body once again counters this rise in blood sugar by upping the production of insulin. It's this constant increase in insulin that eventually leads to insulin resistance and expanded fat cells. At this point, obesity takes on a whole new course and a rollercoaster effect of low and high blood sugar results.

According to a study published in US National Library of Medicine, National Institute of Health, obesity can cause insulin resistance, rendering it ineffective in controlling blood sugar levels. This obviously leads to excess blood sugar levels in our body. However, our body remains oblivious to this fact and continues to produce even more insulin. The kicker is that your body will also begin to break down muscle tissue—in a biochemical process called *gluconeogenesis*—in order to make more sugar (from the muscle), followed by even more insulin and so on, and so on. The ultimate result of this is a predisposition to a whole range of diseases such as diabetes, heart disease, and never-ending expanding fat cells. In essence, controlling blood sugar levels in the first place can steer us away from the risk of obesity and its related complications.

Block the Carbs—Naturally

You already know how important it is to block the rise of sugars coming in from your diet. One of the primary reasons I recommend no more than a 40% intake of the right carbs. But let's face it, people will be people, which means they'll eat too many or the wrong kinds of carbs and fat-burning is just not going to happen with high levels of blood sugar – period.

Since I am not an advocate – in any sense of the word – for side-effect riddled pharmaceuticals, I am always on the lookout for published research on nutrients that either work alone or in combination with other nutrients that can do the same things—and often better—than the drugs. Such is the case with all-natural carb blockers like *white kidney beans, sorghum bran, Mulberry leaf*, and – are you ready for this, *brown seaweed*. Let's take a closer look at what these nutrient wonders can do.

White Kidney Beans

As a food, white kidney beans are known for their health benefits, especially their natural fiber content that helps lower insulin. However, it is what's in the white kidney bean that counts most here. The beneficial compound within white kidney bean extract, *phaseolus vulgaris*, has been shown to disrupt the action of the crucial carb enzyme, *alpha-amylase*. There are two kinds of alpha-amylase: one form is found in the saliva, and another in the small intestine. The latter form, made from the pancreas, carries the brunt of carb digestion. But when it's blocked, some of the carbs in your meal get blocked, while the ones that make it through travel at a slower rate, which, in effect, lowers their glycemic index. This significantly blunts the insulin response, aiding in fat loss.

Conversely, phaseolus vulgaris's biochemical actions have real world results. Research published in *The International Journal of Medical Sciences* found that a 30-day stint of phaseolus vulgaris resulted in significant losses of fat mass and almost 100% retention of calorie-torching muscle.

Phaseolus vulgaris (marketed under the brand Phase 2®) isn't the only carb blocker in town.

Sorghum Bran

In the US, Sorghum Bran had been mainly associated only with cattle and poultry feed until quite recently. With increasing awareness, it has steadily gained popularity to the point that we find it being sold in supermarkets today. The enthusiasm about Sorghum Bran is not unfounded. It is believed Sorghum Bran is among the most potent sources of antioxidants and can also play a major role in reducing obesity.

Sorghum Bran extracts tackle obesity by positively impacting insulin regulation and blood sugar levels. It accomplishes this by helping to regulate the alpha-amylase enzyme (as seen with white kidney bean extract). A study conducted by Hanyang University of Seoul, Korea, and published in the US National Center for Biotechnology Information sheds light on this fact. After in depth research, the study proves, beyond an iota of doubt, that Sorghum Bran improves glucose metabolism and insulin sensitivity.

The best part about this extract is that it has no side effects and is a completely natural way to lose weight.

Mulberry Leaf Extract

Speak of mulberry plants and the first thing that pops up in our minds is silk, as this plant is used for rearing silk worms. However, recent studies have shed light on another vital use for this plant. Mulberry leaf extract is believed to have properties that reduce carb absorption (and reduce blood sugar levels) by inhibiting *alpha-glucosidase* activity in our system. Wondering what this means? In simple terms, alpha-glucosidase—which lives on the thin border that separates your inner intestine and your blood stream—is the enzyme responsible for the conversion of disaccharides (two sugar molecules and starch into glucose. After amylases have done their dirty work, alpha-glucosidase steps in to finish the job. So, when mulberry leaf extracts inhibits the very function of this enzyme, naturally the glucose levels go down, and your fat cells don't need to overact and expand.

Today, there is solid evidence to back the positive impact of mulberry leaf extract on blood sugar levels. Research conducted by Hannam University of Daejeon, Korea, revealed that mulberry leaf extracts not only possess the capacity to inhibit alpha-glucosidase enzymes, but it also does it with almost no side effects such as increased flatulence, which is usually the case with most alpha-glucosidase enzyme inhibitors. As Traditional Chinese Medicine practitioners have known for centuries, the studies are supporting the findings to the extent that researchers are now suggesting mulberry leaf extracts should be tried by diabetic patients for more effective blood glucose control.

Another interesting study on mulberry leaf extracts was conducted by Ewha Womans University of Seoul, Korea. In this study, test subjects were actually first made insulin resistant and then exposed to mulberry leaf extracts. Both the insulin and fat levels in the body of the test subjects were tested continuously for an extended period. The findings proved that after-meal glucose and insulin levels were much lower, which means the insulin sensitivity had increased. It was also found the test subjects had decreased body fat levels as a result of decreased blood sugar and insulin production.

In essence, mulberry leaf extracts can naturally lower blood sugar levels, increase insulin sensitivity, and decrease body fat levels with no serious side effects and are therefore worth trying.

Brown Seaweed Extract

Another natural alpha-glucosidase inhibitor worth mentioning, can be found in two powerful brown seaweeds, *Ascophyllum nodosum*—kelp and *Fucus vesiculosus*—bladder wrack. This combination of brown seaweeds seems to also work well at slowing and hindering carb digestion.

Animal studies using a combination of these two seaweed extracts (marketed under the brand name InSea2®) suggested that 80% of the insulin and glucose spike from a high carb meal is reduced by a single dose of this seaweed combo.

Once you get glucose levels in check, insulin follows suit by trickling into the blood stream. Low insulin levels in turn keep fat-burning pathways running on all cylinders, while blocking fat storage enzymes at the same time – it's a win-win all around.

Blocking Table Sugar?

Yes, there is a carb blocker as well for table sugar (sucrose) and as reluctant as I was to share it with you, I felt you should at least know about it.

L-Aribinose is an ironic supplement. A sugar itself, it actually blocks sugar absorption. More specifically, it blocks table sugar, technically known as sucrose. While refined starches prime the body for fat storage, sugar is even worse. Because of its high GI and propensity for insulin release, not consuming sugar should be a top priority. That's where L-Aribinose comes in. L-Aribinose interferes with *sucrase* – an enzyme needed for the body to take in sucrose.

One study in rats illustrates the potential of L-Aribinose. One group of rats received straight sucrose while the other chowed down on a sucrose/L-Aribinose cocktail. Not only was sucrose absorption inhibited by L-Aribinose, the "lipogenic" (fat creating) enzymes were turned off. The authors concluded that, "Lipogenic enzyme activities and triacylglycerol concentrations in the liver were significantly increased by dietary sucrose, and arabinose significantly prevented these increases."

Japanese researcher recently reviewed the human evidence for L-Aribinose and deduced, "L-Arabinose...reduces the increase of the levels of blood sugar, insulin, triglycerides, and cholesterol by the ingestion of sucrose."

If you're looking for a way to help control your excess glucose and "supplement" your fat-burning efforts, there's no need to turn to unnatural prescription drugs. You can get the same benefits, and even the same mode of action, from nearly side effect free supplements.

CHAPTER 16 – Encapsulated Cocktail

Maria is thrilled about her performance review and the hefty pay raise that her boss gave her. All of her hours working late and through her lunch hour had certainly paid off. However, sitting at her desk, day in and day out, chowing down on asiago cheese bagels with egg, cheese, and bacon has only made her backside as expansive as the new amount in her pay check.

With this new chunk of money coming in monthly now, not only can she join Jenny Craig® and Planet Fitness, but she can also stock up on those diet pills she's read so much about and seen on television.

At the health store, she wanders the aisles looking at all of the labels and promises that each of these supplements make. This one says it'll burn fat. The orange bottle boosts energy. Another one will naturally attack her stress. Oh, and the silver and blue label one will help relax her to get a good night's sleep, which she hasn't had in months.

There's a two-for-one on the Amplified Lose The Love Handles Shake, 70% off the Triple Strength Fish Oil, buy two get one free of the Ultra-Mega-VitaPax, 35% off the Liver and Colon detox cleansing capsules, and a bonus-sized twin pack on all reduced-fat protein bars. She might as well get the three-bottle cocktail of energy boost, appetite suppressant, and vitamin enhancer from the Super-Duper-HyperCutAbove Advanced Weight Loss System. Evelyn in the marketing department was on those pills last summer and lost a ton of weight *and* got engaged.

Maria fills her basket to the rim with supplements, herbs, natural remedies, vitamins, and suppressants. She knows she'll have to give up her beloved cheese bagel, but it'll be worth it when she finally gets a boyfriend once she has her new, sexy, thin shape. And these pills are the secret elixir to get her there.

At the counter, the clerk tallies up her purchases. "That'll be $489.65."

Maria whips out her credit card and smiles, thinking how grateful she is for that raise.

Magic Pills and Potions – the Truth about Supplements

In a way, this book has been a course in basic "metabolismology"—

yes I made that up)—what it is, what it does, and how you can manipulate it to burn fat. With fundamentals in hand, we can now begin our course of advanced studies in metabolismology. That's what this chapter aims to cover. While the cornerstone of a high-speed metabolism is muscle and a well-controlled blood sugar response (as I covered in the last chapter), there's an extra step you can take to push your metabolism into high gear – properly formulated supplements.

Like you learned in Chapter 15, popping prescription meds that promise extreme "weight loss" without having to watch what you eat, what you think, and how you move your body is a recipe for stomach pain, cellular damage, and perhaps even a trip to the morgue. Of course, you can always take the natural route instead and get the same, if not much better, results. However, in the end, it really boils down to what foods you choose to bite down on and at what intervals throughout the day that matter the most. The right supplements are available to help you "supplement" an already well devised dietary and lifestyle strategy.

Sorry – We're Out of Magic Pills at this Time

Taken the right way, supplements can definitely help boost your fat-burning success and make it easier for you to achieve your end goals. Having said that, I need to make one thing very clear before moving any further along: No matter what miracle you may have heard about on the Dr. Oz show this week, there are no silver bullets or magic pills or potions. You still need to make things happen for yourself and that will always take some willpower, dedication, and commitment to making it happen. But trust me when I say, *it is more than worth the effort!*

One of the main ways in which properly-formulated multi vitamin/mineral formulas help with metabolism, is in supporting proper insulin function. Along with insulin resistance, obese people also exhibit some of the highest rates of nutrient deficiencies of any group.

A thought-provoking article written by Tania P. Markovic, MD, Ph.D., and published in the *Medical Journal of Australia,* shines a light on the puzzling issue of how obese people can eat so much, yet be, in many ways, malnourished. She makes sure to note lite foods as a primary culprit. "Foods today are usually defined as 'healthy' on the basis of a reduced content of 'negative' nutrients, such as saturated fat, salt, and sugar, but this provides an incomplete assessment." In other words, people who are overweight tend to eat foods based on what nutrients the food *doesn't have* – not what it does. With a mentality like that, it's no wonder that obese people have such a difficult time losing their fat.

I am an award-winning nutritional formulator as well as a nutritional researcher, so I know what I'm talking about when it comes to supplementation. I hate to be the bearer of bad news, but the bold truth is the majority of "so-called" fat burners, metabolic boosters, or thermogenic aids are nothing more than a ploy to make more money.

Imagine that!

This certainly doesn't mean they're all worthless, but a large percentage of them won't do diddly-squat unless you change your diet and increase your metabolism through Biocizing™, a proper mind set, stress reduction, and deep restorative sleep. Despite the hefty price tag, most metabolism boosters are made with fillers and benign ingredients that were created by people who haven't read the research or understand the science of how these items are supposed to work. The vast majority of these supplements are nothing but brilliantly marketed placebos.

Oftentimes, the manufactures will falsify or exaggerate data to give you the impression there's some sort of science behind their claims. If you've ever had the chance to pick up a body building magazine, you'll see plenty of these ads lining the pages. But if you look closer, you'll find the study they cite was done on individuals who were put on a ridiculously low-calorie diet at the same time as taking the supplement, not exactly the body of evidence to form the basis that their product will perform miracles in your body without starving yourself first.

Some Actually Work – Well!

This isn't to suggest that all metabolism boosters are worthless… they're not. A select few can push your fat loss efforts to another level. Of course, even with the quality supplements (or nutrients) I mention here, the word "supplement" is very apt. No supplement, no matter how good, will ever work as well as the lifestyle principles I've outlined at the end of *Dirty Diets*. With that in mind class, let's begin, shall we?

Let's start with one of the most popular supplements out there: multi vitamin/mineral formulas. Despite upwards of 60% of North Americans being overweight and/or obese, over half of them are currently taking a multivitamin. This is a prime example of how downing a pill can't overcome poor lifestyle choices. That being said, there's merit in taking a properly-formulated multivitamin every day.

Bashing Multivitamins

In December 2013, headlines were splashed across every media outlet possible. You couldn't open a newspaper, listen to a radio news program or watch the 6 o'clock news without seeing and hearing bold statements like: **"Enough is Enough: Stop Wasting Money on Vitamin and Mineral Supplements.'** This was the latest bashing of nutritional supplements that was seemingly driven by the pharmaceutical pundits in an apparent attempt to keep people relying on medications and fearful of natural things like vitamins and minerals. Sure it was written up in the prestigious journal, *Annals of Internal Medicine* to give it enough credit for every media outlet from here to Timbuktu to happily pick it up and run with it, but then again when was the last time you remember the media presenting something positive about vitamins or minerals – I rest my case.

Besides the fact that studies like this are so full of holes a mouse would mistake them as a piece of Swiss, according to Natural Health International (NNH-Intl), an internationally active non-governmental organization that promotes natural and sustainable approaches to healthcare worldwide, studies like this one always seem to use sub-optimal vitamin forms or inadequate combinations (i.e. 100% synthetic versions), treatment periods that are inconstant or too short, wrong doses, inappropriate or poorly characterized study populations and the list goes on.

In other words, before you decide to throw your vitamins away in place of a prescription med, consider who and what is behind the attack and what their end goals may be.

A multivitamin, in the words of Walter Willet, Ph.D., of Harvard University, is "nutritional insurance." Meaning, on days when our diets simply aren't up to snuff, a multivitamin serves as a safety net, making sure our bodies receive at least the bare minimum of the nutrients. There's also a case to be made that many of the current RDAs for vitamins and minerals are outdated. With studies finding that elevated intakes of certain vitamins and minerals help with metabolism, getting a little extra may give you a metabolism boost without the adverse effects from most fat burners. Incidentally, only a few nutrients contained in a multivitamin/mineral formula will do anything for your fat-burning goals.

B Vitamins

B vitamins fit the bill. While the word "metabolism" gets thrown around quite a bit (by me especially), it's a bit of a vague term in and of itself – making it difficult to understand how any nutrient would potentially effect it. In reality, your metabolism is the sum of dozens of pathways, millions of enzymes, and billions of reactions (every second of every day no less), the bulk of which rely on B vitamins. In particular, metabolic enzymes, the metabolism's workhorses, need ample B vitamins to function. If B vitamin levels fall, the rate of these energy-burning reactions starts to wane and metabolism drops. Considering the fact that we're replacing a good amount of the carbs in our diet from fat-creating grains (which are fortified with B vitamins) to roots, shoots, and tubers, taking a multivitamin with high doses of B vitamins is a metabolic necessity. Due to the fact that traditional forms of B vitamins must first be enzymatically-converted in the body in order to be utilized properly, look for metabolically active B formulas (containing *Riboflavin-5-Phosphate* – B2, *Pantethine* – B5 and *Pyridoxal-5-Phosphate* – B6 and *Methylcobalamin* – B12).

Chromium

One of the most research-backed fat-burning nutrients, *chromium*, usually finds its way into multivitamin formulas, although usually at a dose too low to make any difference. However, if you do your homework and find a multivitamin with ample levels of chromium, you'll be rewarded with enhanced fat-burning. University of Texas clinical researchers put chromium's fat-burning abilities to the test in a well-designed placebo-controlled study. The scientists summarized the results by stating the data clearly confirms that by supplementing with chromium, it can lead to significant improvements in body composition resulting from fat loss. Chromium works by making your cells more sensitive to insulin, tapering the insulin response, and controlling excess blood sugar. Do your body a favor and look for natural, plant-derived forms of chromium (like *chromium 454*).

R+ Lipoic Acid

R+ Lipoic acid is a nutrient that could help jump start your metabolism by helping to generate energy-burning within cells. It is also more powerful as an antioxidant than vitamins C and E. It seems that lipoic acid works similarly to chromium (and in conjunction with) –in helping your body's cells become more sensitive to insulin. The action of the most important molecules in insulin sensitivity, Glucose transporter type 4 or GLUT4, is improved by lipoic acid. GLUT4, in the old "insulin is the key" analogy, is the keyhole – sitting on the surface of your cells. In people who are insulin resistant (and if you can't see your toes, you likely are), GLUT4 doesn't work as well. Lipoic acid was shown in a study published in the journal *Metabolism* to increase the expression of GLUT4 on cells, making them instantly less insulin needy.

Vitamin D

One of the most crucial and sorely lacking nutrients in the Western diet, levels of vitamin D tends to be very low in obese people. Scientist aren't sure why, but they think fat actually captures circulating vitamin D (as it's a fat-soluble vitamin), imprisoning it so it can't get to the cells that need it most. Low vitamin D levels are no joke. In the last ten years or so, strong evidence has emerged that low vitamin D up's the risk of cancer, diabetes, and cognitive decline, and now possibly even obesity.

Don't Forget the Alpha

As I touched on in Chapter 13, Ultimate Protein, whey protein—especially high (33%) in alpha-lactalbumin (aka: high alpha whey protein)—is a nutrient density powerhouse. Its amino acids are incredibly well-absorbed and its influence on body composition is well documented. But whey goes a step further to secure its place upon the pedestal of the king of all proteins. Unlike any other protein source, whey contains special and unique antioxidants and immune system boosters that aid metabolism, which is why I'm mentioning it here again.

An interesting study conducted by researchers in the Netherlands illustrates how profound alpha-lactalbumin's effects can be in a short period of time. The researchers took two groups of subjects – one prone to high stress and another more mellow group – and gave them either alpha-lactalbumin or it's less effective cousin *beta-lactalbumin*. After just two days on this diet, the feel-good brain chemical, serotonin rose dramatically.

Why does serotonin matter? High serotonin levels indicate many detrimental stress hormones fallen and cortisol. This is why I was one of the first to isolate alpha-lactalbumin from whey protein and make it available outside of a research lab to the public. Its benefits are too potent to be left to lab coat wearing scientists and research volunteers.

Before you sip on your high-alpha protein shake, be sure to throw in some fiber. Fiber is one of—if not the most—effective compounds for controlling insulin levels. The best part is fiber can blunt insulin levels even before you lose a pound of fat. Researchers out of Finland gave 15 grams of a *guar gum* based fiber source to a group of insulin resistant subjects over the course of a year. At the end of the study, an important indicator of insulin output, *C-peptide*, dropped significantly.

Research on flaxseed and naturally derived fruit and vegetable fibers has found similar results. One study in the *Journal of the American College of Nutrition* noted that daily flaxseeds significantly improved insulin sensitivity over a ten week period. Be sure to avoid the ubiquitous *psyllium* fiber – this cheap, mass-produced fiber source is well-known for causing bloating, gas, and intestinal obstructions.

Fat-burning Nutrients That Actually Work

Finally, there are a select few *thermogenic* (literally *heat creating* or in this case, more appropriately labeled *fat-burning*) nutrients to choose from that'll give your fat-burning a kick in the pants. Unlike most other thermogenics out there, these actually have science and a great deal of in-field testing to back them up. In other words, they actually seem to aid in fat loss when taken as part of a proper fat-burning program (centered around a healthy diet and exercise).

The Two Fat-Burning Spices

Cinnamon is a spice from the inner bark of *Cinnamomum* trees. Sadly, more people around the globe associate it with gooey, delicious, overly-sweet cinnamon buns than a nutrient that can actually help you lose body fat. In fact, cinnamon works so well that I've been using it in my protein shakes religiously for years. It seems like the US Department of Agriculture (USDA) may agree with me on this one. They've been studying cinnamon's ability to lower blood sugar levels for more than ten years and have discovered that compounds within cinnamon may have the ability to increase sugar metabolism by 20-fold.

Extracts from a specific form of cinnamon known as *Cinnamomum cassia* are the ones that perform the best when it comes to regulating blood sugar and insulin levels. They accomplish this by increasing specialized proteins inside the pancreas (where insulin is produced), restoring blood sugar control, and lowering insulin—especially as you age.

Cayenne, the brutally spicy plant, has been shown to increase metabolism in clinical research. In fact, the part of the plant that gives cayenne and other hot peppers their trademark bite, *capsaicin*, dynamically influences metabolism. One Japanese study gave a group of women one of two high-carb meals. One was the typical bland fare you'd find at a roadside diner, while the other was spiced up with copious amounts of capsaicin. Even though the calories and fat were the same between the groups, the spicy meal not only increased the calories needed to digest the meal, but amplified fat-burning as well. However, if you want to actually enjoy your food, the amount of cayenne pepper you'd have to add to a meal to see an effect would be enough to set your mouth ablaze. That's why I prefer a supplement called Capsimax®. It's a top-notch capsaicin supplement, but what separates it from most other supplements on the market is the fact that the product has been run through the rigors of clinical research – and come out a winner. Aside from this, the powerful metabolism-enhancing capsaicinoids in this patented extract are embedded in beadlets that prevent them from causing stomach burning.

Green Tea with High EGCG

As mentioned in the last chapter, green tea extracts, in recent times, have become a very popular aid for weight loss. I touched on their lipase inhibiting actions already; however, there is a lot more to green tea extract than blocking fat. So, I feel this nutrient warrants a deeper look into the research behind its claims.

According to a publication by the South China Institute of Botany, green tea indeed has fat-burning capabilities. The EGCG *polyphenol* component in green tea stimulates thermogenesis, which is a fancy word for heat production, but in this case the heat is coming from burnt body fat. This obviously means that green tea that is rich in EGCG (over 50%) may be an excellent addition in to any fat loss program.

It is also believed that green tea increases fat oxidation, whereby people burn fat more rapidly during exercise (one of the reasons I take a specialized fat-burner with high levels of EGCG prior to Biocizing). Further, green tea extracts are believed to increase insulin sensitivity and reduce overall blood sugar and insulin levels. This belief is strengthened by a study performed by The University of Birmingham in the United Kingdom. The study was performed on 12 healthy men and clearly showed that green tea extracts increase fat-burning and insulin sensitivity while reducing insulin levels.

Research in the *Journal of Clinical Nutrition* tested green tea extract's influence on metabolism. Just three doses of green tea extract significantly enhanced fat-burning and total energy output. As you can see, these studies (and others) tell us green tea is indeed a very potent agent in helping to eliminate excess body fat and support a healthy metabolism in more than one way, especially when it is rich in EGCG.

Yerba Mate

Yerba Mate is a popular South American wonder I've personally been using for years. It is usually consumed in the form of tea, but studies show that compounds within yerba mate (primarily *mateine*) may have positive effects on us that induce weight loss. Aside from its potential metabolism-boosting properties, it also has other beneficial effects such as antioxidant and lipid-lowering properties.

The amazing attributes of Yerba Mate are backed by the research conducted by Taishan Medical University of China. A study was conducted on test subjects that consumed a high-fat diet over a period of time. When they were exposed to Yerba Mate in aqueous (water soluble) form, it was seen that there was a significant reduction in weight gain. Further, other noted results were increased metabolism and antioxidant activity. What this means is that Yerba Mate not only helps in supporting an optimal metabolic rate, but it also goes a step further to keep you healthy and away from ailments like atherosclerotic heart disease (often caused by the deposits of low density lipoproteins or LDL cholesterol).

Another study conducted by Universidade São Francisco of Brazil explains that Yerba Mate not only increases anti-obesity activity within our body, but it also has a modulating effect on gene expressions that are connected to obesity (i.e. epigenetics). According to researchers from the University of Rochester Medical Center in New York, genes play a role in obesity, where parents can pass the trait on to their children. Although epigenetics shows us that a parent's traits (as in being predisposed to obesity and eating a poor diet along with a sedentary lifestyle) can be passed down from one generation to the next, we are talking about a specific set of genes that, when turned on, can lead to excess body fat. It is to be seen in the future, with further studies, whether Yerba Mate can actually repair this gene. For now, however, it is an optimistic wait as you consume this natural obesity-countering supplement that seems to have far-reaching positive health outcomes.

Guarana

Guarana is a plant native to the Amazonian population and is widely consumed in Brazil. It is famed for its potential fat-burning properties and is fast gaining popularity throughout North America. Since extracts of Guarana (containing *guaranine*) are habitually consumed by Amazonians, it only made sense to test the effects of its long-term use in this population. This was the exact motive behind the study conducted by The Federal University of Santa Maria, Brazil. The study was conducted on a total of 637 people over the age of 60, some of whom regularly consumed guarana, while the others had never tried it. The results showed that people who consumed guarana regularly had a comparatively smaller waist circumference. The study further went on to say that guarana had a protective effect against metabolic disorders in the elderly. While this was a study based on a huge population in the open environment, the next study I am about to cite, was conducted in a more controlled environment. The results, however, were similar.

Brazilian researchers at The Institute of Biomedical Sciences in São

Paulo, Brazil, set out to find the truth behind guarana, as it is widely used by athletes in various forms to maintain energy and remain lean. After a study that spanned almost a fortnight, in a controlled setting, it was concluded that guarana indeed plays a part in fat metabolism. The study concluded that guarana possesses this property as it contains *methylxanthine*, which aids in weight reduction.

It's important to note that when it comes to guarana (and even green tea), the presence of caffeine-like substances (xanthine alkaloids) actually increases the fat-burning effects.

Combinations

I have found it is usually best to look for reputable companies that put together nutrients, like the ones mentioned here, in combinations. For instance, formulas that would contain the right extracts of green tea, yerba mate, and guarana might work much better than taking any of these nutrients on their own. These combinations would take advantage of all of the properties found in each nutrient in order to increase the overall fat-burning potential.

And So On

A number of other important nutrients such as vitamin C (a powerful antioxidant), calcium (bone-builder, but also directly involved in fat oxidation), fiber (blunts the insulin response and curbs hunger), folic acid (an essential B vitamin necessary for cell division and also in lowering heart disease risk), and iron (necessary for oxygen transport throughout the body and oxygen equates to most fat-burning) are low in obese individuals.

As you can see, it's entirely possible to eat loads of calories and still not get the nutrients your body needs. Talk about starving to death on a full stomach. The difference between the malnourished person who eats 3,500 + calories per day and the one who eats 2,500 and is in perfect nutritional health, is the nutrient density of the foods they eat.

Nutrient Density

Nutrient density is a relatively new concept in the world of nutrition; therefore, its precise meaning has yet to be defined. In a nutshell, nutrient density refers to the nutrient "bang for your buck" that you get from a particular food. For example, a low-fat bag of baked potato chips has an extremely low nutrient density, despite being fairly low in calories. On the other hand, almonds have an incredibly high nutrient density, even though they're higher in calories than most lite foods. But even if the foundation of your diet is nutrient-dense foods like fresh vegetables, grass fed meats, and nuts, you really can't beat supplements in terms of nutrient density – in fact, they are almost 100% pure nutrients (as long as the multi you are consuming isn't one of those one-a-day 100% synthetic multi's).

In Closing

Please don't interpret this chapter to imply that supplements are fat-burning shortcuts – they're not. Instead, view them as giving your vehicle a new super-charged engine on your road to fat loss.

CHAPTER 17 – Think Lean, Be Lean

Rebecca's friends know how much she loves to read and how she's trying to have a new positive outlook on life now that her divorce is final. So, on her birthday, they shower her with gift cards to her favorite online bookstore.

Unable to hold in her excitement, Rebecca logs in to her account that night and starts her shopping spree. She is in a transitional phase in her life and is destined to do everything she can to stay positive. She's finally going for the things she's always wanted in life including buying that Vespa GTS 300 Super scooter, joining hot yoga, and losing those pesky thirty pounds she put on since graduating college eleven years ago. Okay, add on the extra twelve to that thanks to her divorce. Her husband may have disappointed her, but her boyfriends, Ben and Jerry, never did. Rebecca's always had a negative view of her body and how others see her. It certainly didn't help matters or her self-confidence to find out her husband was cheating on her. That revelation was good for two pints of Chunky Monkey, a *Sex in the City* rerun marathon, and a weekend spent under the bed covers.

However, Rebecca vows to rectify the matter. Today is a new day. She is determined to start this next year of her life out right after blowing out her birthday candles.

At her computer, she peruses the virtual bookshelf, looking at all of the titles that might call out to her. There are books for single women, divorced women, women who are healing from a broken heart, a broken home, a cheating husband, a dying parent, an evil boss, you name it. There are also diet books with magical promises to pray away the pounds or chant them away, there's the yoga diet or the positively think yourself thin one. The cynic in her wants to laugh at the literary promises, but the new Rebecca wants to find that perfect book to help her see herself in a more positive light and get her eating back on track.

Before she knows it, her shopping cart is filled with books on self-confidence, taking charge, battling carbs, fighting calories, and standing up for herself, finding the real person in the mirror, and one that promises how men can be replaced by a few pieces of decadent dark chocolate. She clicks "Buy" and sits back in her chair as the order goes through.

Rebecca glances over at the mirror that hangs on the wall. She smiles, but the grin falters. She wants to be positive, but all she can think about is how her husband chose someone else over her and how if she'd just lost the extra weight things might have turned out differently. Tears start to gather, but she quickly wipes them away and vows not to let her self-loathing thoughts get the better of her. Not this time.

She points at her reflection and warns, "Just you wait until those books get here. I'm going to learn all the secrets and life will be perfect."

There's No Secret

In Chapter 3, I revealed methods to help you overcome the most common roadblocks that obstruct health goals – the mind. Perhaps unfairly, I painted the human mind as an enemy to be defeated. However, if you took the time to incorporate the barrier-busting strategies I provided, you may have found yourself with a mental vacuum – only slightly better than a mind cluttered with self-sabotaging thoughts.

To fill that void (before the dieting industry does), I'm going to introduce to you some extremely powerful mental techniques that will not only accelerate your results, but ensure that they last. If you think techniques like visualization and positive self-talk aren't for you—but should instead remain a mainstay of tree-hugging hippies—stay tuned, because I'm going to introduce some convincing evidence that this stuff flat out works, and just wait until I share with you information on an easy way to actually alter your brain waves so your new thought patterns become a regular part of your daily life. Welcome to the new improved you.

This chapter aims to take having a muscular, healthy, and lean body from something convenient to something you'll be committed to keep.

But before I get into scientific data and practical strategies, let's go over what we're trying to accomplish. In essence, almost every self-help book on the shelf at your local or online bookstore has the same goal: improve your confidence in completing a goal. Whether it's Napoleon Hill's business classic *Think and Grow Rich* (The Ralston Society, 1937) or the spiritual *The Secret* (Atria, 2006) the message is essentially the same: **think you'll accomplish your goals and you will**. If you don't, then you won't. Or as it was eloquently put by John Assaraf, *"If* you're interested, you will do what is *convenient; if* you're committed, *you'll do* what it takes."

Cracking the Nut

To do that, you'll need clear-cut goals and the confidence to achieve them. Goals themselves are fairly straightforward, as long as they're practical and measureable. Confidence on the other hand, is a much tougher nut to crack. Be warned: skipping confidence-building and moving on to healthy eating is like driving cross country in a ramshackle car held together with duct tape. You'll do fine on well-paved roads, but after the first pothole, you'll be stuck. Confidence is what will sustain you when your new, lite food-free lifestyle doesn't go according to plan.

Confidence, or as it's called by researchers, self-efficacy (the ability to produce a desired or intended result), is an integral element of lifestyle change. It took 20 years of watching research subjects drop like flies during weight loss trials to realize there's more to the story than "wanting" to lose weight. That's when nutrition scientists starting calling up psychologists and learning about the remarkable power of self-efficacy.

Karen Dennis Ph.D. and RN of the School of Nursing at the University of Maryland and Department of Veterans Affairs Medical Center in the UK, notes, "Matching obesity treatments to heterogeneous clients is a recent evolution in the development of more effective weight-control programs, yet most interventions emphasize the external features of treatments rather than the internal belief structures of individuals." The conclusion is there's been undue focus on the external environment and too little on the environment in our own head.

This is particularly true in terms of dropout rates when it comes to those trying to lose excess fat. The great majority of people completely abandon their new lifestyle changes after only a few weeks of living with their lean(er) physiques. Indeed, the relationship between fat loss and self-efficacy is less about losing more fat in less time and more about staying with the program.

The Power of Belief

Researchers at the University of Montreal wanted to see whether the action of believing in one's weight loss success resulted in lower attrition rates on a weight loss program. Sixty-two women signed up for the study and were assessed on how confident they were that they'd lose the weight they wanted. After six months, the variable most tied to successful weight loss and continued participation was self-efficacy.

After surveying hundreds of overweight older women, Australian scientist, Rhonda Anderson, Ph.D., has seen the potential for self-efficacy in overcoming inevitable obstacles. "Self-efficacy is our belief that we can produce the result we want to produce, so a person with high dietary self-efficacy believes they can eat healthily no matter what – even when bored, upset, tired, on holiday, or at a party." Many other studies, including well-designed, randomized control trials, have found that self-efficacy is especially important in weight maintenance – which is by far the most elusive and challenging aspect of any fat loss plan.

But how do you all of a sudden get the confidence of a real life James Bond? While self-efficacy is the "what" in your mental fat loss journey, *Cognitive Behavioral Therapy* is the all-important "how." Cognitive Behavioral Therapy, or CBT, is therapy that focuses on positive internal mental dialogue. Unlike traditional psychiatry, where you lie down on a couch and talk about how your relationship with your mother made you fat, CBT is a much more practical and effective approach.

Whether you're aware of it or not, you're almost constantly having a conversation in your mind. Sometimes these thoughts are mundane, such as, "I need to remember to take out the trash tonight" and even occasionally profound, like, "So *that's* the purpose in life." However, most of our thoughts tend to lean toward the everyday and unfortunately many of them are extremely self-deprecating in the vein of "Am I ever fat," or "I don't deserve to be thin." CBT aims to bring conscious awareness to these thought patterns and fix them as needed.

In fact, these thought patterns, which tend to seem spontaneously produced, are actually the result of a consciously or unconsciously learned reaction to a stimulus. Meaning, we can (and do) train our brains. For many—as mentioned above—the training has led people to produce negative thoughts that derail their goals. The objective of CBT is to pinpoint these stimuli and retrain our brain to react in different ways.

The dialogue and thoughts in our heads are incredibly important. Buddha said thousands of years ago that, "We are what we think. All that we are arises with our thoughts. With our thoughts we make the world." Famous German philosopher, Von Goethe, said, "Before you can do something, you must first be something."

While we'll be retraining ourselves to think positively, and thus bring on newfound self-efficacy, CBT shouldn't be confused with the simpler and less helpful "think positive thoughts" approach – which doesn't last and usually results in a reversal to old thinking habits.

The Proof

In obesity interventions, CBT has fared quite well when pitted against our old friend calorie cutting. Forgetting weight and fat for a moment, take a look at these results from a 1995 study that investigated the potential for CBT in helping overcome poor body image – a contributor to binge eating and obesity as you saw in Chapter 3. Eight sessions of CBT significantly improved the way the women in the study felt about their bodies and let's not forget perception equals reality.

A study in the *International Journal of Obesity* followed a group of overweight men and women for a year. Instead of having them meet with a dietitian, they met with CBT specialists. Despite never discussing fat, exercise, or even metabolism, those that underwent CBT lost body fat, lowered their risk of cardiovascular disease, and even exercised more. San Diego State University scientists found similar results when they did a four month trial of CBT on fat loss. In this study, CBT worked: body fat and belly fat both fell dramatically.

CBT's fat reducing benefits aren't limited to adults. CBT trials on teens have been very promising. In fact, one study found that just three months of CBT resulted in an average fat loss of 6% in a group of overweight adolescents. Importantly, the fat loss remained after a full year. Another study found that CBT effectively combats soda drinking, body fat, and large waist circumference in obese kids.

There's little doubt that CBT works. The question becomes, how can you make it work for you? I've spent the last few months picking the brains of some of the best CBT experts the world has to offer. I tend to ask them the same question, "If you were in the shoes of one of my readers, how would you use CBT to overcome mental obstacles that might stand in their way?" In doing so, I've gleaned some pretty amazing golden nuggets from these generous individuals.

Most recommend consulting an expert. The research on CBT and health-related behavior change (diet, smoking, exercise, etc.) suggests that taking advantage of a CBT expert's wisdom goes a long way. Not only do they have CBT down to a science (literally), but you'd be surprised the perspectives you can gain from getting an outside viewpoint on your thought patterns. What may seem "normal" to you might actually be detrimental negative self-talk.

Also, it should be noted that CBT therapy isn't the kind where you visit once a week for ten years to bring out repressed issues. CBT is extremely practical and easy on the psyche – meaning you don't have to reveal painful personal experiences to a stranger to start seeing results (not comfortable at the best of times).

I want to mention something that's particularly impressed me about CBT practitioners. By and large they aim to make themselves obsolete to their clients. Let me explain. Once you're armed with the techniques and strategies that your therapist provides you with, you will ultimately become self-reliant. The exact time it takes to become your own brain's CBT expert varies from person to person, but it's a relief to many that they won't need to rely on another person for their entire adult life.

Life Changing

If you decide to go at it alone, you can still squeeze meaningful benefits from CBT. The first step is to become aware of the "voices in your head." I'm not talking about the devil ordering you to burn your house down; I mean the internal dialogue that has a fabulous impact on your feelings and behavior. You may be able to monitor these thoughts by mentally recording them, but it's much more effective to write your thoughts down, especially negative, or self-defeating ones. The act of writing it down offers a place of unique reflection, tracking, and monitoring that a mental tally can't offer.

Instead of simply taking pen to paper every time a thought enters your mind, most find an organized system works better. Whenever a negative thought pops into your head, make sure to write down: **the thought, the situation, the time**, **how it made you feel**, and **how your feelings changed over time**. It sounds simple, but recording thoughts and feelings on paper is one of the most important aspects of CBT. In fact, many say the effects are nothing short of life changing.

Now it's time to make sense of what you've written down. More often than not, there was something that preceded the thought (known as an *antecedent*). Sometimes you can avoid the antecedent, but this isn't always possible. In that case, it's time to fix your response. Instead of letting the negative, and oftentimes false, dialogue enter your mind, make a conscious effort to think a positive thought. For example, let's say that every time you pass by an ice cream shop, you tell yourself, "I remember when I ate two pints of ice cream there, I'm such a fatty." Replace that thought with something more positive like, "I'm doing an amazing job resisting the fat-forming ice cream." Over the course of days and week, you'll "relearn" your negative response – substituting it with something more positive and beneficial.

Can You See It?

Finally, I highly recommend you start incorporating visualization into your life. The benefits of visualization are hard to overstate. Most importantly, you can start visualization today, without needing the help of any expert. Studies show that visualization, especially when done regularly, is an extremely powerful motivator. Visualization can be used to help you stick with any part of your new healthy lifestyle, whether it's avoiding junk food, exercising, or just thinking thin.

Research has proven that repeated visualizations form new synapses in the brain in a similar fashion as if you had actually done the activity. For example, if you can't seem to avoid the vending machine at work, visualize yourself breezing by it without an ounce of temptation. If done again and again, the next time you see the vending machine; it'll be like you passed by it unscathed hundreds of times before.

With self-efficacy and CBT now at your disposal, the hypnotic draw of lite foods will gradually dissolve – making your goals literally unstoppable.

Retrain Your Brain

Could you imagine if there was some kind of device that could help you—almost effortlessly—reprogram your subconscious? There is. But before I share it with you, let me first set the stage. As I often teach and demonstrate in my lectures, time and time again, your thoughts impact your actions, which impact your results. There are three ways to get results in your health or anything else you want to achieve:

- **Your inner game**
- **Your outer game**
- **The action you take**

In order to be truly successful at anything you achieve in life—including losing fat and having energy for life—you need to focuses on all three:

Your inner game. How you feel about health and wellness, what choices are you making, and what you believe about yourself? Are you happy? Are you sad?

Your outer game. This influences what choices you make. If you're stressed, are you going to give in and go for the junk food cravings or are you going to make the healthy choice? The outer game is what you're doing to help your dietary choices. And the final outer game is the action.

The Action you take. What are you doing? Are you doing the exercising regularly? Are you eating the right foods? Do you have the right mindset?

Surfing Your Brain Waves

For the inner game, when it comes to health and wellness and overall enjoyment of life, Buddha once said, "We create the world with our thoughts." It's pretty safe to say, if you're able to change your thoughts to be more positive, life-empowering thoughts, you will have a better experience. But the trick for centuries has been identifying what is required to help change the thought process and patterns. Of course, you can locate your own CBT specialist and start incorporating CBT's modalities right away, but what if you're just not comfortable enough in pursuing CBT, what then? The good news is there does seem to be another – quite viable – way.

Beta (14-40Hz)

Understanding how our mind functions gives us the tools we need to create the results we desire. Except when we are sleeping, we spend most of our time in the brainwave state of *beta*. Beta is our conscious wide-awake state and the only brainwave state where you can feel pain, fear, anxiety, and stress (and how fat you are).

Alpha (7.5-14Hz)

When we shift to doing something we enjoy or slip off into a daydream, we move into the *alpha* brainwave state. Humans actually spend about 25% of their awake time in alpha. Have you ever looked out a window or driven down the road and then wondered what happened to the time or wondered how you got there. You were in alpha.

Theta (4-7.5Hz)

The great thinkers of the world like Einstein and Tesla used the brainwave state *theta* to find solutions to their problems. That's because theta is the brainwave state we all go through just before sleep. Theta is our creative state, where our mind is free to explore, invent, and create the solutions we are seeking. Theta is also the predominant state of accelerated learning, which is why we spend the majority of our time between the ages of two and six in the theta state.

Reaching the theta brainwave state without intending to go to sleep is referred to as meditation. We all know the benefits of meditation. The relaxation and stress reduction acquired from clearing the mind and letting go of the tension in the world around us is physically and mentally beneficial to the body as well as the mind.

Delta (0.5-4Hz)

I've been lecturing about the *delta* frequency for many years now in association with anti-aging and fat loss. The reason for this is, aside from the fact that delta represents the slowest brain frequency, is it is also the one responsible for *human growth hormone* (HGH) secretion, which is directly related to reduced body fat levels and greater muscle size and activity. Delta is reached when we are in our deepest phase of sleep and also during transcendental meditation, where we are able to detach from our awareness. Since delta is synonymous with greater sleep cycles, its health benefits are too numerous to cover in one section, suffice it to say for your mind's benefit, delta is the doorway of your unconscious mind, and the key to the collective unconscious, where all that negative belief about you is stored. By accessing delta, it is believed we can rewrite our subconscious mind and replace the negative with positive.

Gamma (above 40Hz)

Gamma is not only the fastest of the frequencies, it is also the most recent one to be discovered, which is why we do not know all that much about it yet. One thing we do know is gamma frequencies seem to be associated advanced information processing.

Introducing Brain Wave Entrainment

So just how do we get our inner game, our outer game and our mindset all working together? Recent studies have shown that it is possible to induce responses from the brain through a process dubbed *Brain Wave Entrainment* or BWE. BWE is showing great promise as yet one more tool in helping to control obesity-inducing chemicals like cortisol. At the same time, your brain can literally be tuned to produce healthy chemicals like dopamine and serotonin that give us a positive outlook, which are also allies in combating obesity. To get a deeper insight into BWE, let's begin with the basics and first understand what brain wave entrainment is.

Brain Wave Entrainment refers to the response our brain sends out in the form of electrical impulses or frequencies when subjected to external stimuli such as light and sound. The electrical impulses of the brain can actually be measured by a device called an *electroencephalogram*, more commonly known as EEG. However, the question remains as to how these brain waves can be entrained to fight against obesity, create a sense of positivity, and help us rewrite unhealthy subconscious thoughts.

Our brain communicates with our body through electrical impulses. Some of this communication is obvious to us such as the reflex of pulling our hand away from a hot object. Other communication, such as the production of cortisol in response to stress goes unnoticed. However, the interesting fact is that these electrical impulses or frequencies can be generated through specific external rhythmic stimulus, giving rise to brainwave synchronization.

Brainwave Synchronization

In simple terms, when your brain is constantly exposed to a certain frequency, it responds by producing a similar frequency. This phenomenon is known as *frequency-following response* or FFR. A study published in *National Center for Biotechnology Information* (NCBI) proves this fact. According to the researchers behind this study, when the brain is exposed to a particular frequency through an external auditory source (i.e. headphones attached to your iPod or computer), the brain responds by producing measureable waves of similar frequency. In other words, the brain mimics the frequency (aka: FFR).

Researchers from Ohio State University set out to shed more light on this subject and prove that our brain can and does respond to these frequencies quite easily. In this study, the brains of test subjects were exposed to specific rhythmic frequencies through drum beats and clicks. It turns out their brains indeed responded through brainwave synchronization to this periodic stimulation, which was documented through EEG. More interestingly, the test subject's brains responded to various external frequencies by giving out similar synchronized frequencies in *delta*, *theta*, *beta*, and *gamma* ranges.

Chemicals and Frequencies

The various brain frequencies are directly linked to various chemicals in our body. Dr. Ashok Panagariya, President of the Indian Academy of Neurology of India, explains:

- The *frontal lobe* of the brain is rich in dopamine and creates beta rhythms – responsible for alertness

- The *parietal lobe* is rich in *acetylcholine* and creates *alpha* rhythms – responsible for the speed with which we think or process our thoughts

- The *temporal lobe* is rich in *gamma amino butyric acid* or GABA and produces theta waves – responsible for calming the mind

- The *occipital lobe* is rich in serotonin, creating delta waves – responsible for deep sleep

- The *prefrontal lobe* is rich in *glutamate* and generates gamma waves – responsible for judgment, abstract thinking and reasoning.

Human studies have documented a direct link between beta frequencies and higher cortisol levels. One study from the Netherlands showed that increases in cortisol brought about an increase in beta oscillations, which caused anxiety. Now, since beta range is directly related to stress and anxiety (higher cortisol levels), if it can be controlled through Brain Wave Entrainment, we should be able to effectively control the production of cortisol.

Other research shows that Brain Wave Entrainment can help an individual reach a brain state like theta in under ten minutes, which would normally take someone who practices meditation regularly several years to reach. It has also been shown that brain chemicals like serotonin and endorphins (our natural pain-killers) can be elevated by over 20 percent. Some people who use Brain Wave Entrainment also say that one 20-30 minute session is like getting 1one to four hours' worth of sleep.

So, if you want the ultimate accompaniment to your *Dirty Diets* Program, simply close your eyes, lay back, relax, and let Brain Wave Entrainment change your mind set so you can achieve the results you want for permanent weight loss. And you already know that when you change your mind set, you're set to change your life.

DIRTY DIETS

PART III

CHAPTER 18 – Getting *Clean* with *Dirty Diets*

Dirty Diets Principle #1: Eat the Way Your Ancestors Ate

Your macronutrient (protein, fibrous carbs, and fats) profile should always consist of approximately 40% carbs, 30% protein, and 30% fat. To ensure metabolic success, the most important principle here is to make sure your carb portion does not exceed 40% of your diet throughout the day and that you limit your carb intake in the evenings (more on this below).

Dirty Diets Principle #2: Never Skimp on Protein

Many people don't get enough protein, and if they do, their intake isn't spread out –meaning your body goes hours without a crucial protein source (and remember, the only storage form of protein comes in the form of your very own tissues—primarily muscle – and hopefully I don't have to tell you yet again that isn't a great option). High-quality protein shakes—making up one or two of your daily meals—are an easy way to ensure you are consuming your five or six meals each day, as compliance is of utmost importance when it comes to supporting a healthy metabolism.

Dirty Diets Principle #3: Only Eat *Clean* Carbs

Humans lived without many carbs for millions of years – way before a single grain entered the historical picture. Whole grains should form only a very small part of your diet with refined grains taking up an even smaller place or better yet, none at all. Roots, shoots, and tubers in the form of fruits and vegetables should be the cornerstone of your carb sources (aka: *clean* carbs).

Dirty Diets Principle #4: Say No to "Dirty-Fats" and Yes to "*Clean*-Fats"

You already know that low-fat diets aren't good for your weight, your body composition, or your heart. So choose your fats wisely as they aren't created equal. Monounsaturated fats are, by a large margin, the best fat source. Monounsaturated fats, from fatty fish, extra virgin olive oil, avocados, and nuts are a necessary part of any healthy eating plan and have long made up the majority of our fat intake.

Dirty Diets Principle #5: Never Count Calories Again

If there's one aspect of fat loss that's the most overhyped, it's calories. Study after study shows calorie counting doesn't last and doesn't work. Also, an unhealthy obsession with calories often leads to choosing food based on its calorie content alone – thus ignoring the all-important *food source.*

Dirty Diets Principle #6: Don't Eat These Foods

I know you're probably sick of being told "don't eat this and that," but there are some no-no foods that are too harmful to ignore. In no particular order, here's my junk food most wanted list:

- ✓ Processed desserts
- ✓ Full-calorie soda
- ✓ Anything with high fructose corn syrup in it
- ✓ Agave nectar
- ✓ Anything with the word "lite," "low-fat," "reduced-fat," or "low-calorie" in the title
- ✓ Processed meats (hot dogs, sausages)

Unfortunately, the American and Canadian food supplies are so saturated with crap, this is far from an exhaustive list. As a general rule, if you can't pronounce the ingredients, don't eat the food.

Dirty Diets Principle #7: Limit the Damage When You Eat Out

In reality, it's very difficult to follow most of the principles here if you eat two or more of your meals on the run. Once you step foot out of your kitchen and into someone else's, your knowledge of what the meal is made of, how it's prepared, and where it come from flies out the window. The good news is I've listed a section below that will give you the tips you'll need to stay *clean* in the outside world.

Dirty Diets Principle #8: Make Your "Evening Meal" Low-Carb

It's a few hours after dinner and you're hanging out at home when an earthquake of a hunger pangs hits. Because it's late, you don't feel like preparing anything that requires an ounce of effort. You swing open the cupboard and reach for... the dreaded crackers.

I'm not going to say that late night binging will completely derail your midday efforts, but it can do some serious damage. With a sluggish metabolism preparing for eight-ish hours of slumber, your body is in no way ready to burn off simple *dirty* carbs. You want to avoid *hyper* (and *hypo*) glycemia at all times of the day, but especially at night.

The evening time is when most people ruin their day's fat-burning effects by chowing down on too many carbs. In this case, even the 40% rule flies out the window as evening time should be about maintaining strict insulin regulation so your body is able to burn fat while you sleep and well into the next day.

This is why I have found that limiting your carb percentages for the last two meals becomes most advantageous in terms of successful fat loss. There is nothing wrong—and everything right—in going to bed with nothing but fibrous veggies and protein in your stomach. This shift will keep your metabolism going and increase growth hormone, which is highly effective at maintaining a fat-burning metabolic rate.

No need to go to bed hungry; just try to make sure your last two meals of the day are devoid of any carbs other than fibrous vegetables like dark leafy greens, kale, or any of the other vegetable choices in the *clean* category. In other words, *no* fruit and certainly *no* grains in the evening; only high-in-quality protein and fibrous veggies. In real life, this translates to a big green salad with chicken, turkey, duck, fish, or whatever other *clean* foods (more on this below) that may make your shrinking tummy happy or a shake with loads of greens and protein.

Dirty Diets Principle #9: Shave the Milk Mustache

"Milk... it does a body good." "Got Milk?" These two creative and well-designed ad campaigns by the dairy council quickly turned milk from a fringe beverage into a necessity for growth, bones, and health. The message was, "If you're not drinking milk, something must be (or soon will be) wrong with you."

On the other hand, there are groups like The Physicians Committee for Responsible Medicine who abhors milk and fights tooth and nail to stop the government from promoting it. Their website states that, "Many Americans, including some vegetarians, still consume substantial amounts of dairy products—and government policies still promote them—despite scientific evidence that questions their health benefits and indicates their potential health risks."

With completely dissident messages from both sides, it's no wonder that most North Americans are clueless about milk. What's the truth?

The truth isn't quite as black and white as a dairy cow. It turns out there are two factors that determine whether the milk in your glass is a healthy boon or a detriment: the source and pasteurization.

Like any food, the source and how it's processed makes all the difference. Milk is no exception. You may think "milk is milk," but although all milk may look the same on the surface, it can be completely different under a microscope. In North America, New Zealand, and some parts of Europe, the predominant cow breeds in these areas are called A1 because they contain a protein called *A1 beta casein*. A1 cows, such as Holsteins (the most commonly bred cow in North America) are the result of a relatively recent mutation that occurred about 5,000 years ago. The result of this mutation is it releases a potentially harmful compound called *BCM 7*, which besides throwing off your immune system, causes the trademark phlegm that you sometimes notice after finishing a glass of milk.

On the other hand, older breeds of cows—like Jersey and Guernsey—called A2 (because they contain *A2 beta casein*, which differs from A1 beta casein by only one amino acid) don't have this mutation and may actually stimulate a beneficial immune response.

Whether it's A1 or A2, you definitely want to stay away from pasteurized milk. The pasteurization process, while killing bacteria, also destroys many of the nutrients found in milk. The minute the milk is pasteurized, say goodbye to valuable protein, vitamins, and enzymes.

This is why I use a non-denatured (undamaged) whey protein that is derived from flash pasteurization (which does not damage the delicate protein bonds) coming predominantly from A2 cows as the basis of my High-Alpha Whey Protein formula.

Dirty Diets Principle #10: Water Should Be Your Beverage of Choice

Any way you look at it, you are made mostly of water. The question is, if you take water for granted, aren't you in essence taking yourself for granted? Your brain and muscles are three-quarters water. Your blood and lungs are over 80% water. Even your bones are one-quarter water. Next to oxygen, water is unquestionably the most important nutrient for sustaining life. Then why don't the majority of us drink enough of it?

Well, you might say, "I drink plenty of liquid; juice, coffee, tea, sodas." No, no, no. Nothing can take the place of water. A great many of us may indeed be dehydrated and not even know it. Aging is a process of drying out. Many health researchers and medical experts now believe that water—not just fluid—is essential to our health and well-being, and is one of the keys to an effective metabolism – and helping us lose excess body fat.

Is Tap Water Good Enough?

Have you ever left a few drops of tap water in a glass on your counter only to come back to a dried residue of sediment? Do you actually believe the sediment should be in your body—it shouldn't. Over 60,000 different chemicals are known to contaminate our water supplies and studies indicate we may drink over 450 pounds of raw metal and sediment over the course of our lifetime. The problem is the human body cannot use the majority of these inorganic materials in our tap water.

Aside from this, specialized water channels—called *aquaporins*—only allow the purest of water to travel through their structures to hydrate your 100 trillion thirsty cells. Therefore, it would stand to reason that you should drink only the cleanest sources of properly filtered—not mineralized—water. Water purity is measured in Total Dissolved Solids in milligrams per liter (TDS mg/l) usually referred to as parts per million or ppm. You should do your best to always consume extremely low ppm water. For this reason, I recommend distillation, reverse osmosis filtration, and bottled waters with ppm levels of 30 or less.

Health experts are still not 100% certain regarding exactly how much water is needed by the average person on a day-to-day basis—due to factors including the amount of exercise, heat loss, illness, etc.—but the general consensus is that adults require anywhere from three-quarters to one ounce of water per pound of body weight. In other words, the average 120-pound woman should drink at least eight eight-ounce glasses of fluid per day.

Dirty Diets Principle #11: Get To Know the Glycemic Load

A few chapters back, I discussed the glycemic index (GI) – a measure of how rapidly a carb-based food gets absorbed – and how the GI greatly influences the insulin response (and thereby fat storage). While a valuable tool, the GI is far from complete. Most times, you don't sit down and eat just baby carrots or a slice of bread. You eat a meal. When scientists test the glycemic index of meals instead of individual foods, they find tremendous variations. It turns out the other components of the meal effect the glycemic response to it known as the Glycemic Value.

For example, if you downed a giant bowl of white rice, you can expect insulin to fly out of your pancreas in response to rapidly-elevated blood glucose. But if you add a heaping pile of vegetables, a small portion of chicken, and a handful of nuts, you've got an entirely different beast. While the GI of the meal may be high in theory, the more important and representative value – the glycemic value – may be much lower.

This area of research is relatively new, and with thousands (if not millions) of food combinations to test, we may be years away from getting a hard and fast GI for meals the same way we have a GI for specific foods. That being said, there are a few noticeable and consistent trends that have come out of this early research.

One of the first correlations scientists noted was any food that delayed gastric emptying (the rate food leaves the stomach and enters the small intestine for absorption), lowered the GI considerably. This means healthy fats, protein, and fiber – nutrients well-known to slow this process – should be included in nearly all of your meals.

In 2008, University of Missouri researchers noted the importance of omega-3's in slowing gastric emptying and preventing hyperglycemia. None of this should be earth-shattering news. The foods that form a low GI meal are the cornerstone of the *Dirty Diets* Eating Plan, which I'll discuss next.

The *Dirty Diets* Eating Plan

I've never known anyone to get excited about starting a diet, which is exactly why I wrote this book and designed the *Dirty Diets* Eating Plan. You are going to find out that this plan is about "eating *clean*" again, which means embracing proper foods at the proper times of the day— and **not** about counting calories. That's right, I said there is **no** calorie counting allowed.

The dietary protocols listed here are time-tested and proven to help your metabolism get to where it needs to be and keep it there for life. After all, who wants to count every calorie, every day, for the rest of their lives?

The majority of people throughout North America have trained their bodies to leave its own body fat stores alone and go after other fuels—such as muscle tissue. If you read Chapter 8, His Fat, you are well aware of why men tend to have a much easier time losing weight as women on the same diet —even though women more often than not try harder. It's because of the metabolic advantage men hold over women:

muscle. Men carry on average an extra 30-40 pounds of the stuff, and since muscle is the key metabolic engine of the human body, responsible for allowing you to burn an enormous amount of calories (coming from those billions of storage containers we call fat cells) at rest, men have about a 30% greater ability to burn body fat (please don't shoot the messenger).

I developed the *Dirty Diets* Eating Plan to help you hold onto your precious fat-burning engines by supplying your body with high quality proteins (the building blocks of muscle, bone, skin, hair, and almost everything else the body is comprised of) at regular intervals throughout the day. Most people—especially women—have a tendency to lose almost as much muscle tissue as they do fat on the majority of fad diets these days. I know, I know, you have always believed "weight loss" equals success on a diet. **Wrong!** If you lose too much muscle on an unbalanced program (a.k.a. a fad diet) all you end up doing is creating a smaller—yet still fat—version of your former self (the "Smaller Fat Person Syndrome").

The *Dirty Diets* Eating Plan is designed around fat loss, *not* weight loss. By following the principles behind this program (the same principles have been used successfully by thousands of people around the world who have followed my *Fat Wars*™ and *Losing Fat for Life*™ protocols), your body will become accustomed to using your body fat as its main fuel source—around the clock (yes, even while you sleep). Let me make it clear that your metabolism will become healthy and strong, which equates to a leaner, more energetic, happier you. Couple these eating principles with an effective exercise program (a la Biocize™) and you have a one-two combination punch that can't lose. Your metabolism will never know what hit it.

The reason this plan is so successful at helping you create a healthy and strong metabolism is due to the fact it is based upon portion control—using optimal macronutrient choices (high quality protein, low-glycemic carbohydrates, and good fats) that are effective for your (biochemical and physiological) individuality. After following the *Dirty Diets* Eating Plan for a relatively short period of time, your body will adjust its metabolism to allow the use of its own fat stores to become the *preferred* source of fuel for your body.

It is important to understand that the *Dirty Diets* Eating Plan is all about eating, enjoying, and embracing nutrient dense *clean* foods rather than reducing nutrient intake or avoiding foods all together. In fact, I often hear people commenting on the fact they just can't believe how much food they are supposed to eat on my food plans. Now that's a concept you can sink your teeth into—literally.

Supplement or Necessity?

High-Alpha Whey Protein isolates or Grass-Fed Whey Protein concentrates and/or Organic Sprouted and Fermented Brown Rice Proteins are an integral part of this plan, as they provide high quality protein to your muscles in order to support optimal metabolic function, which is essential to the burning of your body fat stores. As part of the *Dirty Diets* Eating Plan I advise making one to two of these protein shakes every day.

These protein powders can be mixed (as in one-scoop of each) or one may be substituted for the other (i.e. whey protein instead of rice protein). For an extra bonus, try adding in at least five grams (usually one scoop) of a 100% organic fruit and vegetable fiber formula (such as Ultimate FibreLean™) to each of your shakes. These natural dietary fibers—along with the outlined fruits, vegetables, nuts, and seeds—help cleanse the body and support optimal insulin production.

High insulin levels—due to low fiber diets—are a hallmark of obesity. The additional benefit of consuming the recommended nuts and seeds (or nut butters) on this program is they supply high quality fats that actually work to enhance your body's metabolism.

It is also important to understand this plan is designed to educate you on *how* and *what* to eat to build a healthy and strong metabolism for life. This in no way means you can *never* enjoy those so-called "fun foods" (or what I call the "Dirty Foods"), but your goal must be to establish a healthy and strong metabolism (which can take a few months) <u>before</u> you begin to include those "Dirty Foods" in your diet again. Strictly speaking, you need to make a real commitment to getting *clean* this time.

Optimal Nutrition

In order to create a healthy and strong metabolism, boost your energy levels, and build lean muscle tissue (which further enhances your metabolism), it is essential to consume high quality *clean* foods and exercise regularly.

The *Dirty Diets* Eating Plan consists of consuming <u>specialized meals</u> at <u>regular intervals</u> throughout the day. This is why I have always recommended consuming <u>three solid meals</u> and <u>two liquid meals</u> (in the form of protein shakes) per day. To optimize your metabolism, balance blood sugar, keep insulin levels in check, and reduce cravings more effectively, I recommend consuming smaller portions of nutrient-dense foods approximately every **three to four** hours throughout the day (this equates to five balanced meals).

To function, you require a consistent supply of essential nutrients— the majority of which your body is unable to manufacture on its own. Essential nutrients are: water, minerals, vitamins, carbohydrates, fats, and proteins.

Following is a breakdown of these nutrients:

— **Water** regulates *all* functions of the body

— **Minerals** regulate actions within the body that aid in generating enzymes, hormones, skeletal bones, skeletal tissues, teeth, and fluids.

— **Vitamins** help the body produce energy and are required in small amounts to help facilitate the chemical reactions within our cells.

— *Clean* **Proteins** help stabilize blood sugar, promote cell development, and repair and assist in hormone, enzyme (digestive and metabolic), and neurotransmitter production, cell metabolism, body fluid balancing, maintenance of the immune system, and are essential for a healthy and strong metabolism—as they comprise a large portion of muscle tissue.

— *Clean* **Carbs** (low-glycemic) ensure antioxidant protection (in the form of fruits and vegetables) energy production, thyroid conversion, muscular repair and assist in maintaining a proper balance of insulin to glucagon (a fat-burning hormone) to ensure successful fat-burning.

— *Clean* **Fats** with monounsaturated, essential fatty acids—EFA's— and yes, even saturated (see below), leading the way. These *clean* fats are necessary to create energy, build cellular membranes, help detoxify the body, control cell traffic (ensuring that viruses and germs stay out, all the while keeping cell proteins, organelles, enzymes and genetic material in), maintain healthy insulin functions, form red blood cells, lubricate our joints and help maintain a healthy metabolism. EFA's also make sure we burn fat by increasing the quantity of oxygen utilized by the cells in order to create energy. Two types of EFA's are Omega 6 and Omega 3's. Although Omegas 6's are commonly found in our diet, the same cannot be said for Omega 3's.

Omega 9's (part of the monounsaturated family) are also important fats—especially where heart disease is concerned. Omega 9's can be found in olive oil, avocados, and almonds, to name a few. And finally, one more fat I'd like to introduce you to—when it comes to supporting a healthy metabolism—is a saturated fat called coconut oil. Saturated fat? What? I must be crazy! Believe it or not, research shows that some saturated fats are actually health-promoting, and coconut oil seems to be leading the way. All fats are classified as short, medium, or long-chain based on the number of carbon molecules they contain. When it comes to coconut oil, almost two-thirds of the saturated fat is in the form of medium-chain fatty acids (MCTs), and unlike their long-chain cousins, MCTs do not need to be emulsified by bile salts in the small intestine before they are absorbed by the body. This gives MCTs a unique advantage to become immediately available and provide a great source of energy to the body as opposed to being stored as fat.

Building Your *Dirty Diets* Meals

When preparing a *Dirty Diets* friendly meal (which is actually called a **Clean Meal**), it is imperative to ensure that all essential nutrients are present. We know where water comes in, but what about the rest of these nutrients? Vitamins and minerals should come primarily from fruits and vegetables; however, it is important to note that many of today's conventionally-grown foods are often lacking minerals (up to 90% less) than their **organic** counterparts, which is why I always recommend organic produce whenever possible and supplementing with 100% organically-bound natural minerals (the best one I have used can be found at the following website: *www.LeafSource.com*).

The *Dirty Diets* Eating Plan – *Clean*, Murky, and Dirty

The food lists below are simple to follow, but to avoid *any* and *all* confusion, allow me to lay it out here. The *Dirty Diets* **Clean** foods list are those items you can choose to eat every day, as they follow the proper guidelines when it comes to *clean* food choices in each category (protein, carbs, and fats). The *Dirty Diets* **Murky** foods list are foods you can still choose from, but try to minimize their intake to no more than twice a week, as they are not necessarily *bad* choices, but they're not the *best* either. The *Dirty Diets* **Dirty** foods list are foods that should be eliminated from the diet, as they cause the greatest hormonal mayhem and potential toxicity.

This doesn't mean you can *never* eat foods from the dirty list again. It just means these foods are best left alone and every once and a while when you are feeling a little bad yourself, enjoy some of these foods, but use them *only* on designated cheat days once you have arrived at your desired metabolic destination.

In the *Dirty Diets* Eating Plan Recommended Food Choices section below, you will find an overview of which foods fall under the various categories of *Clean* Proteins, *Clean* Carbs, and *Clean* Fats. In this section—along with the **clean food** choices—you will also see a complete list of Murky and Dirty Foods.

Step One: Start with *Clean* Protein

When it comes to building a properly-designed *Dirty Diets* Eating Plan meal (or **clean meal**), it is important to start by fulfilling your protein needs. Remember, protein contains the building blocks of muscle and muscle is the key to converting your metabolism into a fat-burning machine. Your protein source should be the approximate size and thickness of your palm (and no more)—this should equate to roughly **3-4 ounces for a woman** and **4-6 ounces for a man** (there are approximately **6-7 grams** of protein per ounce).

It's also recommended that you start your meal by consuming a few bites of the protein portion first (as long as it is not in a salad or a shake – good luck with that). By taking a few bites of protein at the beginning of a meal, the body is able to stimulate the hormone *glucagon*, which stimulates the HSL enzyme and sets the proper environment for using fat as the primary energy source.

Note: If needed, you can find a list of recommended *clean* protein sample sizes for both men and women at www.DirtyDiets.com.

Always **Remember and** *Never* **Forget**

Now that I've got your attention and even though *Dirty Diets* Principle #8: Make Your "Evening Meal" Low-Carb was clear about this, I need to once again mention the importance of making your last two meals as low carb as possible. So go ahead and follow the *clean* macronutrient ratio principles of 40-30-30 for your first three meals of the day and for meals four and five try to *only* include fibrous veggies with no fruit and absolutely no grains allowed.

Trust me, you'll have more than enough carbs in your system from the first three meals so any cravings for other carbs is just in your head. Follow this principle and I promise you will not only reach your fat-loss goals much faster, you'll continue to stay lean for life.

Step Two: Add *Clean* Carbohydrates

The next step is to fill the **remainder of your plate** with fibrous vegetables (see recommended *Clean* Carbs below). Be creative—you can make many fantastic dishes with your healthy vegetable choices. You do not need to include a salad with every single dinner—your vegetables can be steamed, broiled, baked, or poached. Recommended *clean* carb sample sizes for both men and women are provided below.

Step Three: Don't Forget Your *Clean* Fats

When it comes to adding the healthy fat portion to your *Dirty Diets* Eating Plan, I recommend you use the *Dirty Diets* Eating Plan *Clean* Fat recommendations in the form of healthy salad dressings (i.e. organic olive oil *with* balsamic vinaigrette) or vegetable toppings as in the case of seeds and nuts. Recommended *clean* fat sample sizes for both men and women are provided below).

Protein Shakes

For the greatest results on the *Dirty Diets* Eating Plan, it is best to have two high-quality protein shakes every day (mixed as two separate complete meals). As mentioned, you may choose between *high-alpha whey protein isolate (with 33% alpha-lactalbumin), *grass-fed whey protein concentrate, or *organic sprouted and fermented brown rice protein (more on this protein source below).

Also, if you do choose whey, keep in mind that if you are at all milk sensitive, you will fare much better with the high-alpha whey isolate as isolates are void of *lactose* (the milk sugar) and most *casein* (the predominant milk protein people are sensitive to). Only use whey proteins that are properly processed (with minimal heat) and have no artificial sweeteners.

If you are a vegetarian or vegan, then the next best choice will come from complete plant-based proteins that have as close of a correlation to human milk (like the high-alpha). In this case, the only plant-based protein source that comes close is a 100% organic raw sprouted and fermented whole-grain rice protein.

When constructing a properly-balanced *clean* shake, make sure to include a proper carb and fat source in order to balance the shakes macronutrient ratio.

*For more information for protein sources/brands that offer these unique quality-tested protein formulas, please visit *www.DirtyDiets.com.*

The *Dirty Diets Clean* Way of Life

Below, you will find a snapshot look at a day in the life with the *Dirty Diets* Eating Plan. As you will see, these meals are designed to show you just how easy it is to follow the plan by constructing meals that are *clean*—but even more important—they are fast and delicious, The *Dirty Diets* Eating Plan is not another diet—fad or otherwise. Instead, it is a lifestyle plan that you (or anyone) can follow for the rest of your life.

It is now up to you to use the *Dirty Diets* Eating Plan as a guideline to construct your own *clean* meals, or you can follow them exactly as they appear. Within a few short weeks of preparing these meals, you will find yourself constructing your own *clean* meals easily and without the need of the recommended food lists. However, always remember these lists are here to fall back on, if need be.

Why Choose Organic?

I always suggest choosing organic foods, if given the option, as they supply better nutritional value to your body and are comparable to the foods our ancestors ate. Organic foods are also free from unnecessary hormones and antibiotic residues (in the case of meat and poultry) chemicals, preservatives, contaminants, and other harmful substances, such as pesticides, herbicides, and fungicides. According to the *Journal of Applied Nutrition*, the majority of organic fruits, vegetables, and grains have 90%more minerals than conventionally grown food.

Go Against the Grain

When it comes to grains, it is important to note that many grains cause a rapid rise in your insulin response—which places your body in a fat-storing mode by elevating the powerful fat storage enzyme LPL. This is the main reason the great majority of grains appear on my Dirty Carbs list. Aside from this, many people have a difficult time digesting gluten, which is the protein found in grains. According to the book *Dangerous Grains*, gluten intolerance does not just affect people with Celiac Disease (CD) — an allergic reaction to the grain found primarily in **rye**, **oats,** and **barley** — but a great percentage of our population. In fact, the authors suggest that CD should actually be renamed "gluten sensitivity."

If you suffer from any of the following, the possibility that you are gluten-sensitive may be worth investigating:

- Upper respiratory tract problems such as sinusitis, allergies, or "glue ear"

- Symptoms related to mal-absorption of nutrients such as anemia and fatigue (lack of iron or folic acid), osteoporosis, and insomnia (lack of calcium)

- Bowel complaints including diarrhea, constipation, bloating, and distention, spastic colon, Crohn's disease, and diverticulitis

- Autoimmune problems such as rheumatoid arthritis, bursitis, and Crohn's disease

- Diseases of the nervous system such as motor neuron disease and certain forms of epilepsy

- Mental problems such as depression, behavioral difficulties, and ADD

The *Dirty Diets* Eating Plan Food Choices:

Clean Protein (eat often)	
Whey	High-Alpha Whey Protein isolate or grass-fed whey concentrate
Meat	Grass fed and finished, as well as game
Lamb	Grass fed and finished
Poultry	Free-range and organic: chicken, turkey, duck, goose, or pheasant
Fish	Lowest in mercury and only wild: anchovies, haddock, sardines, sole, Sockeye salmon, flounder, trout, tilapia
Eggs	Free-run and organic
Yogurt	Goat
Cheese and cottage cheese	Goat
Organic hemp, miso, tempeh, rice protein	Organic sprouted and fermented – Ultimate Vegan Protein
Murky Protein (eat occasionally)	
Pork	Commercially raised (of all kinds)
Poultry	Commercially raised (of all kinds)
Seafood	All farmed varieties
Tenderloin	Organic
Milk, cottage cheese, cheese and yogurt, pea protein isolate, fermented soy isolate	Organic
Dirty Protein (try to avoid at all costs)	
Soy	Anything non-organic and processed

Dirty Protein (try to avoid at all costs)	
Wheat	All varieties
Farmed meats	All varieties
Non-organic milk	All varieties
Yogurt and cheese	All varieties
Farmed eggs	All varieties
Shellfish	All varieties

Clean Carbs (eat often)	
Vegetables	Kale, cabbage, broccoli, cauliflower, Bok Choy, Brussels sprouts, collards, fennel, spinach, herbs, radish, garlic, carrots, cucumber, asparagus, zucchini, dark lettuce, artichokes, onions, mushrooms
Fruits	Lemon, lime, cranberry, blackberries, strawberries, raspberries, grapefruit
Grains	Brown, black, or wild rice
Unpasteurized raw organic honey	
Murky Carbs (eat occasionally)	
Vegetables	Sweet potatoes, yam, squash, beets, peas, plantains
Legumes	Black-eyed peas, Beans - Adzuki, Black, Navy, Haricot, Butter, Kidney
Fruits	Cherries, blueberries, apricots, apples, cantaloupe, Kiwi, oranges, nectarines, peach, pear, plums, pineapple, banana, mango, and papaya

Murky Carbs (eat occasionally)	
Grains	Preferably sprouted: oatmeal (steel-cut), quinoa, teff, millet, buckwheat, and amaranth
Pasteurized raw organic honey	

Dirty Carbs (try to avoid at all costs)	
Vegetables	All canned varieties, corn, potatoes, button mushrooms
Fruits	All canned varieties, fruit juices, guava, tangerines, grapes, watermelon, lychees and dried fruit
Grains	All non-organic refined varieties, white-flour and corn meal-based pastas, baked goods

Clean Fats (eat often)	
Saturated	Coconuts, organic virgin coconut oil, grass-fed butter, grass-fed ghee, free-range egg yolks
Omega 3's	Wild cold water fish, molecularly-distilled fish oil, organic cold-pressed flaxseed oil, cold-pressed hempseed oil, raw walnuts and Brazil nuts
Omega 6's and monounsaturated	Raw organic; almonds, cashews, macadamia nuts, pecans, and pistachios, extra virgin olive oil, and avocados

Murky Fats (eat occasionally)
Commercially-raised ghee, butter, palm oil, egg yolks, and bacon

Dirty Fats (try to avoid at all costs)

Commercial lard and shortening, all margarines, peanuts and peanut oil, soy oil, canola oil, corn oil, cotton seed oil, safflower oil, sunflower oil, all trans-fats

Clean Sweeteners (eat often)

Stevia and Xylitol

Murky Sweeteners (eat occasionally)

Organic raw honey, organic maple syrup, organic coconut sugar

Dirty Sweeteners (try to avoid at all costs)

High fructose corn syrup and crystalline fructose, white sugar, brown sugar, pasteurized honey, agave syrup, corn syrup, Aspartame, sucralose, Acesulfame-K

More on *Clean* Sweeteners

There are numerous artificial sweeteners on the market and it is in your best interest to become aware of the pros and cons of all of these. I personally do not believe in the use of any artificial sweetener that is available today as these were never around when our intricate biochemistry was evolving and therefore could possibly present harm to our bodies. The only natural sweeteners I currently advocate are *Stevia* and *Xylitol*, as they are both 100% natural and do not seem to have a negative effect on metabolism.

Your *Dirty Diets* Food Guide

The *Dirty Diets* Eating Plan Food Choices list above is to show you how simple it can be to construct *clean* meals that are properly-balanced for hormonal control and fat-burning just by using your eyes and hands as measurements.

Although this method will help you construct *clean* meals that will help you lose body fat effectively enough, it is by no means an exact science. It is only you who will be fooling yourself if you choose to eat copious amounts of food from each category, so do your best to control your portion sizes.

Shake it Up Once or Twice Each Day

Make whatever food choice you feel from each category in the following manner four to five times each day. Try to incorporate one to two of those meals as liquid protein shakes for best effects. For instance, if you can eat five times each day, make three of those meals solid food choices and two liquid ones using one of the approved protein powder sources.

Obviously, there will be occasions when you'll want to eat some of the Dirty foods, but if you do, try to at least limit some of their destructive powers on your blood sugar and insulin levels by first using one or more of my recommended starch blockers in Chapter 15.

Your *Clean* Carb and *Clean* Fat Sample Sizes

In order to construct the cleanest meals possible, simply choose the appropriate number of servings – per meal – from each category that pertains to your individual needs. For instance, if you're a smaller and/or less active woman, try to choose three **(3)** selections from each of the categories and if you are larger or very active, choose four **(4)** selections. Same with men. The larger and/or more active you are, the larger the portion selections you will need.

It is always best to start off with the smaller portion sizes for greater success and then adjust as needed. After all, you're only fooling yourself if you are taking larger portions when you should be taking smaller ones, but I will leave this up to your discretion.

LADIES: You get to make **3-4** selections per meal from each *Clean* Carb category—for the first three **(3)** meals of the day & **3-4** selections per meal from each *Clean* Fat category for all five **(5)** meals.

MEN: You get to make **4-6** selections per meal from each *Clean* Carb category— for the first three **(3)** meals of the day & **3-4** selections per meal from each *Clean* Fat category for all five **(5)** meals.

Clean Carb Portion Sizes (1 selection = 8-9 grams of carbohydrate)

Popeye Had it Right!

Spinach can actually help you feel full for a longer period of time because it contains tiny membranes called *thylakoids*. These membranes envelop the fat portion of the meal, making it harder for your body to digest. Because of this, spinach stays in your intestinal tract for a longer period of time. This is one of the reasons I highly recommend using organic spinach to make your salads as often as possible.

Vegetables (C = *Clean;* M = *Murky;* D = *Dirty*)	
Artichokes (C)	1 small
Asparagus (C)	12 spears
Beans, most varieties (M)	¼ cup
Beets (M)	½ cup
Vegetables (C = *Clean;* M = *Murky;* D = *Dirty*)	
Bok Choy (C)	3 cups
Broccoli (C)	1 cup
Brussels sprouts (C)	¾ cup
Cabbage, red, green (C)	1 cup
Cauliflower (C)	1 cup
Carrots (C)	1 cup
Celery (C)	2 cups
Cilantro (C)*	3 cups
Collards (C)	1 ¼ cups
Corn (D)	1/3 cup
Cucumber (C)	1 whole
Eggplant (C)	1 ½ cups
Endive (C)	3 cups
Fennel (C)	3 cups
Garlic (C)	Unlimited
Greens like collards, turnips, Swiss chard and others (C)	1 ½ cups
Jicama (C)	1 ½ cups
Kale (C)	1 ¼ cups
Lettuce all varieties (except iceberg)/dark leafy (C)	6 cups

Vegetables (C = *Clean;* M = *Murky;* D = *Dirty*)	
Mushrooms, all varieties (portabella, crimini, oyster, shitake, button, bella, etc.) (C)	3 cups
Okra (C)	1 ½ cups
Onions (including scallions, shallots, leeks) (C)	2/3 cup
Peas, most varieties (M)	2 cups
Parsley (C)	3 cups
Potatoes/white (D)	¼ cup
Potatoes/red and purple (M)	1/3 cup
Potatoes/yam (M)	1/3 cup
Radish (C)	2 cups
Radicchio (C)	1 ½ cups
Rhubarb (C)	1 ½ cups
Spinach (C)	4 cups
Squash/all varieties (M)	1 cup
Zucchini (C)	1 1/3 cups
* This also goes for other herbs like chives, basil, rosemary, thyme, etc.	

Fruits (C = *Clean;* M = *Murky;* D = *Dirty*)	
Apricots (M)	3 whole
Apples (C)	½ of one
Avocados – refer to Fats section	
Bananas (M)	1/3 cup
Blackberries (C)	1 cup

Fruits (C = *Clean;* M = *Murky;* D = *Dirty)*	
Blueberries (C)	½ cup
Boysenberries (C)	1 cup
Cantaloupe (M)	¼ of one
Cherries (M)	8 whole
Coconut	Refer to Fats section
Cranberry (C)	1 cup
Dried fruit (D)	¼ cup
Figs	Refer to Dried fruit
Gooseberry (C)	1/3 cup
Grapefruit (C)	½ of one
Grapes – red and green (D)	½ cup
Guava (D)	½ cup
Honeydew (M)	¼ cup
Kiwi (M)	1 whole
Kumquat (M)	¼ cup
Lemon (C)	1 whole
Lime (C)	1 whole
Lychees/natural (D)	6 whole
Mango (M)	1/3 cup
Nectarines (M)	½ of one
Olive	Refer to Fats section
Oranges (M)	1/3 of one
Papaya (M)	¼ of one
Peach (M)	½ of one
Pear (M)	½ of one

Fruits (C = *Clean;* M = *Murky;* D = *Dirty)*	
Pineapple (M)	½ cup
Plantains (M)	1 cup
Plums (M)	1 whole
Raspberries (C)	1 cup
Star fruit (C)	½ a whole
Strawberries (C)	1 cup
Tomatoes (M)	1 cup
Tangerines (D)	1 whole
Watermelon (D)	¼ cup

Grains (C = *Clean;* M = *Murky;* D = *Dirty)*	
Amaranth/dry (M)	½ ounce
Buckwheat/dry (M)	½ ounce
Cream of Wheat (D)	¼ ounce
Farro (D)	½ ounce
Grits (D)	½ ounce
Millet/dry (M)	½ ounce
Oatmeal/steel-cut (M)	1/3 cup
Polenta (D)	½ ounce
Popcorn/organic popped (M)	2 cups
Quinoa (M)	½ ounce
Rice/black, brown and wild (C)	1/4 cup
Teff (M)	½ ounce

Other (C = *Clean;* M = *Murky;* D = *Dirty)*	
Honey/unpasteurized organic, raw (C)	½ teaspoon
Honey/pasteurized raw (M)	½ teaspoon

Clean Fat Portion Sizes (1 selection = 1.5 grams of fat)

Saturated (C = *Clean;* M = *Murky;* D = *Dirty)*	
Butter/grass-fed (C)	1/3 teaspoon
Coconut (C)	1/4 cup
Coconut oil/organic (C)	1/3 teaspoon
Egg yolk/free-range (C)	½ of one
Ghee/grass-fed (C)	1/3 teaspoon
Palm oil (M)	1/3 teaspoon

Omega 3's (C = *Clean;* M = *Murky;* D = *Dirty)*	
Fish oil/molecularly distilled (C)	1/3 teaspoon
Flaxseed oil/organic cold-pressed (C)	1/3 teaspoon
Hempseed oil/organic cold-pressed (C)	1/3 teaspoon
Brazil nuts/raw (C)	1 whole

Omega 6's & Monounsaturated (C = *Clean;* M = *Murky;* D = *Dirty)*	
Almonds/raw (C)	3 whole
Almond Butter/organic raw (C)	½ teaspoon
Avocado (C)	1 tablespoon

Omega 6's & Monounsaturated (C = *Clean;* M = *Murky;* D = *Dirty)*	
Cashews/raw (C)	2 whole
Macadamia nuts/raw (C)	1 whole
Olives – all varieties (C)	3 whole
Olive oil/virgin & cold-pressed (C)	1/3 teaspoon
Pecans/raw (C)	3 whole
Pistachios/raw (C)	3 whole

Trans Fats

Avoid foods containing trans fats as they have been found to raise LDL cholesterol and triglyceride levels, which are a major cause of heart disease—the number one killer in North America. A whopping 40% of everyday trans-fat intake comes from cakes, cookies, crackers, pies, bread, and the like.

Dining Out *Clean*

Looking for the keys to eating out and being sociable without blowing everything you've worked so hard for? Your success at keeping your metabolism functioning at its peak capacity while eating *clean* foods is largely determined by your lifestyle and dietary choices. In fact, every time you sit down to eat you are either moving one step closer to a wise metabolism or one step closer to losing it. Each and every day, and perhaps each hour, you are in a position to make a choice that advances your goals or sets them back.

Since it has taken most of us years to transform into the shape and health we are presently in, we cannot expect positive transformation overnight. One fat-promoting meal can easily turn into a second and so on, just as one day of lethargy can turn into a second, then a week, and so on. We all have choices. Unfortunately, too many of us take the easy road and end up breaking down long before we reach the end.

It is not always easy to make the right choices, but the bottom line is we all have to live with the choices we make. Some of the hardest ones come in the form of what and when to eat when we are out for dinner or on the road traveling. Far too often, we make food choices unconsciously in an effort to satisfy a need that is not tangible at the time. We need to be preemptive and make sure we plan for behaviors and situations, so we are always one step ahead.

Being on the *Dirty Diets* Eating Plan is about making changes that will transform your life. It is not designed to stop you from enjoying social activities; it is designed to allow you to enjoy the fruits of life with proper food choices that will allow you to live a healthier lifestyle while becoming leaner in the process.

Clean Restaurant Eating

In spite of our good intentions to make healthful meals, our lives are filled with competing interests that draw us to making convenient choices. When eating out either at a trendy restaurant or fast-food outlet, consider these strategies:

- Choose a restaurant with a varied menu. Stay away from places that don't allow you to make a healthful choice such as fish-and-chips diners, fried-chicken outlets, and barbecued-rib joints.

- While at the restaurant, be strategic and choose foods that are wholesome instead of processed. These unprocessed foods will not only provide you with the greatest amount of nutrients, but they will also keep you full longer.

- Ask yourself questions when making food choices at a restaurant. How much unhealthy fat does it have? Does it contain *clean* fats or dirty ones? Fats provide the most calories for the lowest amount of nutrients. This is an important area to consider when deciding how much and what type of fat you will consume. By making the right choice, you may be cutting your total number of calories in half. Even though there is no calorie counting on the *Dirty Diets* Eating Plan, they can still add up.

- When you sit down at a restaurant, sometimes a bread basket gets brought to the table. It is best to ask the waiter not to serve the bread to avoid the temptation altogether. It is extremely rare to find a restaurant that serves somewhat healthful, stone-ground, or sprouted-grain breads, so it is best to just say no. Eating the bread will stimulate the fat-storing high-insulin response, add calories to your meal, and provide you with very little nutrient density. If you are in a situation where others at your table want bread, do your very best to avoid eating it.

- Make sure you choose a main dish that is not starch-based. Choose meals that are high in *clean* protein sources and low in dirty carbs. Most restaurants are very accommodating, so don't be afraid to ask your waiter for what you want.

- Include a good portion of *clean* mixed vegetables with your protein source. For instance, if you are ordering steak, chicken, or fish, try to forgo the baked potato or rice pilaf and instead opt for a nice serving of veggies or a big salad.

Here are a few simple suggestions that will help you construct a healthier meal at any restaurant:

- Request dressings and sauces to be on the side.

- Avoid creamy sauces and opt for broth or vegetable-based ones.

- Always say no to the tempting (even if it's free) bread.

- Choose meals that are poached, steamed, broiled, or baked, but never fried.

- Choose fruit-based desserts. Have the occasional dark chocolate treat, but make it infrequent and small. Foods that contain more fiber tend to fill you up and control the release of insulin.

- Avoid refined rice, white-flour products, including pasta, and stay away from the tortilla chips (again, even if they're gratis).

- Eat a wide variety and hefty portion of vegetables. If necessary, ask for a double serving or a big salad.

- Ask for steamed, broiled, baked, or poached vegetables that are cooked with olive oil instead of butter. There are fewer calories in vegetables because they contain large amounts of water.

- Don't be fooled into the belief that beverages don't contain calories just because they don't contain fat. Alcohol can contain an enormous number of calories and make you feel hungry rather than provide valuable nutrients. Always choose water as your beverage of choice. Although you may go for the glass of red wine once in a while. After all, you are human, aren't you?

The *Dirty Diets* Eating Plan —Tips for Ultimate Success

- Consume five *clean* meals per day (three solid meals and two protein shakes)

- Eat every 2 ½ to 3 ½ hours to maintain blood sugar levels

- *Clean* protein choices must be included in each and every meal (start by taking a few bites of the protein portion of the meal whenever possible)

- Use the recommended *clean* food choices in each category

- Drink plenty of water

- Drink an eight ounce glass of water approximately 20 minutes before each meal

- Try to leave approximately two hours between your last meal and bedtime.

CONCLUSION – Welcome to the New *Clean* You

We're finally here. It's hard to believe that when you first opened this book and started your journey, you might have been snacking on a bag of low-fat pretzels. Beginning with an eye opening expose of the dieting industry and their version of weapons of mass destruction – lite foods – and ending with a set of hard and fast eating principles, I hope *Dirty Diets* was the paradigm-busting book I intended it to be.

However, that doesn't mean you can recite parts of *Dirty Diets* like bible passages... yet. The gamuts of topics I've covered are extensive to say the least. From enzymes, hormones, and brain chemicals involved in storing or releasing fat, nutrients that may give you a winning edge when it comes to boosting your metabolism, a way of actually rewriting your subconscious to a much more positive you, to a highly-effective form of exercising called Biocize™. I don't want you to walk away from *Dirty Diets* with "full glass syndrome" where every new drop of information pushes out the old.

Trust me, now that you've read *Dirty Diets*, you're in the top 1% in terms of nutrition knowledge on the planet (including doctors and dietitians) – with a soon-to-be raging metabolism and lean, muscular body to show for it.

But perhaps most important of all, I hope you finally feel liberated from the shackles of crash diets, empty weight loss promises, and lite foods.

It's my sincere hope that *Dirty Diets* will bring you the freedom and comfort you so richly deserve in creating the ultimate body and mind. For me, there is no better way to sum up what I wish for you other than to borrow a quote from the late and great Oscar Wilde:

> *"To live is the rarest thing in the world.*
> *Most people exist, that is all."*

Welcome to the new, *clean* you!

Please visit us at **www.DIRTYDIETS.com** as we uncover more dietary lies to help you stay *clean* for life.

REFERENCES

CHAPTER ONE

1. Paeratakul, S., et al. (2002) Sex, race/ethnicity, socioeconomic status, and BMI in relation to self-perception of overweight. *Obesity Research*. 10: 345–350
2. Yanovski J, et al. A prospective study of holiday weight gain. *New England Journal of Medicine*, 2000; 342 :861 –86
3. Flegal KM, et al. Prevalence and Trends in Obesity Among US Adults, 1999-2008. *Journal of the American Medical Association*. 2010 January 13, 2009.
4. Ogden CL, et al. Prevalence of overweight and obesity in the United States, 1999-2004. *Journal of the American Medical Association*. 295:1549-1555. 2006.
5. Brownson RC, Boehmer TK, Luke DA. Declining rates of physical activity in the United States: what are the contributors? *The Annual Review of Public Health*. 2005; 26: 421–443.
6. Cutler D, Glaeser E, Shapiro J. Why have Americans become more obese? *The Journal of Economic Perspectives*. 2003; 17: 93–118
7. Reisner R. BusinessWeek Debate Room the Diet Industry: A Big Fat Lie. Business Week.   January   10,   2008.   Available   at http://www.businessweek.com/debateroom/archives/2008/01/the_diet_indust.h tml. Accessed February 1, 2009
8. McNamara M. Diet Industry Is Big Business. CBS News. Dec. 1, 2006. Available at http://www.cbsnews.com/stories/2006/12/01/eveningnews/main222267.shtml. Accessed January 30, 2009
9. Katan MB. Weight-loss diets for the prevention and treatment of obesity. *New England Journal of Medicine*, 2009; 360: 923–925.
10. Tsai AG, Wadden TA. Systematic review: an evaluation of the major commercial weight loss programs in the United States. *Annals of Internal Medicine*, in press.
11. Spector T. Identically Different: Why You Can Change Your Genes. Weidenfeld & Nicolson, Sep 18 2012
12. Allen J. As A man Thinketh. University of California Libraries (January 1, 1913)

CHAPTER TWO

1. Miller B. How The 'Light' Foods Are Conquering America. *New York Times*. January 27, 1982
2. Ello-Martin JA, Roe LS, Ledikwe JH, Beach AM, Rolls BJ. Dietary energy density in the treatment of obesity: a year-long trial comparing 2 weight-loss diets. *American Journal of Clinical Nutrition*. 2007; 85:1465–77
3. Tsai A., Wadden T. Systematic review: an evaluation of major commercial weight loss programs in the United States. *Annals of Internal Medicine*. 2005; 142:56–66
4. Presiding Panel Commercial Weight Loss Products and Programs: What Consumers Stand to Gain and Lose. (1997) Federal Trade Commission Washington, DC
5. Key FDA Food Program on "Starvation Diet". Center for Science in the Public Interest   Website.   2003.   Available   at: http://www.cspinet.org/new/200310291.html. Accessed January 29, 2010
6. Finer N. Low-calorie diets and sustained weight loss. *Obesity Research*. 2001; 9 (suppl 4):290S–292S.
7. Lemmens VE, et al. A systematic review of the evidence regarding efficacy of obesity prevention interventions among adults. *Obesity Review*. 2008; 9:446-455.
8. Albers, S. Being a Mindful Food Shopper in 2010. Psychology Today. January 4, 2010.
9. Katan MB: Weight-loss diets for the prevention and treatment of obesity. *New England Journal of Medicine* 2009; 360:923-925

10. Tierney, J. Health Halo Can Hide the Calories. *New York Times*, December 1, 2008
11. Kahn BE, Wansink B. The influence of assortment structure on perceived variety and consumption quantities. *Journal of Consumer Research.* 2004, 30:519–33
12. Nordmann AJ, et al. Effects of low-carbohydrate vs. low-fat diets on weight loss and cardiovascular risk factors: a meta-analysis of randomized controlled trials. *Archives of Internal Medicine.* 2006, 166:285–293

CHAPTER THREE

1. Wardle J, Parmenter K, Waller J. Nutrition knowledge and food intake. Appetite. 2000;34:1–8
2. Selby. A Love-Hate Relationship. psychologytoday.com. December 15, 2009. Available at http://www.psychologytoday.com/blog/overcoming-self-sabotage/200912/love-hate-relationship. Accessed February 15, 2010
3. Wilbert W. Fattitudes: Beat Self-Defeat and Win Your War with Weight. New York. Martin's Press ;2000
4. Stonsy. Emotional Eating: All Diets are from Hell. psychologytoday.com. March 24, 2009. Available at http://www.psychologytoday.com/blog/anger-in-the-age-entitlement/200903/emotional-eating-all-diets-are-hell. Accessed February 20, 2010
5. Pinaquy S, Chabrol H, Simon C, Louvet JP & Barbe P 2003 Emotional eating, alexithymia, and binge-eating disorder in obese women. *Obesity Research.* 11 195–201
6. McIver S, McGartland M, O'Halloran P. Qual Health Res. 2009 Sep;19(9):1234-45. "Overeating is not about the food": women describe their experience of a yoga treatment program for binge eating.
7. Omalu BI, Ives DG, Buhari AM, et al. Death rates and causes of death after bariatric surgery for Pennsylvania residents. 1995–2004. *Archives of Surgery.* 2007;142(10):923–928.
8. Kodama K, Noda S et al. Depressive disorders as psychiatric complications after obesity surgery. *Psychiatry & Clinical Neuroscience.* 1998;52(5):471–476.
9. Wing RR, Jeffery RW. Benefits of recruiting participants with friends and increasing social support for weight loss and maintenance. *The Journal of Consulting and Clinical Psychology.* 1999 Feb;67(1):132-8
10. Maltz, M.; Psycho-Cybernetics, Pocket Books, New York, NY, 1969.

CHAPTER FOUR

1. Cordain, L et al. Plant-animal subsistence ratios and macronutrient energy estimations in worldwide hunter-gatherer diets. *American Journal of Clinical Nutrition.* (2000) 7 : 682-692
2. Cordain L. Cereal grains: humanity's double edged sword. *World Review of Nutrition and Dietetics.*1999;84:19-73.
3. Arner, P. 1996. Regulation of lipolysis in fat cells. *Diabetes Review.* 4:450-463.
4. Magré, J., et al. 1998. Human hormone-sensitive lipase: genetic mapping, identification of a new dinucleotide repeat, and association with obesity and NIDDM. *Diabetes.* 47:284-286
5. Gross LS, Li L, Ford ES, Liu S: Increased consumption of refined carbohydrates and the epidemic of type 2 diabetes in the United States: an ecologic assessment. *American Journal of Clinical Nutrition* 2004, 79:774-779
6. Meckling, K. A., O'Sullivan, C. & Saari, D. (2004) Comparison of a low-fat diet to a low-carbohydrate diet on weight loss, body composition, and risk factors for diabetes and cardiovascular disease in free-living, overweight men and women. *Journal of Clinical Endocrinology & Metabolism.* 89:2717-2723.
7. Due A, et al: Comparison of 3 ad libitum diets for weight-loss maintenance, risk of

cardiovascular disease, and diabetes: a 6-mo randomized, controlled trial. *American Journal of Clinical Nutrition* 2008, 88(5):1232-1241

8. Ludwig, D. S. (2000) Dietary glycemic index and obesity. *Journal of Nutrition.* 130:280S-283's.

9. Leidy HJ, Carnell NS, Mattes RD, Campbell WW. Higher protein intake preserves lean mass and satiety with weight loss in pre-obese and obese women. *Obesity* (Silver Spring) 2007;15:421–9

10. Foster-Powell K, et al. International table of glycemic index and glycemic load values: 2002. ajcn.nutrition.org

11. Jacobson MF. High-fructose corn syrup and the obesity epidemic. *American Journal of Clinical Nutrition.* 2004 Oct;80(4):1081.

12. King B. Fructose and Fat Cells. *Alive* Magazine, January 2005

CHAPTER FIVE

1. Kolota. ESSAY; True Secret Of Fad Diets: It's Calories. NYTimes.com. January 18, 2000. Available at: http://www.nytimes.com/2000/01/18/health/essay-true-secret-of-fad-diets-it-s-calories.html?pagewanted=1. Accessed February 17, 2010

2. Frankenfield DC, et al. Limits of body mass index to detect obesity and predict body composition. *Nutrition.* 2001; 17: 26–30.

3. Devlin K. Top 10 Reasons Why the BMI Is Bogus. NPR.org. July 4, 2009. Available at http://www.npr.org/templates/story/story.php?storyId=106268439. Accessed March 17, 2010

4. Kreitzman, SN (1992) Factors influencing body composition during very-low-calorie diets. *American Journal of Clinical Nutrition.* 56, 217S–223's.

5. Martin CK, et al. (2007) Effect of calorie restriction on resting metabolic rate and spontaneous physical activity. *Obesity* (Silver Spring) 15: 2964–2973.

6. Hare-Bruun H, Flint A, Heitmann BL. Glycemic index and glycemic load in relation to changes in body weight, body fat distribution, and body composition in adult Danes. *American Journal of Clinical Nutrition*, 2006;84:871–9

7. Leidy HJ, Carnell NS, Mattes RD, Campbell WW. Higher protein intake preserves lean mass and satiety with weight loss in pre-obese and obese women. *Obesity*, (Silver Spring) 2007;15:421–9

8. Due A, Larsen TM, et al: Comparison of 3 ad libitum diets for weight-loss maintenance, risk of cardiovascular disease, and diabetes: a 6-mo randomized, controlled trial. *American Journal of Clinical Nutrition*, 2008, 88(5):1232-1241

9. Kraemer WJ, et al. Physiological adaptations to a weight-loss dietary regimen and exercise programs in women. *Journal of Applied Physiology*, 1997; 83: 270–279.

10. Hunter GR, et al. Resistance training conserves fat-free mass and resting energy expenditure following weight loss. *Obesity*, (Silver Spring). 2008;16:1045–1051.

CHAPTER SIX

1. Sayre C. A New Diet Equation - The Science of Appetite. Time.com. undefined. Available at http://www.time.com/time/specials/2007/article/0,28804,1626795_1627112_16 26457,00.html. Accessed February 21, 2010

2. Bloom, S. 2007. Hormonal Regulation of Appetite. Short Science Review. Foresight Tackling Obesities: Future Choices. *Obesity Reviews*, 8(s1):63–65

3. Marano H. Chemistry and Craving. psychologytoday.com. October 1, 2009. Available at http://www.psychologytoday.com/articles/200910/chemistry-and-craving. Accessed February 21, 2010

4. Kalra SP. 2004 NPY and cohorts in regulating appetite, obesity and metabolic syndrome: beneficial effects of gene therapy. *Neuropeptides*, 38:201–211

5. Wright K. Consuming Passions.

http://www.psychologytoday.com/articles/200802/consuming-passions. November 17, 2008. Available at http://www.psychologytoday.com/articles/200802/consuming-passions. Accessed February 21, 2010

6. Cummings DE, et al. Plasma ghrelin levels after diet-induced weight loss or gastric bypass surgery. *New England Journal of Medicine*, 2002;346:1623-1630

7. Epel E, Lapidus R, McEwen B, Brownell K. 2001 Stress may add bite to appetite in women: a laboratory study of stress-induced cortisol and eating behavior. *Psychoneuroendocrinology*, 26:37–49

8. Wansink B, Painter JE, North J: Bottomless bowls: Why visual cues of portion size may influence intake. *Obesity Research,* 2005, 13(1):93-10

9. Herman, C. P. (2005). Lessons from the bottomless bowl. *Obesity Research, 13,* 2.

10. Al Awar R, Obeid O, Hwalla N, Azar S. 2005 Postprandial acylated ghrelin status following fat and protein manipulation of meals in healthy young women. *Clinical Science,* (Lond) 109:405–411

11. Stahre L, Hällström T. A short-term cognitive group treatment program gives substantial weight reduction up to 18 months from the end of treatment. A randomized controlled trial. *Eat Weight Disorders.* 2005 Mar;10(1):51-8

12. Liao K.L.: Cognitive-behavioral approaches and weight management: an overview. *The Journal of the Royal Society for the Promotion of Health.* 120, 27-30, 2000.

CHAPTER SEVEN

1. Cappuccio, FP, Taggart, FM, Kandala, NB, et al. Meta-analysis of short sleep duration and obesity in children and adults. *Sleep.* 2008;31:619–26

2. Patel, SR & Hu, FB. Short sleep duration and weight gain: a systematic review. *Obesity,* (Silver Spring) 2008;16:643–53

3. Taheri S. Does the lack of sleep make you fat? bristol.ac.uk. December 20, 2004. Available at http://www.bristol.ac.uk/news/2004/1113989409. Accessed February 28, 2010

4. Davis J. Sleep Loss Feeds Appetite. WebMD.com. December 6, 2004. Available at http://www.webmd.com/diet/news/20041206/sleep-loss-feeds-appetite. Accessed February 28, 2010

5. Van Cauter E, Knutson K, Leproult R, and Spiegel K. The impact of sleep deprivation on hormones and metabolism [Online]. Medscape Neurology Neurosurgery 7, 2005

6. Gordon S. Starved For Sleep? Watch Your Waistline. Health.com. March 16, 2008. Available at http://news.health.com/2008/03/16/starved-for-sleep-watch-your-waistline/. Accessed March 1, 2010

7. Spiegel, K. et al. Brief Communication: Sleep Curtailment in Healthy Young Men Is Associated with Decreased Leptin Levels, Elevated Ghrelin Levels, and Increased Hunger and Appetite. *Annals of Internal Medicine.* December 7, 2004. 141:846-851.

8. Greene G. To Med or Not to Med . psychologytoday.com. December 13, 2009. Available at http://www.psychologytoday.com/blog/insomniac/200912/med-or-not-med. Accessed March 1, 2010

9. Saul S. Sleep Drugs Found Only Mildly Effective, but Wildly Popular. NYTimes.com. October 23, 2007. Available at http://www.nytimes.com/2007/10/23/health/23drug.html. Accessed March 2, 2010

10. Rabin RC. New Worries About Sleeping Pills. *New York Times* (on-line). March 12, 2012

11. Gami AS, Caples SM, Somers VK. Obesity and obstructive sleep apnea. *Endocrinology and Metabolism Clinics of North America.* 2003;32:869-9

12. Chang, Y. F.; Hernandez, M. F.; Myslinski, N. R., Enhancement of hexobarbital-induced sleep by lysine and its metabolites. *Life Sciences,* 1981, 28, (4), 407-13

13. Ruddick JP, et al. (2006). "Tryptophan metabolism in the central nervous system: medical implications." *Expert reviews in molecular medicine,* 8 (20): 1–27.

14. Schmitz M, et al. Comparative study for assessing quality of life of patients with exogenous sleep disorders (temporary sleep onset and sleep interruption disorders) treated with a hops-valarian preparation and a benzodiazepine drug. *Wiener Medizinische Wochenschrift*, 1998;148(13):291-8.

15. Garfinkel D, Laudon M, Nof D, Zisapel N. Improvement of sleep quality in elderly people by controlled-release melatonin. *Lancet*. 1995;346:541-544.

16. Birdsall TC. 5-Hydroxytryptophan: a clinically-effective serotonin precursor. *Alternative Medicine Review*. 1998 Aug;3(4):271-80

17. Yanagisawa E. Study of effectiveness of mixed processed food containing Cucurbita pepo seed extract and soybean seed extract on stress urinary incontinence in women. *Japanese Journal of Medical Science & Biology*. 2003; 14(3):313-22.

18. Després J-P, et al. The Association Between Sleep Duration and Weight Gain in Adults: A 6-Year Prospective Study from the Quebec Family Study. *Sleep*. 2008 April 1; 31(4): 517–523.

19. Dr. Gifford-Jones: Pumpkin seeds for ultimate bladder control. Body and Health, *The Windsor Star*, Windsor, Ontario, Canada. February 6, 2014

CHAPTER EIGHT

1. Esposito K, et al. Effect of lifestyle changes on erectile dysfunction in obese men: a randomized controlled trial. *Journal of the American Medical Association*. 291:2978–2984, 2004

2. Andersen I, Heitman B, and Wagner G. Obesity and sexual dysfunction in younger Danish men. *Journal of Sexual Medicine*. 5:2053–2060, 2008

3. Janiszewski P. The Fatter we Get, the Less We Seem to Notice. obesitypanacea.com. November 2009. (Accessed March 25, 2010).

4. Thompson, J, Manore, M.M. Predicted and measured resting metabolic rate of male and female endurance athletes. *Journal of the American Dietetic Association*. 96(l):30-4, 1996

5. Weight-control Information Network (WIN). Overweight and Obesity Statistics. win.niddk.nih.gov.   February   2010.   Available   at: http://win.niddk.nih.gov/statistics/ Accessed February 5, 2014

6. Silberstein L, et al. Behavioral and psychological implications of body dissatisfaction: Do men and women differ? *Sex Roles*. August 1988, Volume 19, Issue 3-4, pp 219-232.

7. Burns CM, Tijhuis MAR, Seidell JC. The relationship between quality of life and perceived body weight and dieting history in Dutch men and women. *International Journal of Obesity and related Metabolic Disorders*. 2001;25:1386–1392.

8. Halkjaer J, et al. Intake of macronutrients as predictors of 5-y changes in waist circumference. *American Journal of Clinical Nutrition*. 2006, 84:789-797

9. Blokstra A, Burns CM, Seidell JC. Perception of weight status and dieting behaviour in Dutch men and women. *International Journal of Obesity and related Metabolic Disorders*. 1999; 23: 7-17

10. Rebuffe-Scrive, M., Marin, P., & Bjorntorp, P. Effect of testosterone on abdominal adipose tissue in men. *International Journal of Obesity*, 15, 791-795. 1991

11. Ang H. Effects of Eurycoma longifolia Jack on sexual qualities in middle aged male rats. *Phytomedicine*. 2004;6 590-593

12. Tenover, JL. Male hormone replacement therapy including "andropause." *Endocrinology and Metabolism Clinics of North America*. 1998;27:969–987.

13. Loebel, C.C., & Kraemer, W. J. A brief review: testosterone and resistance exercise in men, *Journal of Strength and Conditioning Research, 12*(1), 57-63, 1996

CHAPTER NINE

1. Blokstra A, Burns CM, Seidell JC. Perception of weight status and dieting behaviour

in Dutch men and women. *International Journal of Obesity Related Metabolic Disorders.* 1999; 23: 7-17

2. Burns CM, Tijhuis MAR, Seidell JC. The relationship between quality of life and perceived body weight and dieting history in Dutch men and women. *International Journal of Obesity Related Metabolic Disorders.* 2001;25:1386–1392.

3. Green MW & Rogers PJ (1995) Impaired cognitive function during spontaneous dieting. *Psychological Medicine,* 25, 1003-1010.

4. Bennet J. Why Skinny Models Could Be Making Us Fat. Newsweek.com. February 8, 2007. Available at http://www.newsweek.com/id/113689. Accessed March 27, 2010

5. Rothblum, E. D. The stigma of women's weight: social and economic realities. *Feminism & Psychology.* 2: 61–73. 1992

6. Özcelik A. An Evaluation of Fast-Food Preferences According to Gender. *Humanity & Social Sciences Journal.* 2 (1): 43-50, 2007

7. Evans R. Want to control cravings? Have some chocolate. MSNBC.com. October 3, 2008. Available at http://www.msnbc.msn.com/id/26601848.

8. Presiding Panel (1997) Commercial Weight Loss Products and Programs: What Consumers Stand to Gain and Lose. Federal Trade Commission Washington, DC

9. Epel E, Lapidus R, McEwen B, Brownell K 2001 Stress may add bite to appetite in women: a laboratory study of stress-induced cortisol and eating behavior. *Psychoneuroendocrinology.* 26:37–49

10. Kluger J. Why Men Are Better Dieters Than Women. Time.com. January 19, 2009. Available at:http://www.time.com/time/health/article/0,8599,1872584,00.html. Accessed March 28, 2010

11. Scott J. Craving Clues: Gender's Role in Food Cravings. About.com. January 7, 2010. Available at http://weightloss.about.com/cs/cravings/a/cravingclues.htm. Accessed March 28, 2010

12. O'Sullivan AJ. Does oestrogen allow women to store fat more efficiently? A biological advantage for fertility and gestation. *Obesity Reviews.* 2009; 10: 168-177.

13. Kabat GC, et al. Urinary estrogen metabolites and breast cancer: a case-control study. *Cancer Epidemiology Biomarkers & Prevention.* 1997;6(7):505-9.

14. Lila M.A., Raskin I. 2005. Health related interactions of phytochemicals. *Journal of Food Science.* 70: 20-37

15. Rogan E.G. 2006. The natural chemopreventive compound indole-3-carbinol: state of science. In vivo 20: 221-228. PMID: 16634522

16. Guiliano M. *French Women Don't Get Fat.* New York. Random House. 2004.

CHAPTER TEN

1. Okie S. Fed Up! Winning the War Against Childhood Obesity. The Joseph Henry Press: Washington DC; 2005

2. Ogden CL, Carroll MD, Flegal KM (May 2008). "High body mass index for age among US children and adolescents, 2003-2006". *Journal of the American Medical Association.* 299 (20): 2401–5

3. Dietz WH. Overweight in childhood and adolescence. *New England Journal of Medicine.* 2004;350(9):855–7

4. Copleman P. Clinical Obesity in Adults and Children: 2nd Edition. Wiley-Blackwell: New York; 2005

5. Favaro A. Obese kids have arteries of 45-year-olds: study. CTA.ca. November 11, 2008. http://www.ctv.ca/servlet/ArticleNews/story/CTVNews/20081111/kids_arteries_081111/20081111?hub=TopStories. Accessed April 4, 2010

6. Daines R. Obesity and Sugary Drinks. *New York Times.* March 20, 2010. Letters Section.

7. James J, Kerr D. Prevention of childhood obesity by reducing soft drinks. *International Journal of Obesity* (Lond). 2005;29 (Suppl 2):S54–7

8. King B. Fructose and Fat Cells. *Alive* Magazine. January, 2005.
9. Davis B, Carpenter C (December 2008). "Proximity of Fast-Food Restaurants to Schools and Adolescent Obesity". *American Journal of Public Health* 99: 505
10. Rideout V. Report: Generation M2: Media in the Lives of 8 to 18-Year-Olds. A Kaiser Family Foundation Special Report. January 2010.
11. Kotz K, Story M. Food advertisements during children's Saturday morning television programming: are they consistent with dietary recommendations? *Journal of the American Dietetic Association.*1994; 94 :1296 –1300
12. Batada A, et al. Nine out of 10 food advertisements shown during Saturday morning children's television programming are for foods high in fat, sodium, or added sugars, or low in nutrients. *Journal of the American Dietetic Association.* 2008;108(4):673-8.
13. Halford JCG, et al. Effect of television advertisements for foods on food consumption in children. *Appetite.* 2004;42 (2):221-5
14. Associated Press. Many parents of fat kids in denial, study finds. MSNBC.com. December 25, 2007. Available at http://www.msnbc.msn.com/id/22391071/. Accessed April 7, 2010
15. Simmons A., et al. (2008) Nutrition and Physical Activity in Children and Adolescents. Barwon-South Western Region. Sentinel Site Series. Report 6: Lessons learned from Colac's *Be Active Eat Well* project. 2006: Department of Human Services
16. Videon TM, Manning CK (2003). "Influences on adolescent eating patterns: the importance of family meals". *Journal of Adolescent Health,* 32 (5): 365–73.
17. Children Now. Obesity: Facts & Figures. http://www.childrennow.org. Accessed, February 8, 2014.
18. Coe DP, et al. Effect of physical education and activity levels on academic achievement in children. *Medicine & Science in Sports & Exercise,* 2006, Aug. 38, 1515-1519.

CHAPTER ELEVEN

1. Smith M. Going Against the Grain. Contemporary Books. New York: 2002.
2. Cordain L. Cereal grains: humanity's double edged sword. *World Review of Nutrition and Dietetics.* 1999;84:19-73
3. Simopoulos AP. The importance of the ratio of omega-6/omega-3 essential fatty acids. *Biomedicine and Pharmacotherapy.* 2002;56:365–79
4. Thompson, L. U. Potential health benefits and problems associated with antinutrients in foods. *Food Research International.* 1993. 26:131-149
5. Cordain, L et al. Plant-animal subsistence ratios and macronutrient energy estimations in worldwide hunter-gatherer diets. *American Journal of Clinical Nutrition.* 2000. 7 : 682-692
6. *Huang B, et al.* Acculturation and prevalence of diabetes among Japanese-American men in Hawaii. *American Journal of Epidemiology. 177:674–681,* 1996
7. Mead, J. R., Irvine, S. A., Ramji, D. P. (2002) Lipoprotein lipase: structure, function, regulation, and role in disease. *Journal of Molecular Medicine.* 80,753-769
8. Lindeberg S, et al. A Palaeolithic diet improves glucose tolerance more than a Mediterranean-like diet in individuals with ischaemic heart disease. *Diabetologia,* 2007, 50(9):1795-1807
9. Mourao DM, Bressan J, Campbell WW, Mattes RD. Effects of food form on appetite and energy intake in lean and obese young adults. *International Journal of Obesity (Lond).* 2007; 31: 1688–1695
10. Miller WC, et al. Dietary fat, sugar, and fiber predict body fat content. *Journal of the American Dietetic Association.* 1994;94:612–5
11. Slavin JL. Dietary fiber and body weight. *Nutrition.* 2005;21:411-8
12. Parker H. A sweet problem: Princeton researchers find that high-fructose corn syrup prompts considerably more weight gain. Princeton.edu. March 22, 2010.

http://www.princeton.edu/main/news/archive/S26/91/22K07/. Accessed April 5, 2010

13. Nagai et al. The Role of Peroxisome Proliferator-Activated Receptor γ Coactivator-1 β in the Pathogenesis of Fructose-Induced Insulin Resistance. *Cell Metabolism*, 2009; 9 (3)

14. Mercola J. Shocking! This 'Tequila' Sweetener is Far Worse than High Fructose Corn Syrup. Mercola.com. March 30, 2010. http://articles.mercola.com/sites/articles/archive/2010/03/30/beware-of-the-agave-nectar-health-food.aspx. Accessed April 7, 2010

CHAPTER TWELVE

1. Simopoulos AP. Evolutionary aspects of diet, the omega-6/omega-3 ratio and genetic variation: nutritional implications for chronic diseases. *Biomedicine & Pharmacotherapy*. 2006;60:502–7

2. The Human Brain -Fats. FI.edu. 2004. Available at http://www.fi.edu/learn/brain/fats.html. Accessed April 3, 2010

3. Danaei G, Ding EL, Mozaffarian D, et al. The preventable causes of death in the United States: comparative risk assessment of dietary, lifestyle, and metabolic risk factors. *PLoS Medicine*. 2009;6:e1000058-e1000058

4. Shils M. Modern Nutrition in Health and Disease: 10th Edition. Lippincott Williams & Wilkins. Philadelphia: 2005.

5. Ornish D. Can lifestyle changes reverse coronary heart disease? The Lifestyle Heart Trial. *Lancet*. 1990 Jul 21;336(8708):129-33

6. Howard BV, Van Horn L, Hsia J, et al. Low-fat dietary pattern and risk of cardiovascular disease: the Women's Health Initiative Randomized Controlled Dietary Modification Trial. *Journal of the American Medical Association*. 2006; 295:655-66.

7. Stein R. Low-Fat Diet's Benefits Rejected. Washington Post. February 8, 2006.

8. Taubes G. What if It's All Been a Big Fat Lie? NYTimes.com. July 2, 2002. Available at http://www.nytimes.com/2002/07/07/magazine/what-if-it-s-all-been-a-big-fat-lie.html?scp=1&sq=Gary%20Taubes%20Magazine&st=cse. Accessed April 1, 2010

9. Siri-Tarino PW, Sun Q, Hu FB, Krauss RM. Meta-analysis of prospective cohort studies evaluating the association of saturated fat with cardiovascular disease. *American Journal of Clinical Nutrition*. 2010 [Epub ahead of print, January 13].

10. Enig M. The Skinny on Fats. westonaprice.org. January 1, 2000. Available at http://www.westonaprice.org/The-Skinny-on-Fats.html. Accessed April 2, 2010

11. Michikawa M. Cholesterol paradox: is high total or low HDL cholesterol level a risk for Alzheimer's disease? *Journal of Neuroscience Research*. 2003; 72: 141–146.

12. Golomb BA. Cholesterol and violence: is there a connection? *Annuls of Internal Medicine*. 1998; 128: 478-487

13. Gisella Mutungi, et al. Dietary Cholesterol from Eggs Increases Plasma HDL Cholesterol in Overweight Men Consuming a Carbohydrate-Restricted Diet. *Journal of Nutrition*, February 2008; 138: 272-276.

14. Piers, LS, et al. (2003) Substitution of saturated with monounsaturated fat in a 4-week diet affects body weight and composition of overweight and obese men. *British Journal of Nutrition*. 90:717-727

15. Sampalis F, et al. Evaluation of the effects of Neptune Krill Oil on the management of premenstrual syndrome and dysmenorrhea. *Alternative Medicine Review*. 2003, 8:171-179

16. Hecht HS, Harmon SM. Aggressive Versus Moderate Lipid-Lowering Therapy in Hypercholesterolemic Postmenopausal Women. *American Journal of Cardiology*. 2003; 92:670-676

17. C. Gorman, A. Park, "The Fires Within," *TIME*, February 15, 2004.

CHAPTER THIRTEEN

1. Machello, M Ph.D. Palatability and Nutrient Composition of Grass-Finished Bison. bisoncentre.com. undefined. Available at http://bit.ly/9dpJYk - Accessed April 8, 2010

2. Larick DK, Turner BE. Influence of finishing diet on the phospholipid composition and fatty acid profile of individual phospholipids in lean muscle of beef cattle. *Journal of Animal Science.* 1989;67:2282-2293.

3. Medeiros LC, Busboom JR, Field RA, Williams JC. Nutritional content of game meat. Cooperative Extension Service, University of Wyoming, Laramie, WY 82071, 1992

4. Cordain L, et al. Fatty acid analysis of wild ruminant tissues: Evolutionary implications for reducing diet-related chronic disease. *European Journal of Clinical Nutrition.* 2002;56:181-91.

5. Ponnampalam EN, Mann NJ, Sinclair AJ. Effect of feeding systems on omega-3 fatty acids, conjugated linoleic acid and trans fatty acids in Australian beef cuts: potential impact on human health. *Asia Pacific Journal of Clinical Nutrition.* 2006;15(1):21-9.

6. Layman DK, Boileau RA, Erickson DJ, et al. A reduced ratio of dietary carbohydrate to protein improves body composition and blood lipid profiles during weight loss in adult women. *Journal of Nutrition.* 2003;133:411–7

7. Brehm BJ, Seeley RJ, Daniels SR, D'Alessio DA: A randomized trial comparing a very low carbohydrate diet and a calorie restricted low fat diet on body weight and cardiovascular risk factors in healthy women. *Journal of Clinical Endocrinology and Metabolism.* 88 :1617 –1623,2003

8. Bernhard Bettler, et al. Molecular Structure and Physiological Functions of GABAB Receptors. *Physiology Review.* Jul 2004; 84: 835 – 867.

9. Anwar F, Latif S, Ashraf M (2007) Moringa oleifera: A Food Plant with Multiple Medicinal Uses. *Phytotherapy Research.* 21: 17–25

10. Halton TL, Hu FB. The effects of high protein diets on thermogenesis, satiety and weight loss: a critical review. *Journal of the American College of Nutrition.* 2004;23:373–85.

11. Esterterp KR, Wilson SAJ, Rolland V: Diet induced thermogenesis measured over 24 h in a respiration chamber: effect of diet composition. *International Journal of Obesity.* 23 :287 –292,1999

12. Layman DK, Evans EM, Erickson D, Seyler J, Weber J, Bagshaw D, Griel A, Psota T, Kris-Etherton P: A moderate-protein diet produces sustained weight loss and long-term changes in body composition and blood lipids in obese adults. *Journal of Nutrition.* 2009,139:514-21.

13. Luhrmann P.M. Herbert B.M. Neuhauser-Berthold M. Effects of fat mass and body fat distribution on resting metabolic rate in the elderly 2001 *Metabolism: Clinical and Experimental.* 50 (8), pp. 972-975.

14. Akhavan T, et al. The Effect of Whey Protein on Post-Meal Blood Glucose and Insulin. *FASEB Journal.* 23: 545.2

15. Bouthegourd JC, et al. A pre-exercise alpha-lactalbumin-enriched whey protein meal preserves lipid oxidation and decreases adiposity in rats. *American Journal of Physiology, Endocrinology & Metabolism.* 2002 Sep; 283(3):E565-72.

16. Markus CR, Olivier B, de Hann EH. Whey protein rich in alpha-lactalbumin increases the ratio of plasma tryptophan to the sum of the other large neutral amino acids and improves cognitive performance in stress-vulnerable subjects. *American Journal of Clinical Nutrition.* 2002 Jun; 75(6):1051-6.

17. Markus CR, et al. Alpha-lactalbumin improves sleep and morning alertness in participants with mild sleep problems. *American Journal of Clinical Nutrition.* 2005 May; 81(5):1026-33.

CHAPTER FOURTEEN

1. A Geliebter, et al. Effects of strength or aerobic training on body composition, resting metabolic rate, and peak oxygen consumption in obese dieting subjects. *American Journal of Clinical Nutrition.* Sep 1997; 66: 557 - 563.
2. Kathryn H Schmitz, et al. Strength training and adiposity in premenopausal women: Strong, Healthy, and Empowered study *American Journal of Clinical Nutrition.* Sep 2007; 86: 566 - 572.
3. Trapp EG and Boutcher SH. Fat loss following 15 weeks of high intensity, intermittent cycle training. Fat Loss Laboratory, Faculty of Medicine, University of New South Wales, Sydney, Australia
4. Kokkinos, P. F., & Hurley, B. F. Strength training and lipoprotein-lipid profiles: A critical analysis and recommendations for further study. *Journal of Sports Medicine.* 9, 266-272. 1990
5. S. Ryan, R. E. Pratley, D. Elahi, and A. P. Goldberg. Resistive training increases fat-free mass and maintains RMR despite weight loss in postmenopausal women *Journal of Applied Physiology.* Sep 1995; 79: 818 - 823.
6. Eric T. Poehlman, et al. Effects of Resistance Training and Endurance Training on Insulin Sensitivity in Nonobese, Young Women: A Controlled Randomized Trial. *Journal of Clinical Endocrinology and Metabolism.* Jul 2000; 85: 2463 - 2468.
7. Tjonnas AE, Lee SJ, Rogonmo O, et al. Aerobic interval training vs. continuous moderate exercise as a treatment for the metabolic syndrome: a pilot study. *Circulation.* 2008;doi:10.1161/circulationaha.108.772822.
8. LaMonte MJ, Barlow CE, Jurca R, et al. Cardiorespiratory fitness is inversely associated with the incidence of metabolic syndrome. *Circulation.* 2005; 112:505-512.
9. Abbie E Smith, et al. Effects of β-alanine supplementation and high-intensity interval training on endurance performance and body composition in men; a double-blind trial. *Journal of the International Society of Sports Nutrition.* 2009; 6: 5
10. Whyte LJ et al. Effect of 2 weeks of sprint interval training on health-related outcomes in sedentary overweight/obese men. *Metabolism.* 2010 Feb 11. [Epub ahead of print]
11. Babyak M, et al. Exercise treatment for major depression: maintenance of therapeutic benefit at 10 months. *Psychosomatic Medicine.* 2000; 62: 633–8

CHAPTER FIFTEEN

1. Caballero B. Talking With Patients About Weight Loss. win.niddk.nih.gov. December 2007. Available at http://win.niddk.nih.gov/publications/talking.htm. Accessed April 18, 2010
2. Flocke SA, et al. Exercise, diet, and weight loss advice in the family medicine outpatient setting. *Family Medicine.* 2005; 37: 415-421
3. Flocke SA, Stange KC. Direct observation and patient recall of health behavior advice. *Preventative Medicine.* 2004;38:343-9
4. University of Liverpool. March 18, 2010,. Anti-obesity drugs unlikely to provide lasting benefit, according to scientists. *Science Daily.* Retrieved May 6, 2010, from http://www.sciencedaily.com /releases/2010/03/100316112448.htm
5. Rucker D, et al. Long term pharmacotherapy for obesity and overweight: updated meta-analysis *British Journal of Clinical Pharmacology.* Nov 2007; doi:10.1136/bmj.39385.413113.25
6. Viner, R.M., et al. Rise in anti-obesity drug prescribing for children and adolescents in the UK: a population-based study. *British Journal of Clinical Pharmacology.* 2009
7. Gotfredsen A. Influence of Orlistat on bone turnover and body composition. *International Journal of Obesity.* (2001) 25, 1154-1160
8. Torgerson J, Hauptman J, Boldrin M, Sjöström L (2004). "Xenical in the prevention

of diabetes in obese subjects (XENDOS) study: a randomized study of Orlistat as an adjunct to lifestyle changes for the prevention of type 2 diabetes in obese patients." *Diabetes Care.* 27 (1): 155–61

9. Janeczko LL. Phentermine/topiramate extended-release may help obese patients on antidepressants lose weight. Reuters Health News. Dec 5, 2013

10. RXList: The Internet Drug Index. QSYMIA. www.rxlist.com/qsymia-drug.htm

11. Lean MEJ (1997). Sibutramine: A review of clinical efficacy. *International Journal of Obesity.* 21(Suppl 1): S30–S36.

12. Bruce Japsen (13 March 2005). "FDA weighs decision on Meridia; Health advisory likely for Abbott obesity drug." Chicago Tribune. Chicago, Illinois. pp. 1.

13. Prescription Medications for the Treatment of Obesity. Weight Control Information Network (WIN). http://win.niddk.nih.gov/publications/prescription.htm

14. Olshansky SJ, et al. A Potential Decline in Life Expectancy in the United States in the 21st Century. *New England Journal of Medicine.* 2005; 352:1138-1145

15. Kahn SE, Hull RL, Utzschneider KM. Mechanisms linking obesity to insulin resistance and type 2 diabetes. *Nature.* 2006 Dec 14; 444(7121):840-6.

16. Grundy SM. Pre-diabetes, metabolic syndrome, and cardiovascular risk. *Journal of the American College of Cardiology.* 2012 Feb 14; 59(7):635-43.

17. Bjornholt JV, Erikssen G, Aaser E, et al. Fasting blood glucose: an underestimated risk factor for cardiovascular death. Results from a 22-year follow-up of healthy nondiabetic men. *Diabetes Care.* 1999 Jan; 22(1):45-9.

18. How the Blood Sugar of Diabetes Affects the Body. Web MD. http://www.webmd.com/diabetes/how-sugar-affects-diabetes (accessed February 13, 2014)

19. Celleno L, et al. A Dietary Supplement Containing Standardized *Phaseolus vulgaris* Extract Influences Body Composition of Overweight Men and Women. *International Journal of Medical Science.* 2007; 4:45-52

20. Hargrove JL, Greenspan P, Hartle DK, Dowd C. Inhibition of aromatase and α-amylase by flavonoids and proanthocyanidins from Sorghum bicolor bran extracts. *Journal of Medicinal Food.* 2011 Jul-Aug;14(7-8):799-807. doi: 10.1089/jmf.2010.0143. Epub 2011 May 25.

21. Heon Park JI, et al. Sorghum extract exerts an anti-diabetic effect by improving insulin sensitivity via PPAR-γ in mice fed a high-fat diet. *Nutrition Research and Practice.* 2012 August; 6(4): 322–327.

22. Kim GN, Kwon YI, Jang HD. Mulberry leaf extract reduces postprandial hyperglycemia with few side effects by inhibiting α-glucosidase in normal rats. *Journal of Medicinal Food.* 2011 Jul-Aug;14(7-8):712-7

23. Kim JY, et al. Mulberry Leaf Water Extract Ameliorates Insulin Sensitivity in High Fat or High Sucrose Diet Induced Overweight Rats. *Journal of the Korean Society for Applied Biological Chemistry.* 54(4), 612-618 (2011)

24. Zhang J, Tiller C, Shen J, et al. Antidiabetic properties of polysaccharide-and polyphenolic-enriched fractions from the brown seaweed Ascophyllum nodosum. *Canadian Journal of Physiology and Pharmacology.* 2007 Nov; 85(11):1116-23.

25. Apostolidis E, Lee CM. In vitro potential of Ascophyllum nodosum phenolic antioxidant-mediated alpha-glucosidase and alpha-amylase inhibition. *Journal of Food Science.* 2010 Apr; 75(3):H97-102.

26. Glucose management: high potential of a blend of algal phlorotannins for inhibiting key human digestive enzymes. Technical note. Rimouski, Québec, Canada: innoVactiv Inc; 2011:1-3.

27. Paradis ME, Couture P, Lamarche B. A randomised crossover placebo-controlled trial investigating the effect of brown seaweed (Ascophyllum nodosum and Fucus vesiculosus) on postchallenge plasma glucose and insulin levels in men and women. *Applied Physiology Nutrition and Metabolism.* 2011 Dec; 36(6):913-19.

28. Seri K, et al. L-arabinose selectively inhibits intestinal sucrase in an uncompetitive manner and suppresses glycemic response after sucrose ingestion in animals. *Metabolism.* 1996; 45:1368–1374

CHAPTER SIXTEEN

1. Ferrarai N. Multivitamins: Should you buy this insurance? www.health.harvard.edu. 2006. Available at https://www.health.harvard.edu/healthbeat/HEALTHbeat_120606.htm#art1. Accessed April 25, 2010

2. Kaats G.R., Blum K., Fisher J.A., Adelman J.A. Effects of chromium picolinate supplementation on body composition: A randomized, double-masked, placebo-controlled study (1996) *Current Therapeutic Research - Clinical and Experimental.* 57 (10), pp. 747-756.

3. Bustamante J, et al. Alpha-lipoic acid in liver metabolism and disease. *Free Radical Biology and Medicine.* 1998;24(6):1023-1039

4. Khamaisi M. et al. Lipoic acid reduces glycemia and increases muscle GLUT4 content in streptozotocin-diabetic rats (1997) *Metabolism: Clinical and Experimental,* 46 (7), pp. 763-768.

5. Julie A Pasco, Margaret J Henry, Mark A Kotowicz and Geoffrey C Nicholson || Barbara Depczynski. Paradoxical nutritional deficiency in overweight and obesity: the importance of nutrient density *Medical Journal of Australia.* 2009; 191 (1): 44-45. [Letters]

6. Liel Y, Ulmer E, Shary J, Hollis BW, Bell NH. Low circulating vitamin D in obesity. *Calcified Tissue International.* 1988; 43:199–201.

7. Marshall K. *Therapeutic applications of whey protein. Alternative Medical Review.* 2004; 9:136-156. 24

8. Broadhurst L, Polansky MM, Anderson, RA. Insulin-like biological activity of culinary and medicinal plant aqueous extracts in vitro. *Journal of Agricultural and Food Chemistry.* 2000 Mar; 48(3):849–52.

9. Cao H, Graves DJ, Anderson RA. Cinnamon extract regulates glucose transporter and insulin-signaling gene expression in mouse adipocytes. *Phytomedicine.* 2010 May 27.

10. Anderson RA, Broadhurst CL, Polansky MM, et al. Isolation and characterization of polyphenol type-A polymers from cinnamon with insulin-like biological activity. *Journal of Agricultural and Food Chemistry.* 2004 Jan 14;52(1):65-70

11. Qin B, Nagasaki M, Ren M, Bajotto G, Oshida Y, Sato Y. Cinnamon extract prevents the insulin resistance induced by a high-fructose diet. *Hormone Metabolism Research.* 2004 Feb; 36(2):119-25.

12. Yoshioka M, et al: Effects of red pepper added to high-fat & high-carbohydrate meals on energy metabolism & substrate utilization in Japanese women. *British Journal of Nutrition.* 1998; 80: 503–510.

13. Abdul G Dulloo, et al. Efficacy of a green tea extract rich in catechin polyphenols and caffeine in increasing 24-h energy expenditure and fat oxidation in humans. *American Journal of Clinical Nutrition.* Dec 1999; 70: 1040 - 1045.

14. Gao H, et al. Beneficial effects of Yerba Mate tea (Ilex paraguariensis) on hyperlipidemia in high-fat-fed hamsters. *Experimental Gerontology.* 2013 Jun; 48(6):572-8.

15. Arçari DP, et al. Antiobesity effects of yerba maté extract (Ilex paraguariensis) in high-fat diet-induced obese mice. *Obesity* (Silver Spring, MD). 2009 Dec;17(12):2127-33

16. University of Rochester Medical Center. Obese Parents Influence Children's Weight.

17. Costa Krewer C, et al. Habitual Intake of Guaraná and Metabolic Morbidities: An Epidemiological Study of an Elderly Amazonian Population. *Phytotherapy Research.* 2011 Feb 22

18. Lima WP, et al. Lipid metabolism in trained rats: effect of guarana (Paullinia cupana Mart.) supplementation. *Clinical Nutrition.* Edinburgh, Scotland. 2005 Dec;24(6):1019-28

19. Heck, CI, de Mejia, EG. Yerba Mate Tea (Ilex paraguariensis): a comprehensive review on chemistry, health implications, and technological considerations. *Journal*

of Food Science. 72(9):138-51, 2007

20. ANH-Intl Feature: "Enough is enough": vitamin bashing with the same old hammer. Natural Health International website.

21. Kounang N. Are multivitamins a waste of money? Editorial in medical journal says yes. CNN. 9:15 AM EST, Tue December 17, 2013

22. Shixian Q, VanCrey B, Shi J, Kakuda Y, Jiang Y. Green tea extract thermogenesis-induced weight loss by epigallocatechin gallate inhibition of catechol-O-methyltransferase. *Journal of Medicinal Food.* 2006 Winter;9(4):451-8

23. Venables MC, Hulston CJ, Cox HR, Jeukendrup AE. Green tea extract ingestion, fat oxidation, and glucose tolerance in healthy humans. *American Journal of Clinical Nutrition.* 2008 Mar;87(3):778-84

24. Kim JJY, Tan Y, Xiao L, Sun YL, Qu X. Green Tea Polyphenol Epigallocatechin-3-Gallate Enhance Glycogen Synthesis and Inhibit Lipogenesis in Hepatocytes. *BioMed Research International.* 2013; 2013: 920128

CHAPTER SEVENTEEN

1. Bernier M, Avard J. Self-efficacy, outcome and attrition in a weight-reduction program. *Cognitive Therapy Research.* 1986; 10: 319–338.

2. Dennis K.E., Goldberg A.P. Weight control self-efficacy types and transitions affect weight-loss outcomes in obese women (1996) *Addictive Behaviors.* 21 (1), pp. 103-116.

3. High. *Science Daily.* Retrieved May 12, 2010, from http://www.sciencedaily.com /releases/2008/05/080502082735.htm

4. Foreyt JP, Goodrick GK. Evidence for success of behavior modification in weight loss and control. *Annals of Internal Medicine.* 1993;119:698-701

5. Rosen J.C., Orosan P. Reiter J. Cognitive behavior therapy for negative body image in obese women (1995) *Behavior Therapy.* 26 (1), pp. 25-42

6. Rapoport L, Clark M, Wardle J. Evaluation of a modified cognitive-behavioural programme for weight management. *International Journal of Obesity Related Metabolic Disorders.* 2000; 24: 1726–1737

7. Cooper Z, Fairburn CF, Hawker DM. Cognitive-behavioral treatment of obesity. A clinician's guide. New York, NY: Guilford Press, 2003

8. Mefferd K, Nichols J, Pakiz B, Rock C. A cognitive behavioral therapy intervention to promote weight loss improves body composition and blood lipid profiles among overweight breast cancer survivors. *Breast Cancer Research and Treatment.* 2007; 104:145-52.

9. Brennan L, Wilks R, Walkley J, Fraser S, Greenway K. Efficacy of cognitive behavioural therapy in the treatment of overweight and obese adolescents. *Obesity Review.* 2006;7:87–89

10. Batra R, Kuwada S, Maher VL. The frequency-following response to continuous tones in humans. *Hearing Research.* 1986; 21(2):167-77.

11. Will U, Berg E. Brain wave synchronization and entrainment to periodic acoustic stimuli. *Neuroscience Letters.* 2007 Aug 31; 424(1):55-60.

12. Panagariya A. Living longer living happier: My journey from clinical neurology to complexities of brain. *Annals of Indian Academy of Neurology.* 2011 Oct-Dec; 14(4): 232–238.

13. van Peer JM, Roelofs K, Spinhoven P. Cortisol administration enhances the coupling of midfrontal delta and beta oscillations. *International Journal of Psychophysiology.* 2008 Feb; 67(2):144-50.

CHAPTER EIGHTEEN

1. Mercola D. Avoid this Popular Beverage Until You Learn the Shocking Details. Mercola.com.   April   27   2010.   Available   at

http://articles.mercola.com/sites/articles/archive/2010/04/27/does-drinking-milk-cause-upperrespiratory-congestion.aspx. Accessed May 1, 2010

2.   Lanou AJ, Berkow SE, Barnard ND. Calcium, dairy products, and bone health in children and young adults: a reevaluation of the evidence. *Pediatrics.* 2005;115(3):736-43.

3.   W. Barclay, et al., "Glycemic index, glycemic load, and chronic disease risk—a metaanalysis of observational studies," *American Journal of Clinical Nutrition.* vol. 87, no. 3, pp. 627–637, 2008

4.   Hodak SP, Verbalis JG. Abnormalities of water homeostasis in aging. *Endocrinology and Metabolism Clinics of North America.* 2005 Dec;34(4):1031-46, xi.

5.   Miller M. [Aging and water metabolism in health and illness] *Archives of Gerontology and Geriatrics.* 1999 Jul;32 Suppl 1:I20-6.

6.   King B. Fat Wars Action Planner. Wiley & Sons, Toronto, Ont. 2003

7.   King B. Fat Wars: 45 Days to Transform Your Body. CDG Books. Toronto, Ont. 2002. (pg.11)

8.   Ravaglia G, et al. Determinants of functional status in healthy Italian nonagenarians and centenarians: a comprehensive functional assessment by the instruments of geriatric practice. *Journal of the American Geriatric Society.* 1997 Oct;45(10):1196-202.

9.   Krucoff C. Making Muscle a Thing of the Present: New Guidelines Urge Older Exercisers to Put Emphasis on Strength Training. The Washington Post, Jan. 26, 1999; Pg. Z28

10. Linnane AW et al. The universality of bioenergetic disease. Age-associated cellular bioenergetic degradation and amelioration therapy. 1998. *Annals of the New York Academy of Sciences.* 854: 202-213.

11. King, B & Schmidt, M; BIO-AGE: Ten Steps To A Younger You, CDG Books Canada, 2001.

12. Willix, RD; The Shocking truth About the Water You Are drinking Now...and the lethal Effect it may have on Your Health; Doctor's Special Repo

13. MS Bray, et al. Time-of-day-dependent dietary fat consumption influences multiple cardiometabolic syndrome parameters in mice. *International Journal of Obesity* (Lond). 2010 Mar 30. [Epub ahead of print]

ABOUT THE AUTHOR

Brad King, M.S., M.F.S., is a nutritional researcher, performance nutritionist and one of the most sought-after authorities on nutrition, obesity and longevity. Brad is an inductee into the prestigious Canadian Sports Nutrition Hall of Fame, and a recipient of the Health Motivator/Educator/Public Speaker - Best in Canada Award. He has authored 11 books, including the international bestsellers, *Fat Wars* and *Beer Belly Blues,* and has been profiled in numerous national magazines, newspapers, and television programs throughout North America including the *Today Show* and *Canada AM.*

www.DirtyDiets.com